BROWN v. BOARD
AND THE TRANSFORMATION OF AMERICAN CULTURE

BROWN v. BOARD

AND THE TRANSFORMATION OF AMERICAN CULTURE

EDUCATION AND THE SOUTH IN THE AGE OF DESEGREGATION

BEN KEPPEL

LOUISIANA STATE UNIVERSITY PRESS
BATON ROUGE

Published by Louisiana State University Press

Manufactured in the United States of America
FIRST PRINTING

DESIGNER: Barbara Neely Bourgoyne
TYPEFACES: Brix Slab and DIN Schrift, display; Chaparral Pro, text
PRINTER AND BINDER: Maple Press

Library of Congress Cataloging-in-Publication Data
Keppel, Ben.
Brown v. Board and the transformation of American culture : education and the South in the age of desegregation / Ben Keppel.
pages cm
Includes bibliographical references and index.
ISBN 978-0-8071-6132-6 (cloth : alk. paper) — ISBN 978-0-8071-6133-3 (pdf) — ISBN 978-0-8071-6134-0 (epub) — ISBN 978-0-8071-6135-7 (mobi) 1. United States—Race relations—History—20th century. 2. Popular culture—United States—History—20th century. 3. School integration—Southern States—History. 4. Brown, Oliver, 1918–1961—Trials, litigation, etc. 5. Topeka (Kan.). Board of Education—Trials, litigation, etc. 6. Coles, Robert. 7. Cosby, Bill, 1937– 8. Cooney, Joan Ganz. I. Title. II. Title: Brown versus Board and the transformation of American culture.
E184.A1K425 2015
305.800973′0904—dc23

2015008670

Chapter 3 is an expanded version of an essay published previously in *Race and Science: Scientific Challenges to Racism in America,* edited by Paul Farber and Hamilton Cravens (Corvallis: Oregon State University Press, 2009). It is used by permission.

The paper in this book meets the guidelines for permanence and durability of the Committee on Production Guidelines for Book Longevity of the Council on Library Resources.
∞

CONTENTS

Acknowledgments · vii

1 An Invitation to a Historical Reenactment · 1

2 A Culture Goes to School: An Integrative Revolution in a Developing Country · 30

3 Robert Coles as Domestic Goodwill Ambassador of the Second Reconstruction · 64

4 William H. Cosby, Victorian Reformer, and the Integrative Properties of Humor · 93

5 Joan Ganz Cooney's *Sesame Street* and the Rebroadcasting of Social Change · 132

6 Lessons from a Historical Reenactment · 165

Notes · 181

Index · 215

ACKNOWLEDGMENTS

Although this is my second book, its beginnings lead far back into my own early years. I spent my childhood and youth in Sacramento, the capital of California, at a time when educational reform and property tax relief were on a long-term, and ultimately disastrous, collision course with one another. When I began conceiving of a book about the symbolic place of children in the civil rights movement, I did not realize how close to home I would ultimately have to travel.

In my first years out of UCLA, as a history PhD working outside the academy I hoped someday to join, I was fortunate to meet Eric Gordon, who shared with me the story behind the song "Black and White," which became a hit in the summer of 1972 for Three Dog Night. Eric was then in the early stages of a book on Earl Robinson, who, along with David Arkin, actually wrote that song. My appreciation for the iconography which suffuses American discussions of race was made deeper by Franklin U. D. Westbrook, a graphic artist who also became a friend while he, Eric, and I worked together at the Social and Public Art Resource Center in Venice, California.

The archival research for this book began nearly twenty years ago in Birmingham, Alabama; Washington, D.C. (and College Park, Maryland); and Fayetteville, Arkansas. The research was funded by one of two Junior Faculty Research Grants that I received from the College of Arts and Sciences (of which Paul B. Bell was an outstanding dean) at the University of Oklahoma, where I started my career as a tenure-track faculty member. As the number of these positions falls every year, I am reminded that this book might never have been completed had I not been fortunate enough to land at the University of Oklahoma in 1994. The Arts and Sciences Committee on Teaching and Research also made it possible for me to present parts of this research before audiences at the annual meetings of the Mid-America Conference on History, the Organization of American Historians, the American Historical Association, and the Society for the Study of the History of Children and Youth.

My location at the University of Oklahoma no doubt helped me obtain early support from the National Endowment for the Humanities and the Rockefeller Archive Center. In addition, I was able to work with administrators such as Lee Williams and Kelvin Droggemeyer, who supported my occasional needs for "reasonable accommodation" as I traveled to present papers and do research without ever having to be reminded of the Americans with Disabilities Act. I am also forever grateful to John M. Rhea and Sara Eppler-Janda, who helped find and copy a dizzying array of articles for me in the years before the arrival of the digital age.

Archivists are the historian's indispensible partners, and I owe a debt to several of these skilled professionals. As the focus of my work matured and changed over time, Lin Fredricksen (Kansas State Historical Society), Jim Baggett (Birmingham Public Library), Joan Barker (Topeka High School Historical Society), Jeffrey Bridgers (Library of Congress), Anna Cartier (John F. Kennedy Presidential Library), Faith Coleman (Ford Foundation Archives), Bryan Giezma and Tim Hodgdon (University North Carolina, Chapel Hill), Brenda Hearing (Carnegie Corporation Papers, Columbia University), Jennifer Mandel (Ronald Reagan Presidential Library), and Robert W. Morrow (Public Broadcasting Archives, University of Maryland), Rick Pifer (Wisconsin State Historical Society), Anne Marie Rachman, David Cooper, Peter Berg, and Ben Dettmar (Michigan State University), and Rosemarie Truglio (Children's Television Workshop Video Archives, New York City) often found ways to help me extend my reach beyond what my budget of time and money would allow.

At the University of Oklahoma, H. Wayne Morgan took my wife, Katherine A. Pandora, and me under his strong and capacious wing and mentored us through some very difficult times at the university. I have worked with three departmental chairs, and, of these three, Morgan had the toughest job, helping me in my first semester of teaching, which included an introduction to the institutional procedures associated with academic misconduct by students. (If I had been told back in late 1994 that I would not need round-the-clock psychiatric care after twenty years of handling such issues with a relatively small number of offenders, I would not have believed it. Wayne's advice is the main reason I can laugh about that now.) Rob Griswold picked up where Wayne left off, providing consistent encouragement and support as I worked on this book while juggling too many other things. Jamie Hart, who currently chairs our department, has continued this tradition.

The vast majority of my students at the University of Oklahoma have given me thousands of reasons for optimism and hope for the future. To the extent I now see the civil rights years as a flawed collective experiment in an often unwilling process of historical reenactment, it is because rich and lively conversations with students over the last twenty years have made me see this truth much more clearly.

This book is better because of the friendship and good advice of several colleagues I am honored to also count on as friends. Michael Alexander (now a faculty member in the Religious Studies Program at the University of California, Riverside) read some of my first work on this manuscript. Much later, I sought and promptly received the wisdom of other colleagues at Oklahoma and elsewhere: David Chappell, Hamilton Cravens, Paul Farber, Rob Griswold, Sandie Holguin, Catherine E. Kelly, Kathryn Schumaker, and Werner Sollors offered sound advice at key points. To this group, I am proud to add Fay Yarbrough, whom I met for the first time while we were both presenting papers at a conference at Oregon State University in the spring of 2006. I will always be grateful that she joined our department for an important seven years in its history before she returned to teach at her undergraduate alma mater, Rice University.

In the last several years, as my manuscript grappled more closely with questions of public education, I was fortunate to have capable guides in the University of Oklahoma's Jeannine Rainbolt College of Education. John Covaleskie, Brian Corpenning, Susan Laird, Goldie Pollard Thompson, and Mirelsie Velazquez introduced me to some highly relevant works in education theory.

One of the pleasures of working on more recent history is the opportunity it sometimes provides to meet the people you are studying.

In the course of research I interviewed Joan Ganz Cooney, the founding mother of the Children's Television Workshop, social critic Robert Coles, and former vice-president Walter Mondale, who were each generous with their time and recollections. My work with Coles and Mondale would have been much more difficult without a major grant from the University of Oklahoma Research Council. Those funds not only paid for my travel but for the professional transcription of those interviews.

As this manuscript took shape, Jon Holloway, Ellen Herman, Hamilton Cravens, Dan Wickerg, and George Lipsitz offered essential support, for which I will always be grateful. As the manuscript entered its last phase, Jean Hurtado gave me priceless advice about how to turn what I had written into something others might actually want to read. As I entered the publishing marketplace, Deborah Gershenowitz, Richard Weiss, David Wrobel, and Gary Nash provided frank and helpful advice to navigate the rapids. Weiss and Nash continued as role models and mentors to me going back to UCLA. Jeffrey Prager, another mentor at UCLA, also deserves special mention. He first returned to this project indirectly when I read *School Desegregation Research: New Directions in Situational Analysis,* which he coedited with Douglas Longshore and Melvin Seeman. I have had the book on my shelf at home since he gave me an inscribed copy in his office many years ago during a conversation about Kenneth B. Clark. Only in the last few years, however, did I finally read this book with the care it deserved. Through it, I was introduced to the ideas of John U. Ogbu, an anthropologist whose ethnographic writings on public schooling have aided my own thinking. Prager's more recent work also introduced me to the writing of Danielle S. Allen, whose reflections on the significance of *Brown v. Board* to American public life provided another moment of useful discovery for me.

Getting this book in its final shape took time, and I owe a great debt to others. Jade Chan, Michelle Iodice, and Kristine Seale were indispensible in creating a clean reader-friendly text. When I my manuscript reached home, at Louisiana State University Press, Rand Dotson was there to welcome it. He coordinated a review process which has further improved my analysis. I am especially grateful to "Reader One," who insisted that I be more explicit about my historical assumptions and my framework. This counsel was especially decisive in bringing chapters one, two, and four into sharper focus. Finally, I owe special thanks to Stan Ivester, who gave to this manuscript a final dose of tender loving care.

This book comes from deep within my own experience as an American who first encountered this culture when I was eight years old and came upon a bumper sticker on a car in the parking lot of Starr King Exceptional School in the late 1960s: "America: Love It or Leave It." My first reaction, frankly, was to want to leave. I have spent my life thinking about those words and the emotions they represent. This book is part of that effort. To the degree that I have been unable to do all that I hoped or promised here, I can assure the reader that I am committed to learning from my mistakes in my future contributions.

To the extent that I have struck a chord of truth in what I have written, it comes directly from the love, understanding, and support given to me over many years by my wife, Katherine, and our daughter, Harper. This book is dedicated to Harper, and to her generation, who are already busy contributing both value and values to our world.

BROWN v. BOARD
AND THE TRANSFORMATION OF AMERICAN CULTURE

1

AN INVITATION TO A HISTORICAL REENACTMENT

> In the evening of the day of the inauguration, another new experience awaited me. The usual reception was given at the executive mansion, and though no colored persons had ever ventured to present themselves on such occasions, it seemed, now that freedom had become the law of the republic, and colored men were on the battlefield, mingling their blood with that of white men in one common effort to save the country, that it was not too great an assumption for a colored man to offer his congratulations to the President with those of other citizens.
>
> —FREDERICK DOUGLASS, 1892

The words that open this invitation come from Frederick Douglass's final autobiography. What followed Douglass's decision to attend the reception for President Lincoln in the East Room of the White House was certainly an outrage, but it may not have qualified as a surprise. Although Douglass was the best-known African American of his century and although he would be greeted by the president himself as "my friend Douglass," Douglass was denied admission twice before a white colleague interceded to take him to Lincoln. Douglass's own reaction was both wise and pragmatic: it had been "a new experience for me, and a new experience for the country, to see a person like myself present on such an occasion."[1]

This scene—an old yet robust ritual of antipathy coexisting in close proximity with a new ritual of ambiguous welcome and qualified acceptance—has been, and continues to be, reenacted in the life of the United

States. This ritual was reenacted and innovated upon in the second great period of self-conscious Reconstruction, which I call the Age of *Brown*. It was formally begun, of course, by the Supreme Court's decision in *Brown v. Board* to overturn the doctrine of "separate but equal" in the provision of education at public expense.

When Americans want to chart change along the racial fault line within the United States they most often look to statistics of various kinds to see whether historically rooted separations are being maintained, increasing, or growing closer—demography, encounters with the criminal justice system, employment, levels of political participation, and differences in partisan preference. While I have gleaned much from these kinds of studies, I am especially interested in a different dimension of historical experience: how self-selected individuals seek to lead, guide, or embody the specific steps or measures that a given change requires. Such people do not necessarily initiate a change, although we might usefully classify them as a particular kind of cultural "first responders" who take it upon themselves not just to advocate the necessity for change but also to seek to represent its practical attainability as "participant symbols" working with resources immediately at hand, accessible to them and to the rest of us.[2]

During the Age of *Brown*, three influential public figures dedicated themselves to helping Americans cultivate what political theorist Danielle S. Allen has called "new habits of citizenship" anticipated by *Brown* and the civil rights movement.[3] Psychiatrist and social critic Robert Coles, comedian Bill Cosby, and television producer Joan Ganz Cooney each took upon themselves the responsibility for meeting the preeminent challenge on the American homefront: educating American leaders and voters about the collective work required to finish the cultural work begun so tentatively by Douglass and Lincoln.[4]

They performed this work in a popular culture in which the thematic counterpart to a preoccupation with new threats and responsibilities abroad was, according to historian Rebecca de Schweinitz, the glorification of a particular picture of "domestic life"—symbolized by the affluent two-parent family in which the mother was the "homemaker" and the husband was out in the world working as the "breadwinner" for the family. Part and parcel of the "baby boom" that was at the center of this cultural moment were "very clear conceptions about what constituted a proper childhood," with a particular emphasis on fostering early intellectual development.[5]

Coles, Cosby, and Cooney spoke especially to the culture-wide debates over what the phrase "public education" meant and what it required of an advanced, even exceptional, democracy. Over the early years of the twentieth century, according to legal scholar Derrick Bell, the public school had emerged as a "far more compelling symbol of the evils of segregation than segregated railroad cars, restaurants and restrooms."[6] Coles, Cosby, and Cooney each spoke with special force and conviction about what Americans should do and what they needed to know about creating a national culture in which differences in race, ethnicity, and income no longer meant an inferior quality and experience of citizenship. As such, they were integral figures in attempting to convert a sporadic and episodic concern with a "racial crisis" or a "Negro problem" into something more comprehensive. Coles, Cosby, and Cooney became part of something hoped for by historian and civil rights activist Howard Zinn: that, in the aftermath of the lessons suggested to the nation by the events of the Freedom Summer in Mississippi, a new and more expansive debate might take place—"a national equivalent to the excitement of the civil rights movement, one strong enough in its pull to create a motivation for learning that even the enticements of monetary success cannot match." Could the boundaries of the public mainstream be pushed out sufficiently that "it [would] be possible to declare boldly that the aim of the schools is to find solutions for poverty, for injustice, for race and national hatred, and to turn all educational efforts into a national striving for these solutions?"[7] That often-heated argument has continued at the center of American politics over the last generation, with some moments being more socially inclusive and more intellectually and politically wide ranging than others.

Speaking to different yet distinctly overlapping segments of the national polity, Coles, Cosby, and Cooney made specific efforts and contributions within their fields of expertise: Robert Coles, a Harvard-trained physician with unique credibility as a participant-observer of the consequences of poverty and racism, sought to take political leaders and their constituents inside the struggle to desegregate public schools and to reform institutions to better serve all the members of this multiracial society; comedian Bill Cosby used his talents to suggest what a reconstructed nation might look like. The thrust of the Cosby message, conveyed on records, on television, in books, and in films was to suggest that the basic and fundamental tools for this achievement were much closer at hand than many in his audiences realized. As national audiences watched, and Americans in Mississippi and other places debated what Project Head Start should be and do in their states, television producer Joan Cooney traveled the country exploring how what was then known as "Educational Television" (or ETV) might intervene early enough in a child's life to "make a difference" that some children in some communities might receive in no other way and through no other medium. Viewed together and in tandem, Coles, Cosby, and Cooney are key figures in understanding the Age of *Brown*.

THE AGE OF *BROWN*

The origins and long-term consequences of *Brown v. Board* have produced some outstanding books.[8] *"Brown v. Board" and the Transformation of American Culture* aims to capture something broader by considering how *Brown* interacted with other cultural developments to force a franker public debate about the real politics and social mechanics required to provide the kind of universal public education fitting and consistent with the nation's commitment to equality of opportunity. Well before *Brown v. Board*, the military necessities of two world wars had exposed shortcomings in many local school systems which, for a majority of students, ended well before the twelfth grade. And certainly the ideological consequences of a world war against fascism played a strong part convincing a large number of Americans that the price of upward mobility—a promise so central to the national identity—was steeply rising, a trend that would require much more from schools, teachers, parents, and students.

The holding in *Brown* was but one powerful cornerstone moment in the ascension of a new theme in American folk wisdom: in the words of John H. Fischer, "to limit a man's education is to limit his freedom."[9] Even as the judicial and political momentum for pursuing more innovative ways for making desegregation a pathway toward a deeper feeling of closeness and connectedness some called "integration" between white and nonwhite Americans, the American polity had to face a fact even larger than *Brown* and its legal progeny: the nation's recent history, as Deborah Meier argued in 1995, put the American polity on record as having "an obligation to educate all students to equally high standards."[10]

The struggle over how to meet this standard became a "school of affliction" that, like the Civil War to which Frederick Douglass first applied this phrase, revealed both the very best and the very worst in the American polity.[11] A people committed to the goal of equal opportunity, and yet deeply averse to considering how the "free market" might interact with social antipathies to create the opposite, have been forced by the debates of the last sixty years to face an uncomfortable fact: "education sits at center stage . . . of . . . conflicts . . . about what this society really is."[12]

The author of those words, educational theorist Michael W. Apple, goes further still in describing a reality firmly at the center of American social politics: when Americans debate the specifics of resourcing education and allocating resources within schools and districts, they are using debates over education policy as a "proxy for debates that, too often in the nation's history have been seen as 'un-American': larger battles about what our institutions should do, whom they should serve and who should make these decisions."[13]

To approach the Age of *Brown* as an experiment in historical reenactment does not require us to ignore or to devalue human innovation, determined effort over time, or even the importance of chance in the making of history. As this distinct period of change took fuller and more coherent form, new leavening agents appeared in the mix. Even as familiar resistance remained strong, there was now a large young constituency for participating in a "revolution of regeneration," a term used by the actor and cultural activist Ossie Davis: "[I]n schools, colleges and universities . . . there's a tremendous hunger among blacks and whites for truth about the black experience in this country."[14]

New ideas have the potential to alter existing patterns and create new rituals. As political philosopher Danielle S. Allen argues, that most powerful conception of membership in the American polity—from many, one—commanded the creation of a certain kind of unity in the long aftermath of the Civil War. The priority to claim a new universal conception of citizenship did not lead to a rigorous effort to create institutions in which unequal treatment and its consequences were acknowledged and structured into their daily operations. In practice, the variety of nationalism promulgated between the Civil War and World War II required certain groups to establish alternative institutions and to be "subject to different laws." Adding institutional insult to this civic injury, these Americans were also treated very differently by institutions allegedly required to treat all citizens equally. Thus, membership in the American union required that they acquiesce to their invisibility as citizens with a different yet equally legitimate claim to respect and full participation. Under this regime of citizenship, these Americans "often had radically different experiences of legality in America." In the final analysis, this cultural and political regime "taught habits of domination and acquiescence" as the price of membership.[15]

From the Second World War onward—with special emphasis on the years between 1954 and 1964—legal and political reforms gave legitimacy to a new conception of citizenship. By 1964, a new phase was begun in which "minorities gained mainstream public voices and vocalized the perspectives of citizens who had for decades lived 'beyond the pale' . . . of the 'one people.'"[16] This new ideal of citizenship encouraged broad-based public participation by stressing the "wholeness" of citizenship rather than its (often forcible) contribution to a superficial national unity.

Allen is absolutely clear that this process remains both manifestly incomplete and deeply controversial. School desegregation provided a formative test of how these "new habits of citizenship" might work in day-to-day life and how they might relate to a less inclusive and participatory tradition. In testimony given in 1970 before the Senate Select Committee on Equality of Educational Opportunity, M. Hays Mizzell, director of the South Carolina Community Relations Program of the American Friends Service Committee, described his successful efforts to bring teachers together in preparation for school desegregation: "These were black and white teachers who thought they knew each other very well [but who discovered that] . . . they did not know each other at all, and [that] they harbored all the usual suspicions, hostilities and myths about each other. They were in the session for four days, and they said some fairly rough things to each other . . . but at the end of the four-day period, they were at the beginning of being able to work together and have some kind of communication. At the end of four days, they stood around a hotel room holding hands in a circle while they listened to Ray Stevens [sing] 'Everything Is Beautiful' on a record player."[17]

As real as this moment may have been, there was much going on outside the frame of this picture. As a detailed, multiyear, ethnographic analysis disclosed about life in an elementary school in neighboring North Carolina in the mid-1970s, old patterns of separation and avoidance retained great power. First, the administrative leaders of the school, joined in sentiment by several members of the school board, made no effort to hide their resistance to federal mandates to end "racial isolation" and achieve a new "racial balance."[18] At school, among black and white teachers and students, the formal public cooperation required by a school environment in which "social race has been deemphasized" did not lead to "informal cooperation" either within or beyond the school setting.[19] As one anonymous informant told this research team: "I don't want to be black. I don't want to know things only blacks are interested in. Where I used to teach I had a good friend who was black. I'd invite her to do things outside of school, and she'd invite me, but we never had anything in common socially."[20] Such a reaction is not a familiar part of the national narrative about the return to the work of Reconstruction in the long aftermath of *Brown v. Board*. To highlight these resistances is not to call into question the reality of Allen's claim for "new habits"; rather it underlines a point of agreement about the uneasy and fragile nature of the agreements reached during the First and Second Reconstructions.

To get a further sense of new habits comingling with old, let us go to another scene from the Age of *Brown*. In July of 1960, a camera crew for *CBS Reports* traveled to the Republic of Guinea with a delegation of American college students. This delegation, led by William Sloan Coffin, was part of Crossroads Africa, a nonprofit program that would become one model for incoming President John F. Kennedy's Peace Corps. Once a French colony, Guinea was now a "left-leaning new nation" at the center of the Cold War. The students, representing "an All-American melting pot," were there to build a community center with, as luck would have it, cement imported from the Soviet Union. Midway through Howard K. Smith's report, the camera enters a classroom where the Americans are leading a conversation with a group of young adults from the surrounding area. At the center of their lesson plan is a song, "Black and White," an American folk song written in the mid-1950s by David Arkin and Earl Robinson to honor *Brown v. Board.*

Arkin and Robinson were two "fellow travelers" whose lives had been shadowed by the Red Scare of the 1950s. Their original lyrics offered a compact history lesson, including the action of the nine judges ("Their robes were black / Their heads were white. . . . Nine judges all set down their names to end the years of shame"). By this great decision, Americans "could plainly see the alphabet of liberty." Now Americans could stand before the world confirming the creation of a "beautiful sight," acknowledging the depth of a universal truth: "The whole world knows / This is the way that freedom grows."[21] For these goodwill ambassadors from the United States, the song speaks to what they believe to be a truth of their time: racial segregation is now a "Southern problem," but the American people and their government are "on the side of change."[22]

This piece of film represents yet another scene of historical reenactment. Were Frederick Douglass and Abraham Lincoln able to stand as witnesses to this scene in the nuclear-powered Cold War of the twentieth century, they might agree with historian Howard Zinn, who christened the members of this generation who joined the Student Non-violent Coordinating Committee as the "new abolitionists" (explicitly acknowledging that they were engaged in an experiment in historical reenactment). Looking back to 1860 from the vantage point of 1960, we can easily imagine that Douglass and Lincoln might well have been reminded of the New Englanders who journeyed south to staff the Port Royal Experiment and other initiatives to educate the free people.

The story of the song "Black and White" does not end here. The song resurfaces in the late summer of 1972 when, according to *Billboard* magazine, "Black and White" became the top of the "Hot 100."[23] In this, the "Rock version," all references to the Supreme Court's action in *Brown v. Board* and the conflict it provoked are gone. Revised, the song focuses exclusively on the children sitting together—leaving the impression that this new arrangement was a happily accomplished fact: "A child is black, a child is white . . . together they learn to read and write . . . the whole world looks upon the sight . . . a beautiful sight."[24]

These deletions should bring to mind the process by which peoples reconstitute their "imagined communities" after a rupture. This softening of historical memory into a warmly remembered myth is not unprecedented and requires that we look beyond the immediately satisfying explanation that this bit of amnesia through editing was a simple concession to what we politely refer to as "commercial consideration." It must be remembered that "Black and White," as a song, was first heard by millions of Americans, not in the mid-1950s, when it was written by Arkin and Robinson, nor in October 1957, during the crisis over the desegregation of Little Rock's Central High School—when it was first released as a "single" record by the B'nai B'rith featuring the voice of Sammy Davis Jr.—but in the summer of 1972.

As turbulent as the early seventies were, they nonetheless stood at a "safe" distance for millions of Americans from the most searing images of resistance to school desegregation and racial equality generally—nearly ten years removed from the fire hoses, police dogs, and church bombings in Birmingham.[25] In this sense the version of "Black and White" that gained such wide popularity in the early 1970s had the same charm as the nineteenth-century scene of "imagined community" to which it is related. Consider the words of political scientist Benedict Anderson: "It remained for Mark Twain to create in 1881, well after the 'Civil War' and Lincoln's Emancipation Proclamation, the first indelible image of black and white as American 'brothers': Jim and Huck companionably adrift on the wide Mississippi. But the setting is a remembered/forgotten antebellum in which the black is still a slave."[26]

Here too, a painful struggle has been softened and simplified ("humanized" or "brought down to earth") in the service of a "new habit of citizenship" still in the future. In the same way that Twain's classic existed in the same political and cultural universe with more powerful and popular civic emotions—a feeling among white Americans of the nineteenth century that the Civil War and Reconstruction must now be declared closed chapters—the song "Black and White" ascended amid a sense that "enough was enough." Here again the celebration of a "new habit of citizenship" coexists in intimate proximity with contrary signs, rooted in the past and vibrantly alive in the present. At the time of its release and for its few weeks at the top of the charts, this song provided unacknowledged background music as Americans—black and white—registered a strong disagreement over "busing." The question placed before the nation by recent Supreme Court decisions was this: could children be transported to schools beyond their neighborhoods in order to end the racial isolation of black and white students from each other? On this question, blacks and whites gave opposing answers: by margins as high as 80 percent, whites said "No." In contrast, majorities of African Americans supported such measures. [27]

Lincoln and Douglass, as veterans of many a public campaign waged across this land, might have recognized this division as well as the race-baiting rhetoric that some elected leaders invoked against the prospect of busing, even in places where there was no possibility of it actually happening. They might also have had deep insight about the origins of the rubric by which progress was being measured. Among the big stories of 1970 was that whites in all parts of the country were now more receptive to sending their children to school with "a few" blacks."[28] Despite the vast expansion of suffrage beyond the white majority, this was still a "white country" whose most successful leaders would have to follow Lincoln's example and bow to such an emphatically majority sentiment.

This sentiment was reflected not only in the opposition to virtually any court-ordered busing; it was at the very heart of strategies of compliance. A substantial body of meticulous scholarship reminds us that, as in the nineteenth century, this was no coming together of equals to chart a shared journey forward. The focus on a new civic ideal—children sitting side by side in the same classroom—led inexorably to a quite lopsided program of student transfers to schools outside their neighborhoods. Although the populist opposition to busing in the 1970s was powered by the assumption that whites would be denied the right to attend schools in neighborhoods that their families had sacrificed mightily to afford, the sacrifice most often worked the other way. It was black parents and their children who did most of the moving into unfamiliar territory.

We can see these social dynamics in motion in a couple of key scenes from the early 1970s. In those years Florida's Democratic governor, Reuben Askew (first elected in 1970), gained considerable attention as a potential candidate for national office when he emerged as one of the few politicians in the country to make an argument for busing:

> I recognize and regret the inconvenience, the disruption and the hardship it often creates for many of our parents and our children. I am not without

> feeling for them. . . . Busing is an artificial and inadequate instrument of change. It should be abandoned as soon as we can afford to do so. Yet by the use of busing and other methods, we've made real progress in dismantling a dual school system of public schools in Florida. . . . Until we can find alternative ways of proving an equal educational opportunity for all . . . until we can be sure than an end to busing will not lead to a return to segregated schools . . . we must not unduly limit ourselves. . . . I would really hope that we can all work together to find ways other than busing to guarantee that no one in this country is denied an equal opportunity to grow and develop in a non-segregated society.[29]

Askew expressed the hope that, by leading the way in school desegregation, through busing where it was necessary, "the people of the South are not merely going to join the Union. They're going to be faced with the opportunity—perhaps even the responsibility to lead it."[30]

In the same vein, consider the words of Wilson Riles, who also ran in 1970, but in California for the statewide office of superintendent of public instruction against his former boss, the nationally known incumbent and conservative firebrand Max Rafferty. The contest was already seen as historic because the low-key and soft-spoken Riles was black. As he began his fall campaign, Riles garnered national attention in his race against Rafferty by testifying before the Senate Select Committee on Equal Educational Opportunity about innovative strategies to achieve greater integration in the schools. Riles advocated moving decisively forward by appealing to the self-interest of child-centered parents who "visualize that [their children] will go to Yale, Harvard or Princeton. . . . I would make [inner-city schools] such fine schools . . . that no one would dare move away. . . . I know that middle-class people, regardless of color, want their children in fine schools and if you can put a little edge on that when they know they are getting the best, then you can cut down on this transition and tipping."[31]

These educational arrangements have come to be known as "magnet schools" and are squarely within the tradition of American social provision in which the small help given to the "have-nots" is legitimized by giving even more resources to those who are already "haves." Those who fought to implement *Brown v. Board* to the fullest extent possible were seeking, in the words of Alan David Freeman, "change in [the] practical conditions" in which black students (and, presumably, also their teachers) required the historically favored whites assume an "over burden" to achieve equality in substance—that historically black schools be the beneficiaries of substantial new resources and that white students be the ones taking the first steps into new schools and classrooms in which they might, perhaps for the first time, be in the minority.

It must be said that to bring such plans effectively into being would have required a mobilization of resources and social commitment unprecedented in American history. In the actual circumstances of the Second Reconstruction, such plans were as impossible as a systematic plan of land redistribution had been in the first. To press forward down this freedom road would have led "to hostility and instability which only coercive force can contain."[32] At that precise moment this "new world" democracy begins to act very much like an embattled bound regime of the "old world."

If we are really to reckon with meeting the high cost—in tangible resources such as highly trained people with years of experience—how do we explain the closure of historically black schools and the firing of many of their teachers and administrators (often on the grounds that they were now not properly or insufficiently credentialed)?[33] According to legal scholar Derrick Bell, embedded in the logic of the NAACP's litigation in the Age of *Brown* was the assumption that "blacks must gain access to white schools because 'equal educational opportunity' means integrated schools and only school integration will make certain that black children receive the same education as white children." There is finally a deeper question, rooted in class and reinforced by institutional racism: Does the education of some children—those whose parents want them to go to college—matter more than that of others who do not? "In the course of seeking racial balance," Bell asserts, there is "all too little attention to making black schools educationally effective."[34]

The coming together of white and black in the Second Reconstruction remained what it had been in the First Reconstruction, a coming together of two parties, one with significantly more power than the other: whites who, as a group, retained power and advantage, and blacks who, as a group, accepted an equalization of educational opportunity whose terms and conditions were determined by others. Understanding why this is so requires that we look back to before the First Reconstruction.

ANOTHER LINCOLN-DOUGLASS DEBATE

Generally, when Americans speak of the "Lincoln Douglass Debates" they are referring to the political argument between two white men—Abraham Lincoln and Stephen A. Douglas—seeking in 1858 to represent their home state of Illinois in the U.S. Senate. Here I present the early years of a debate between Lincoln and the antebellum black political establishment (represented most famously by the abolitionist leader Frederick Douglass). Looking back to this discourse exposes the roots of a continuing difference in answering a central question of modernity: what does the phrase "public education" require of the rest of us?[35]

If Douglass and Lincoln shared the nineteenth-century reformers' simple faith in the transforming power of suffrage and a deeply held sense of how slavery undercut every virtue of human civilization, Douglass and the free people for whom he spoke most cogently looked past the unavoidable starkness of slavery to the ways in which the social atmosphere, even where slavery was entirely absent, was inimical to creating a biracial society and republic. Only as an advocate for the removal of African Americans from the United States did Lincoln address the high level of unremitting white hatred of black Americans, whether free or enslaved. And his message was a simple one: "It is better for us both . . . to be separated."[36]

When Abraham Lincoln looked out upon the social mechanics of his nation, he saw a society of free white men working in harmony with a beautifully self-governing machine. Looking back on the lessons taught him by experience, Lincoln saw the following life cycle naturally at work: "A young man finds himself of an age to be dismissed from parental control; he has nothing for his capital save two strong hands that God has given him, a heart willing to labor, and a freedom to choose his own mode of work and the manner of his employer; he has got no soil nor shop, and he avails himself of the opportunity of hiring himself to some man who has capital to pay him a fair day's wage for a fair day's work. . . . He works industriously, he behaves soberly, and as a result of a year or two's labor is a surplus capital. Now he buys his own hook; he settles, he marries, begets sons and daughters, and in the course of time, he too has enough capital to hire some new beginner."[37]

As a candidate for the Illinois state legislature in 1832, Lincoln echoed an already venerable theme of American political culture when he said, "[Education is] the most important subject which we as a people can be engaged in. That every man may receive at least a moderate education, and thereby be able to read the histories of his own and other countries, by which he might duly appreciate the value of free institutions appears to be an object of vital importance even on this account alone, to say nothing of the advantages and satisfaction to be derived from all being able to read the scriptures and other works. . . . For my part, I desire to see the time when education, and by its means, morality, sobriety, enterprise and industry, shall become more general than at present."[38]

Those words faithfully reflected both the expert knowledge and the common sense of those days. Education, as John Dewey would later remind twentieth-century educators, was primarily gained and confirmed through work. In the nineteenth century, and for much of the first half of the next, education was not, for the great majority of Americans, a stand-alone obligation—it competed with (and often lost out to) helping one's family earn its living. Throughout his life, Abraham Lincoln embodied the truth of this time: that the rudiments of rising to a new station in life required little formal schooling beyond "*readin,' writin,' and cipherin'* [*sic*]. . . . If a straggler supposed to understand latin [*sic*], happened to sojourn in the neighborhood, he was," Lincoln remembered, "looked upon as a wizzard [*sic*]" (emphasis in original).[39]

Free blacks who attempted to speak to this "whites only" nation had a message which both strove to demonstrate solidarity with some reigning national values while underlining the fact of a sharp, painful, and persistent difference in how American society and its institutions regarded them and acted upon them. First, like white Americans, free blacks spoke ardently in favor of labor as socially sacred work. A resolution passed by "colored freedmen of Pennsylvania" declared: "Labor is the natural source of wealth, and is not only right in the sight of God, but honorable in the eyes of all good men."[40]

That offering of agreement with a key cultural value did not obscure for those there assembled the existence of a deep difference in life experiences and social prospects between whites and blacks. As historian John Ernst has demonstrated, the free blacks of the nineteenth-century convention movement well understood that they would achieve very little if they simply imitated white models and repeated their pieties. These members of "an imagined nation within a fallen nation . . . faced fundamentally different obstacles" from white Americans of similar economic background and education. The work of schools and churches was meant to accomplish more than individual salvation or social rise, but instead "broad scale social change."[41]

Education, fully understood and appreciated, was fundamentally a matter of skills learned in the context of values essential to life within a thriving community founded on a shared kinship in the human race. For Wm. R. Topp, S. Myers, and E. N. Hall, the three members of the Committee on Education of the "State Convention of the Colored People" of New York State, gathered in Albany in the summer of 1851, the liberating potential of education (broadly conceived) was clear to all who wished to see it: "Education . . . properly understood has to do with all the laws and principles that regulate our progress in this life, and only answers its legitimate duty when it seeks to elevate, to liberalize, to Christianize. To this end it gives its subjects a clearer vision and a greater power to bring out hidden virtues and to combat those errors and prejudices that only live as they are able to pervert men's minds and to make them low and groveling."[42]

Such insight had been painfully won through a harsh experience in American society and culture:

> These truths are clearly seen in the facts that surround us on every side, in the great struggle now being waged between the oppressor and the oppressed. In the community about us, we are realizing daily the bitter evidence, that an education given in a one-sided direction and continued for a series of years from father to child, grows up into a system all powerful in the accomplishment of its ends, and subduing to its aims well nigh every mind that receives it. Dictated by the self-love that delights to claim superiority and exercise its rule, we see the social and school education of the land fattening [*sic*] upon the hideous error that God has created a noble and an ignoble race, and that by virtue of this he has given a right to the strong to tyrannize the weak—to load his body with chains and shut him up from the revelations of light and love guaranteed to him in the very ground work of his being."[43]

This mission of cultural education was understood to be a responsibility borne by the tax-paying public. As J. H. Townsend, a delegate from San Francisco, told a large gathering in Sacramento, California, six years after statehood, the first plank of any program for education must begin with securing "the removal from the Statute Book of the law which deprives our children of common schooling, and get them into Common Schools."[44]

Achieving this goal left an even bigger struggle ahead. As an editorial (published simultaneously in Douglass's newspaper, the *North Star,* and in the *National Anti-Slavery Standard* on September 5, 1850) warned the escaping slave looking for sanctuary and a new start in life: "Send not your children to the schools which the malignant and murderous prejudice of white people has gotten up exclusively for colored people. As valuable as learning is, it is too costly if it is acquired at the expense of such self-degradation."[45]

The records of the African American convention movement convey a subtle understanding not only of the social and political necessity of education, but also of the way it can be misdirected to institutionally reinforce inequality and prejudice. Long before words such as "stereotype" and phrases such as "inferiority complex" first entered the lexicon of twentieth-century social science and then moved out into popular culture, the findings quoted here anticipate much of what progressive social scientists would have to say in the twentieth century about the role of culture as a weapon of the strong in the confinement of the weak.

In the end, as we remember Mr. Lincoln's expressed belief in the incorrigible nature of the separateness between blacks and whites, we are left to puzzle and to guess over the extent of his own capacity to learn from his experiences within the "school affliction" of which Lincoln, as president, was the headmaster. Had Lincoln lived, how would the final and most tangible symbols of his hope for the future—the Thirteenth, Fourteenth and Fifteenth amendments—have been made to fit within this national culture? As things turned out, we do know this much with considerable certainty: Americans living in 1965 or 2015 would have no trouble recognizing the crisis of their times either in the words above, or in the words that follow, uttered by Mr. Douglass back in 1865: "What relation shall this five million of people sustain to the American Government and to the American people? What condition shall they hold? What condition shall they occupy? Shall it be one of elevation or degradation? Shall they be made a blessing to American people and to this country, or a curse, a blot? Shall their influence be beneficial or malignant? It is with the American people to say. It is now their opportunity to decide."[46]

In the final analysis, the struggle over strengthening the egalitarian promise of public education after the Second World War had an impact on politics in the 1960s and 1970s much like that ascribed to the Civil War by Frederick Douglass: it was both a necessary and "salutary struggle" which became for many participants also a "school of affliction"—the source of much disappointment. Looking back on those struggles from the vantage point of this century, it is remarkable how little has changed. As George Lipsitz, an important pioneer in the field of cultural studies, forcefully reminds us, we remain a society organized and structured around a rigid and thoroughly institutionalized racial hierarchy:

> People of different races in the United States are relegated to different physical locations by housing and lending discrimination, by school district boundaries, by policing practices, by zoning regulations, and by the design of transit systems. The racial demography of where people live, work, play, shop, and travel exposes them to a socially-shared system of exclusion and inclusion. Race serves as a key variable in determining who has the ability to own homes that appreciate in value and can be passed down to subsequent generations; in deciding which children have access to education by credentialed teachers in safe buildings with adequate equipment; and in shaping differential exposure to polluted, air, water, food and land.[47]

Lipsitz's stark account of the continued entrenchment of inequality at every point in American life enables us to more clearly see the Age of *Brown* as a historical reenactment following a familiar script. If we focus too much on the gross statistics of social and economic change, we are likely to miss the way in which the order of things has not changed much between the Age of Lincoln and the Age of *Brown*. As the first entry of *Star Trek* into American popular culture reaches its fiftieth anniversary, we must reckon with how far we are from the egalitarian cosmopolitanism epitomized in its many "generations": the reality on the ground, in the aftermath of the murder of Trayvon Martin, is that "space is the final frontier."[48]

THE FIELD OF RE-ENACTMENT IN THE AGE OF *BROWN*

That concentrated and centralized power is dangerous, and that governmental authority should be reserved to those closest to receiving its direct impact, are two ideas closely linked and deeply revered in the American political tradition—this intellectual combination has well served dissenters across the ideological spectrum. This belief in "localism" is an intimate part of the American "imagined community" of democracy in its most idyllic expression—think of the New England town meeting as represented on canvas by Norman Rockwell.

Taking her inspiration from political scientist Benedict Anderson's assumption that, at the intellectual and emotional center of modern nationalism is an idealization of community life, an "imagined community," Deidre Cobb-Roberts asks us to apply this concept to the politics of American public education. We see the school as both a neighborhood and a neighborly institution "where children, teachers and parents gather with a shared sense of purpose." When we subject this "first glance" to closer examination, we are forced to recognize that, at the core of where we would like to find consensus, we inevitably also find sources of discord. As the social history of the United States over last sixty years has taught Americans (as if for the first time), schools do not "always work as the communities we often imagine them to be."[49] The consequences of intervening in local school affairs have been especially magnified in the American case by the very close linkage between that place where most people have made their most significant long-term capital investment (their home) and the attendance zones which formally open the doors of local public schools to the surrounding residents.[50] Thus, whether we look back to the Age of *Brown* or look around this age of "No Child Left Behind," we not only *know* but we readily and immediately *feel* the heat of the continuing debate over what is the "proper community of a school."[51]

This long tradition of local control—this sense that local communities owned and possessed the public schools in their neighborhoods has sometimes supported reform, as illustrated by the career of Marcus Foster. Here, however, it is important to remind ourselves of a more familiar history—how deference to local majorities made desegregation difficult to initiate, much less to sustain over time. The federal district judges vested in 1955 with implementing *Brown v. Board* worked within the same system, which governed the lives of Frederick Douglass, Abraham Lincoln, and other Americans in the nineteenth century. Even in wartime, Lincoln discovered something that political scientist Gary Orfield summarized a century later in the Age of *Brown*: "federal officials were 'without the strength to successfully dominate' and thus, had no choice but to come to terms with local centers of power."[52] As war gave way to Reconstruction, the same equation was in force.

American college students, when they read about post-Civil War Reconstruction, learn how fleeting strong federal intervention was and how the southern old guard was able to return to power within a relatively few years. In the Second Reconstruction, which was announced in the 1950s but not really attempted until the 1970s, a similar survival of the old guard occurred. As Orfield pointed out in 1969, the institutional arrangements of the federal system insured that any change would be slow and grudging. Whether by inaction or through the details of implementation, the preeminence of certain powerful locals was accommodated by the judicial process. The "crucial responsibility" of seeing this Second Reconstruction through was placed "on the shoulders of . . . men who were very much a part of a region where eighty percent of fellow whites opposed the Supreme Court's decision." More than this, these judges had not so long ago "been active in the community and political life of their states."[53]

Confirming the importance of making preemptive peace with powerful locals, historian Tony A. Freyer has found that the nine justices, despite the unanimity of their vote to overrule *Plessy*, harbored reservations about how much compliance they could expect. According to Freyer, "Publically the court ascribed its flexible standards to the enormous difficulties inherent in enforcing uniformity across hundreds of local school boards. Privately, however, the justices expressed concerns that local resistance could result from requiring immediate desegregation."[54] In practical terms, this led to a "locally centered compliance process [that] enabled both Arkansas governor Orval Faubus and the Eisenhower administration to eschew enforcement responsibility. Only a federal district court decision against the school board or public disorder precipitating intervention by state and/or federal chief executives could upset the balance of diffused authority."[55]

In 1865, President Lincoln, in language that was both richly imaginative while also leaving much to the imagination and the initiative of others, announced the First Reconstruction with these words: "With malice toward none, with charity for all; with firmness in the right as God gives us to see the right, let us strive on to continue the work we are in, to bind up the nation's wounds, to care for him who have borne the battle, and for his widow and his orphan—to do all which may achieve a just and lasting peace, among ourselves, and with all nations."[56]

Ninety years later, Chief Justice Earl Warren, in similarly cautious words, elaborated ever so sparingly on a decision of the previous year, which had announced a return to "the work we are in." In this time and place in American history, the public school was at center stage, positioned to both lead and follow in a movement away from a formal regime of racial separation spelled out in many cases by legislative enactments and, in every case, backed by some degree of popular and elite sentiment: "The judgments below . . . are accordingly reversed, and the cases are remanded to the district courts to take such proceedings and enter such orders and decrees consistent with this opinion as are necessary to admit to public schools on a racially nondiscriminatory basis with all deliberate speed the parties to these cases."[57]

These announcements of renewed civic purpose are unified across the years by their careful accommodation of deep divisions in the territory, making the transformation of this surviving past into a new frontier of possibilities difficult but not impossible. These were not calls to cultural transformation, much less political revolution; they were instead injunctions to completing the fuzzily defined yet necessary work of what social scientists used to call "political modernization." Both Lincoln and Warren are advocating change within a seemingly loose-fitting constitutional framework that, as the price of its textual economy, cannot easily be modified. Each of these cautiously tendered injunctions to change had only the moral power of argument behind them, which would mobilize armies of people who had been working for opposing social visions, one having more strength, especially in the nineteenth and in the first half of the twentieth century. These are, in fact, efforts to manage or contain the consequences of a change that Lincoln and Warren did not initiate and for which their support was mixed with unease about the "school of affliction" that lay ahead for their country.

The questions abound; in Lincoln's time: What, beyond the treatment of wounded human bodies, was to be the national work to which Lincoln alluded? How was a severely wounded body politic to be healed? What did it require of each of us and of all of us? In Warren's time: What exactly did the Supreme Court expect to achieve with "all deliberate speed?"

How jurists, attorneys, parents, and school board members in various cities and towns answered that and other related questions is the largest part of the historical record created by *Brown v. Board*. Beyond this record is something very important but more difficult to establish; how did *Brown v. Board* strike the rest of the citizenry, especially those Americans coming of age in the world to which the Supreme Court spoke? The work of Robert Coles will enable us to have a very close look at some of the children who were at the very center of this national drama.

But what about those young Americans whose leadership became more publically visible and recognized in adulthood? The evidence—admittedly fragmentary—is that *Brown* was well remembered in the clash between the civics-book picture of American institutions and a more complicated and sordid reality. Sara Lawrence Lightfoot, who has become a leading educational theorist, was ten years old when *Brown II* was announced on May 17, 1954. For Lightfoot and her family, who lived in the North, that first decision confirmed the validity of a public promise that was finally being kept: "The evening news reported the uncompromising, strong words of the Supreme Court justices that segregation in schools was illegal, unjust and wrong. Jubilation, optimism and hope filled my home. Through a child's eyes, I could see the veil of oppression lift from my parents' shoulders. It seemed they were standing taller. And for the first time in my life, I saw tears in my father's eyes. 'This is a great and important day,' he said reverently to his children. . . . I truly believed at that moment, that my black brothers and sisters in Southern schools would now have an equal chance, taste the sweetness of the American pie, and learn to value their black skin, their history and their children."[58]

It did not take long for Sara Lawrence to be schooled by the actual practices of her society; "clarity and decisiveness" were replaced by the "messiness, ambiguities, and complexities" that arose with the announcement of *Brown II* on May 30, 1955, and the spirit of defiance—politically sanctioned lawlessness—which met the prospect of actual enforcement. Back at her white-majority school, young Sarah Lawrence still had to contend with the "subtle exclusion and micro-aggressions that [she] experienced daily in [her] all-white Northern middle-class school."[59]

In Pike County, Alabama, a somewhat older John Lewis received the news of *Brown* at the end of his freshman year of high school. His expectations were high but more readily described: "Everything was going to change now. No longer would I have to ride a broken down bus almost forty miles to attend classes at a 'training' school with hand-me-down book and supplies. Come Fall I'd be riding a state-of-the-art bus to a state-of-the–art school, an integrated school."[60]

Instead of acting on these expectations, the state's political establishment joined others in "derisively referring to the day of that Supreme Court decision as Black Monday and making clear that they had no intention of obeying the ruling." A lifetime of experience with racial segregation also tempered the reaction of Lewis's parents. "My parents," Lewis wrote in his autobiography, "despite their enthusiasm about the Supreme Court ruling, were disapproving of people trying to push things, no matter how justified the cause. Right or wrong didn't matter to them as much as reality. . . . We heard stories all the time about black men being arrested . . . for one offense or another and being physically manhandled, even beaten. As far as my parents were concerned, anyone who was arrested for any reason was 'riffraff,' and that was that. 'Decent' black folks stayed out of trouble. It was that simple."[61] Like ten-year-old Sara Lawrence, fourteen-year-old John Lewis was about to get schooled by his culture and its people. The bottom-line lesson was simple: John Lewis never rode in the new school bus or attended the more modern racially integrated school that he had understood as the promise implied in the court's ruling. In reality, "nothing in my life had changed."[62]

Brown v. Board was so important a symbol that it even provided the lens through which many Americans interpreted the meaning of the murder of Emmett Till. As historian Stephen Whitfield found, if the date of the first ruling in *Brown* became "Black Monday" for many white southerners, especially those enrolled in or allied with the Citizens' Council movement founded to defy the high court, the acquittal of Till's killers on September 23, 1955, became "Black Friday" for those who supported the court's action. The death of Till also awakened a generation of southern black youths, close in age to Till, to the need for more militant action against the Jim Crow social order.[63]

Historian Tomiko Brown-Nagin has beautifully described the connection between the failure of effective follow through on *Brown*, the importance of Till's murder as a symbol of the depth of individual and institutional white resistance to equality, and the rise of student protest for "Equality Now!": "Using the streets as their courtroom, the public as their jury, and the liberal and alternative media as their judges, the students demanded an end to Jim Crow in every facet of life."[64] It would be nearly another decade before other events in Mississippi—the Freedom Summers of 1964 and 1965—would have a similar impact among the same generation of white Americans.

To assess the more general cultural impact of *Brown*, think, for instance, about how directly the images of domestic conflict that most represent the postwar years are connected to *Brown v. Board*: Elizabeth Eckford calmly defying a mob of her peers, or of Ruby Bridges being escorted to a New Orleans elementary school by national guardsmen on the first day of the 1960–61 school year—each recalling for us what was at stake in the last great push for reform in the American century. Consider as well another scene: the film of Alabama governor George C. Wallace placing himself symbolically "in the schoolhouse door," thus launching one of the most significant national careers of the later twentieth century. Each of these is fixed in our "collective electronic memory" as the essence what we have gone through together. Each of these images speaks to the impact of *Brown* beyond the courtroom in popular culture itself. None of these images would have been possible had the Supreme Court not acted as it did in 1954.[65]

Think also about the imagery of one of the most important works of fiction of this period—Harper Lee's *To Kill a Mockingbird*. We do not know if Elizabeth Eckford's solitary walk was among the forces that moved Lee to write the novel, but it seems quite probable. We see evidence in that book of a sensibility not too far from the feelings of Sarah Lawrence and John Lewis—children confronting a deep cultural contradiction and deciding not to simply look past it. In one of the most unforgettable scenes in both the novel and the film, Scout's forthright questioning of a lynch mob causes it to dissolve. Scout's warm summons to decency not only dissolved a mob; her intervention forced each of its members to decide whether they wished to become individuals again, each accountable for his actions.[66]

We are thus also led to wonder: did the many readers who picked up the book between its publication in July of 1960 and its general release as a film nearly three years later see any connection between this memory of a 1930s lynch mob and events transpiring in their own time? When readers saw Norman Rockwell's portrait of Ruby Bridges entering Franz Elementary School as its lone black student, did they remember Scout too?

To Kill a Mockingbird, as remarkable a first novel as it is, and as remarkable as its longevity in print and on film is, must be seen as part of a broader cultural ambiance. Frank and fearless accounts of life within American schools were also provided by Jonathan Kozol and Bel Kaufman, to name just a few. If the images created for us by Richard Wright, Walker Evans, and James Agee help us to understand that the New Deal was something far greater to Americans than one man's program of action—but a mood, a temperament, and a frame surrounding a people's historical experiences—then we also owe it to ourselves to look back at how *Brown* became a dynamic inspiration that some people embraced and others rejected.[67]

Finally, let us return to the somewhat more prosaic world of day-to-day electoral politics—not meant for recapture in any history book, not because they are illicit and exciting, but exactly because they are not—they seem indistinguishable from other noise. As far back as the contest between John F. Kennedy and Richard M. Nixon, candidates for president had to opine on how best to provide federal aid to education (as opposed to whether or not it should be provided). The crisis of school finance was so acute by the 1970s that it shaped the political calculations of national leaders. In early 1972, the year of his historic reelection, President Richard M. Nixon gave "the crisis of school finance and property taxes" prized space in the State of the Union Address of 1972, the year of his reelection.[68]

Meanwhile, on the other side of the political aisle, Senator Walter Mondale, a prominent Democrat with presidential ambitions (and also up for reelection in 1972), found himself worrying about the political implications of property taxes. As chair of the Senate Select Committee on Equal Educational Opportunity between 1970 and 1972, Mondale learned firsthand the costs of delving deeply into education reform, especially the mechanics of school desegregation. As his reelection campaign geared up, Mondale instructed his staff to stay away from any discussion of property taxes in the committee's final report: "I don't want to come out with a report recommending taxes at the local level. . . . I don't want to [raise] property taxes . . . or [to revise] property taxes. It's something we just don't know [about], and, secondly, it would be a hell of a good issue [to use] against me."[69]

NATION BUILDING ON THE HOME-FRONT OF THE COLD WAR UNITED STATES

Whatever Americans think of the Reconstruction of the southern states after the Civil War, we do not have any difficulty in retroactively seeing it as an example of "nation building" in the American homeland. The need to reestablish the union of the states within a legal framework through the Thirteenth, Fourteenth and Fifteenth amendments is easy to see. At the same time, we have yet to fully appreciate that the Age of *Brown* represents another experiment in nation building, this one occurring on the home front of the Cold War United States.

The physical manifestations of material and technological progress make the United States seem to be the epitome of modernity. Indeed, as anthropologist Arturo Escobar has pointed out, the Americans who thought most about nation building looked outward to a postcolonial world whose newest members suffered from "under-development." These social scientists considered its most salient factors and specific requirements as a "technical problem. . . . Instead of seeing change as a process rooted in the interpretation of . . . history and cultural traditions . . . these professionals sought to devise mechanisms and procedures to make societies fit a pre-existing model that embodied the structures and functions of modernity."[70]

Such an approach does not yield much that is unfamiliar, new, or challengingly human, no matter where we are looking. I propose a thought experiment in which we think about what the United States of the 1950s and 1960s would look like if we could look out from the windows of its rural schoolhouses, and the imposing brick and stone structures of its urban schools, and from the stucco and cement grounds of its growing number of suburban schools. How do the resources and the work in these places stand in relation (developmentally) not only to the nation's official aspirations but to its technological and other material achievements?[71]

The activities within these diverse public settings became central to a larger national discussion of a need to reconstruct and "modernize" this country. The seemingly reflexive need of many Americans to interpret domestic nation building as being the exemplary labor of a people inhabiting a "City on a Hill" makes the fundamental nature of this home-front challenge very difficult to see. Yes, it is true that having a global audience looking in on American society did help to legitimize protest and change, but something was also lost in the overly exuberant celebration of American prowess and advancement by rank-and-file Americans as well as political elites. Perhaps it is far too much to ask of any proud polity to, for a sustained period, look past pride in itself to see struggles shared with others. Nonetheless, in our lack of capacity to see ourselves as struggling beside other peoples to solve essential problems, we have lost something of high potential value.

Within this context, Coles, Cosby, and Cooney can be thought of as "modernizers" who seek to bring new tools, ideas, and technologies to bear in an effort to close a racial divide between Americans that, more than a century after the Civil War and Reconstruction, remained deep and wide. I recognize that, by using the term "modernizers," I am taking a problematic and outmoded piece of equipment from the kit of the American social scientist and working as a participant observer—and occasionally an active architectural consultant—in the nation building of people in faraway places.

However, I invoke the term here for the same reason as Kwame Ture (then known as Stokely Carmichael) and Charles V. Hamilton invoked it in their 1967 classic call to arms, *Black Power: The Politics of Liberation in America*: to help Americans realize that their society was not as advanced or as enlightened as the Cold War political culture portrayed. Though Coles, Cosby, and Cooney no doubt disagreed with important parts of the program outlined in *Black Power,* they did concur with the authors that, in the United States, a "modernization of structures" was "essential." At its core, modernization was needed because the base of political participation was far too narrow.[72]

If Coles, Cosby, and Cooney shared some part of their mission with these and other more radical figures, they were themselves reformers. When they first set out on their work in the early 1960s, they shared in key elements of the national consensus of the high Cold War years as identified by sociologist Doug McAdam. According to McAdam, the years prior to the civil rights movement were infused with the sense that Americans "were a 'can-do' people, who accomplished whatever we set out to do. We had licked the Depression, turned the tide in World War II, and rebuilt Europe after the war."[73] And, of course, the initial reaction among major civil rights leaders to *Brown v. Board*—that a milestone had been reached and that desegregation and its fruits were just down the road—is further evidence of this attitude.

Coles (born in 1929), Cosby (1937), and Cooney (1930) shared a national sense of confidence in the soundness and effectiveness of their nation's basic political institutions. Both Coles and Cooney came from the same upper middle class that produced the white college students who spent the summers of 1964 and 1965 in Mississippi. And Robert Coles was directly linked through marriage to the New England abolitionist tradition. Although the life of Bill Cosby is exceptional in many ways, these details should not distract us from how he is connected to the student activists who were only a few years younger than he was.

For all of Cosby's writing and speaking on his family life, this extensive published record yields few details. Cosby, however, does provide enough illumination that we can discern that, like the black students who made up the majority of SNCC's members, he came from the black working class whose fathers, Howard Zinn reminds us, were "for the most part janitors and laborers, their mothers maids and factory workers."[74] And one needs hardly any imagination at all to see William H. Cosby Sr. speaking the words used by a black worker in an East St. Louis meat packing plant, circa 1960, as reported by sociologist Theodore V. Purcell: "I wouldn't want a kid of mine to have a job like this. I'll try to educate 'em. I wouldn't want 'em even to *live* around here. [He laughs.] If I can ever get them through high school . . . and through college—I'll try my best to send 'em on further up. . . . Because anything they can do, I want 'em to do it . . . I'd never want to see any child of mine . . . work here."[75] These words light the road ahead because they indicate that public education had become, for twentieth-century African Americans, what the phrase "forty acres and a mule" represented to their nineteenth-century southern ancestors—the key to fulfilling the promise of upward mobility that drives the ideal of the "American Dream."

As college-trained young Americans venturing out in the early 1960s, Coles, Cosby, and Cooney shared the view of one of the most eminent historians of nationalism, Hans Kohn, that "what Karl Marx regarded as the central issue of modern European history, the struggle of the bourgeoisie against the aristocracy and of the proletariat against the bourgeoisie, has hardly had a counterpart in American reality."[76] They would also accept as a given that the American political system represented the "civic culture" and the "open polity" at their best.[77] And, finally, they started out their own experiments in educating the public with some confidence that sharp conflicts in experience and vision could be ameliorated, for, as two experts of the time reminded their cosmopolitan readers, "generation after generation of the children of immigrants have been socialized with considerable effectiveness into the mainstream of American life."[78]

It is this last placidly moving image—deeply rooted in both American popular culture and accepted expert knowledge—that is most immediately and lastingly shaken up by the political and social turmoil of the 1960s, by the local knowledge that was made national through the work of social activists. At the same time, dissatisfaction with the status quo within their country might well have led Coles, Cosby, and Cooney to at least appreciate words from the young SNCC leader John Lewis, words meant to be spoken at the March on Washington in 1963 but ordered deleted by the senior leadership. As transcribed for us by Howard Zinn, they read as follows: "We all recognize the fact that if any radical social, political and economic changes are to take place in our society, the people, the masses must bring them about. In the struggle we must seek more than civil rights; we must work for the community of love, peace and true brotherhood. Our minds, souls and hearts cannot rest until freedom and justice exist for *all people*" (emphasis in original).[79]

It would please me to affirm that these words were merely "ahead of their time," and that the American polity has collectively weathered enough storms to make these words less jarring to the collective ear. It does sometimes seem that the compass needle of American political culture has moved "left" just enough that they at least are less likely today to "awaken tremors in the pilots [of the civil rights movement] themselves."[80] And yet the reflexive apprehension about thinking about what lies "beyond civil rights," even for simply acknowledging the legitimacy of organizing to question long-accepted economic arrangements, remains deep in the marrow of the body politic.

Fidelity to reality and the ritualized language of this "post–civil rights" era requires that I also remind you that John Lewis, the author of those once-censored words, is, at this writing, the U.S. Representative from Georgia's Fifth District. I am happy to do so, and to acknowledge that this is real progress. Furthermore, he has not either sold himself to others or been co-opted by them.

And yet, the history of the last two generations teaches that the transformation of existing institutions is, to retrofit a metaphor utilized by Warren I. Susman, a pioneering analyst of Depression-era popular culture in the United States, still "not in the cards"—not among the options within which Americans define a "Square Deal," a "New Deal," or a "Fair Deal."[81] The problems addressed by the young John Lewis, and still struggled over by the older man, remain both enduring and threatening, as they were in the time of Douglass and Lincoln.

When Americans were forced by protest and necessity to return to these long-held disagreements, they did so on a new field of conflict. Even as the inequalities that the "forty acres and a mule" doctrine was meant to address continued in force. The new center of struggle—the new "school of affliction"—was over both the meaning and the ways and means of providing "public education."

2

A CULTURE GOES TO SCHOOL

AN INTEGRATIVE REVOLUTION IN A DEVELOPING COUNTRY

> If the general strike is the classic political expression of class warfare, and the coup d'état of the struggle between militarism and parliamentarianism, then the school crisis is becoming the classical political—or para-political—expression of the clash of primordial loyalties.
>
> —CLIFFORD GEERTZ, 1963

> To call that period of struggle a civil war will probably seem like an exaggeration, given how the history of the civil rights movement is typically told. The outcome of events allows us to peddle a softer version of the tale than the origin of those events points to. At the very least . . . large groups of citizens had decided to no longer obey a fair portion of the laws of their states. And citizens on each side of the ethnopolitical divide had difficulty imagining a future together.
>
> —DANIELLE S. ALLEN, 2004.

When anthropologist Clifford Geertz wrote in 1963 that "the school crisis is becoming the classical political—or para-political—expression of the clash of primordial loyalties" about events in post-colonial Indonesia, Pakistan, Nigeria, the Philippines, and Morocco, was he also thinking about the "school crisis" as a symbol of change and conflict in his own homeland? My own investigation into his public writings turned up no tantalizing clues.[1] The more recent reflections of political philosopher Danielle S. Allen on what was at stake in the 1950s and 1960s drive the point home: *Brown v. Board* "began a series of civil wars within each of the former Confederate states."[2] Together, these quotations help to provide a view of postwar American politics—not from the bird's eye afforded us by the Telstar satellite first launched into outer space in 1963, but from the grounds of different American neighborhood schools, as (to use Geertz's language from that same year) "primordial sentiments" rooted in the "gross actualities of blood, race, locality or tradition" conflicted with pressure from both within and without to finish the creation of "a reasonably large, independent, powerful, well ordered polity" with a substantively comprehensive commitment to equal citizenship.[3]

Do these words not apply to the American attempt at an "integrative revolution"? Did not some Americans fear their "domination by some other rival ethnic, racial or linguistic community that is able to imbue with the temper of its own personality?" Do not such fears still divide us?[4]

"AMERICA'S OWN UNDERDEVELOPED AREA"

One of the most important lessons of the Second Reconstruction was that the racism and institutional incapacity that complicated, and in some cases derailed, desegregation were national in origin and character. To open a discussion that is national in scope in the South is only to begin where the conflict between local values and the civic claims was most visible. As some American scholars looked outward at the struggles of new nations, others saw the mid-twentieth-century American South as an underdeveloped area.

Understanding the unique forces that underlay political participation (and a seemingly voluntary withdrawal) on the part of large numbers of Negroes was, political scientists Donald R. Matthews and James W. Prothro wrote in 1965, "almost as demanding (if not nearly so exotic) as to test them in India or Thailand." Matthews and Prothro believed themselves to be among those in their discipline who were "rightly preoccupied with problems of change and 'modernization' in a world desperately in need of both," yet they felt compelled to react against a tendency to "study these phenomena in other cultures and ignore the revolutionary changes that are occurring in America's own 'underdeveloped area.'"[5]

Matthews and Prothro were not alone. The northern students who traveled to Mississippi with the Student Nonviolent Coordinating Committee (SNCC) in the summer of 1964 brought a curriculum that among its many innovations asked whether the South was an underdeveloped country and used this question as point of entry into a unit on the South as a closed society in which federal constitutional guarantees of political membership and participation in it meant very little on this particular American ground.[6]

Like the student workers for SNCC, Matthews and Prothro provided an essential service to the nation by documenting the pragmatic realism and well-justified fear that lay behind the frequent public comment by African Americans that politics is "the white man's business." This belief explained the high number of southern Negroes among Americans who had been erroneously classified by social scientists as "apolitical" in voter surveys taken in the 1950s.[7] As the voting rights revolution unfolded across the South over the next generation, black voters gave redundant evidence through their actions that they had never been apathetic; they had simply known that their participation was unwelcome, and that it could be life-threatening. This record of active engagement not only changed the present but also forced scholars to reexamine what they had quite recently concluded about the state of political integration within the American South.

When political scientists Gabriel Almond and Sidney Verba visited the region in the fall of 1960 as part of the field research for their classic study in comparative politics, *The Civic Culture,* they found what seemed to be a widespread degree of contentment with the American political system. They also found evidence of significant progress in the area of religious toleration. In 1928, Democratic presidential candidate and New York governor Alfred E. Smith met strong opposition in the South because he was a Catholic. A generation later, in 1960, southern voters, especially the youngest, seemed to have little problem defying the advice of their Protestant ministers and voting to elect John F. Kennedy as the first Catholic to serve as president of the United States.[8]

In other respects, Almond and Verba missed the dissatisfaction and restiveness that lay just beneath a deceptively quiet social surface. What they missed was that widespread political disengagement among African Americans, that apathy-concealed "hopelessness and indifference," an unwilling concession to the fact that, "for these Americans, a civic culture had not yet arrived."[9] Of particular relevance is the case of "Mr. F.," an aging African American coal miner in an unnamed southern state (possibly West Virginia or Kentucky).

Mr. F. was classified as an "allegiant subject" who "is relatively satisfied with governmental output, and has no desire for a greater participant role."[10] According to his own testimony, he has "just a little" interest in politics and has never voted because, no matter what actions he takes, "what will be will be, anyway." Mr. F. finds the functioning of local government to be "adequate" to his needs. "He does wish for some improvements in housing and general living conditions" and hopes that the national government under the Democrats might bring some change, but to hope for that kind of help from the local government "would be like daydreaming. I mean, they are not much concerned about the people." As to his own political philosophy, his painful memories of the Great Depression and his gratitude for "Social Security protection" have made him a strong Democrat and a strong opponent of Communism. He is also at pains to report that his life has been good because "'I know my place,' as the old saying goes." He declares that the United States is "a free country" where anyone "can work anywhere and buy what you want with your money."[11]

It is not difficult to see why Almond and Verba classified Mr. F. as an allegiant subject; looking back now with the clear and obvious benefit of fifty years' hindsight, we can perceive something else just a few moments away from seeming to invade the public stage of that time. Mr. F.'s statements confirm him as a public fatalist. However, as Almond and Verba imply, this man placed faith in people and in a world beyond his immediate reach. The nonvoting Mr. F was a daily reader of the newspaper and a consumer of news on both radio and television. He counted himself as a staunch admirer of both Dr. Martin Luther King Jr. and President Dwight Eisenhower. Almond and Verba see Mr. F as someone who chooses "obedience and passivity" in public life while, at home, he "enjoys learning about the outside world."[12]

Perhaps Mr. F.'s comments were expressions of the last years of "racial diplomacy," which, as historians Tomiko Brown-Nagin and Adam Fairclough have observed, was losing its legitimacy among African Americans. This practice required African Americans—from the coal miner to the college president—to publically acknowledge, through their words as well as their physical conduct and demeanor, that racial inequality was the way of the world.[13]

ANTIQUATED SYSTEMS OUTSIDE THE SOUTH

It is easy from this evidence to decide that the South was cordoned off from the rest of the nation as less "developed" than the rest of the United States. The choice of many southern leaders to engage in varieties of very public resistance reinforces this inclination. Nonetheless, it is now possible to avoid this too-well-traveled path and instead pursue another route. Obscured by the political exhibitionism of a George Wallace, a Ross Barnett, or an Orville Faubus in the face of an "integrative revolution" is the more nationally salient fact that the school systems of the United States were still relatively young (or underdeveloped) as compulsory and thus universal institutions.

There is no question that the local systems of public education established in the nineteenth century did provide an unprecedented number of Americans with literacy. Over the next century, the speed of technological change accelerated, further raising educational requirements for upward mobility. While the United States still shared with other much newer nations serious and fundamental challenges in its national development, the systems that were in place were unable to accomplish something quite basic: to ensure that every school met minimums standards for the safety and habitability of its physical plant.[14]

The degree to which the modernization of the United States was also held back by antiquated systems outside the South has not been given the weight it deserves. In Detroit, a major city of American technological and cultural modernity, the school and the political systems intersected in the millage or property tax election. Between the late 1940s and the late 1960s, the city of Detroit lost 350,000 residents to the surrounding suburbs while its schools gained 65,000 students, many of them poor African Americans.[15] As young families left the city for the suburbs, the tax base to support city schools went with them. This "white flight" caused property taxes to rise precipitously, encouraging further departures and a continuing annual erosion of the city's tax base. In 1970, with white flight entering its third decade, the city received $700,000 less in revenue than it had been receiving fifteen years earlier, while its costs had greatly increased.[16]

In the 1968–69 academic year, the Detroit school tax was the lowest among the twenty communities surrounding it, perhaps in response to outmigration;[17] yet the tax assessed to pay the cost of city services was, by far, the highest in the same group, creating a heavy additional "overburden" to be borne by property tax payers.[18] This overburden led to increased voter opposition to raising property taxes or approving school bonds. Between 1957 and 1968, Detroit voters turned down four of seven efforts to raise more money through higher property taxes.[19]

As we think about those factors which effectively close a political system to large numbers of its own registered voters, let us also take account of the hurdles the political system placed in the way of a much-needed increase in resources. First, although only a simple majority was needed to raise the tax, the right to vote in this part of the election was restricted to property owners.[20] In addition, the mechanics of voting were so complex that large numbers of voters in the most economically hard-pressed neighborhoods registered blank votes. In 1968, with a high presidential-year turnout of 78.8 percent, fully 32.3 percent of the votes cast citywide in the millage election were blank, eclipsed only marginally by the 37.5 percent of eligible voters who elected to raise the millage or property tax rate.[21] The reasons for voter disenfranchisement differed between Detroit and the states of the Deep South, but the practical result was the same: whether created by a racial bias in the election system or an unstated institutional bias against the participation of the poor in Detroit, these systems were in need of fundamental repair.

This example from a major city in the industrial North highlights a more general fact well before some communities had to address a mandate to desegregate: Many local educational systems were already being severely tested. Now that school was no longer an optional affair, the question was what to do with all these people, of whatever race or ethnicity, who had been judged uneducable. The increasing requirement for compulsory school attendance was creating a "cold war between students and teachers," complete with an iron curtain of class conflict and cultural difference.[22] There were also many unexpected consequences of bringing so many adolescents together in one place. Until the publication of sociologist James S. Coleman's intensive study of the American high school, few people considered the degree to which students would create their own social world and that the social priorities of this world would coexist and often compete with the school's formal academic mission.[23]

According to Charles G. Spiegler, principal of the Food Trades Vocational High School in New York City, these students required that middle-class, college-educated teachers look past their own preconceptions about the impossibility of reaching "children born into homes at [the] cultural ebb tide . . . where the bedtime story has rarely been heard . . . where the television set has replaced the reading lamp . . . the talk is on 'who's gonna win the fight tonight.'"[24]

Increasing numbers of students did require more money, and even during the boom years of the 1960s, American schools were struggling to meet the needs of the increasing numbers of students. In 1961, for example, American public schools served 1.5 million students more than could be accommodated in classrooms if each were capped at thirty students. So crowded were some local school systems in the peak years of the baby boom that five million students across the nation were forced to attend school in "curtailed sessions."[25]

At the same time, well before the tax revolt of the late 1970s, groups of angry taxpayers—from Levittown, New York, to Los Angeles—showed their determination to keep the schools not only on a short financial tether but on a shorter political one as well, with a narrower educational and cultural mission than envisioned by some educators.[26] Long before the Tea Party movement of the Obama years, prominent conservatives such as California State School Superintendant Max Rafferty had to push back against the reflexive tendency among some of their most devoted followers to say "we may not be able to hog tie [President] Lyndon [Johnson], but we can sure hog tie our own school board." Rafferty confessed that, in his "old hometown of Los Angeles, this sort of shortsightedness" led to severe overcrowding.[27]

These comments by Rafferty are especially illuminating when placed beside sociologist Clarence Y. H. Lo's close examination of anti–property tax campaigns in Los Angeles before the passage of Proposition 13 by California voters in June of 1978. Much of the current thinking about California between the 1940s and the early 1960s emphasizes the positive attributes of a rising economic tide and dramatic increases in suburban populations. Major attention has been paid here and elsewhere to what happens to cities such as Detroit when their populations (and the tax revenues they contribute) fall off exponentially over a relatively few years.

Very little attention has been paid to the "fiscal overburden" that was created when the needs created by growth outstripped the ability of working-class and middle-class homeowners to pay, especially when their tax bill was tied to the steeply rising value of their homes. Between 1949 and 1958, property taxes rose by 126 percent in Los Angeles County and rose again by 71 percent by 1968 and again by 65 percent by 1978. As Lo demonstrates quite convincingly, these increases provoked popular anger.[28]

The mobilizations before Proposition 13 were ignored by the elected leaders of Los Angeles County government because these activists did not have the means of more affluent homeowners to spend large amounts of time on political organizing and protest. It is also worth noting that the solutions advocated by these leaders aimed to preserve a system which had favored the small homeowners over large businesses and commercial developers.[29]

Only when the taxing system was made more systematic by computerization did high-income homeowners begin to feel a financial burden comparable to that felt earlier by less wealthy and less politically connected homeowners. It was the activation of this high-income group in the mid-1970s that, according to Lo, finally created "the white brigade that had the energy and commitment to contact neighbors, gather signatures and attend protest meetings."[30] These efforts propelled a very regressive reform forward with broad support because, for working-class and middle-class voters, it was the one most immediate and reliable form of relief available from what had become a general crisis.

NATION BUILDING IN AMERICAN SCHOOLS OF THE 1960S AND 1970S

As academics, social critics, and other cultural contributors surveyed the American scene in the generation after World War II, what they discovered on a close inspection often alarmed them. Well before the launch of a Soviet satellite in late 1957 added a well-known chapter to the twentieth-century (and now twenty-first-century) trend of episodic panic over the quality of public schools within an economy and a culture that are also seen to be in decline, if not in crisis, the early returns on the first generation of systematic education research suggested some weakness in the foundations of the common American school experience. Whether it was being able to read, successfully mastering the basics of math and science, or even reciting and understanding the Pledge of Allegiance as their country prepared to go to war against Nazi fascism, American students and teachers seemed to be missing some key ingredients beyond an ever-present shortage of basic funding.[31]

The pioneering educational ethnographies produced by Jules Henry, John U. Ogbu, and Ray C. Rist found school systems engaged in the domestic equivalent of the "containment" that was a centerpiece of Cold War foreign policy. American schools were quite good at teaching the "unwritten rules" of American life, which stressed competition and conformity. If students could be labeled early as either "problems" or "stars" based on scanty and impressionistic evidence, the systems of the classroom, the school, and the district often ensured that they were. Schools often sanctioned and rewarded a fierce competition among students for the approval of authorities. Models of learning that emphasized exploration and cooperation were nowhere to be found.[32]

In the larger political culture, a roughly similar case was being made, and judging by the book sales garnered by its best-known participants, it was reaching a large public audience. If the photographs taken for the Farm Security Administration during the New Deal, accompanied by the words of social critic James Agee, represent the discovery of injustice and human struggle during the Great Depression, the literary vehicle for continuing this conversation during the 1960s and 1970s was the teacher memoir. Best-selling examples such as Bel Kaufman's documentary novel, *Up the Down Staircase,* Jonathan Kozol's *Death at an Early Age,* and Herbert Kohl's 36 *Children* each sent similar messages of school systems that had given up on many students on the basis of scanty evidence.[33] John Holt, one of the most widely read and insistently provocative educational writers in those years, offered a most disturbing suggestion. Whether schools had sufficient resources or not was one problem. Another major problem in classrooms of all kinds was that

> What goes on in class is not what teachers think. . . . Those who most needed to pay attention, usually paid the least. The kids who knew the answer to whatever you were asking wanted to make sure that you knew they knew, so their hands were always waving. Also, knowing the right answer, they were in a full position to enjoy the ridiculous answers that might be given by their less fortunate colleagues. . . . What of the unsuccessful majority? Their attention depended on what was going on in class. Any raising of the emotional temper made them prick up their ears. If an argument was going on, or someone was in trouble, or someone was being laughed at for a foolish answer, they took notice. . . . But most of the time, when explaining or questioning, or discussing what was going on, the majority of children paid little attention or none at all. Some daydreamed and no amount of calling them back to earth with a crash . . . could break them out of the habit. Others wrote and passed notes, or whispered, or held conversations in sign language, or made doodles or pictures on their papers or desks, or fiddled with objects.[34]

At the same time that a federal report mandated by Section 402 of the Civil Rights Act of 1964 asserted, upon a surprisingly cursory and superficial examination, that financial disparities between schools and regions were not as great as had been believed, and that such conditions did not have as direct an impact on student performance as was once confidently believed.[35] To make their crucial qualitative comparison of school facilities, the final report by James S. Coleman and his several teams of researchers "merely presents the information derived from questionnaires completed by principals and teachers regarding the facilities, special services, curriculums, programs for exceptional children, pupil evaluation methods, and extracurricular activities available in their schools."[36]

While this kind of data collection is an indispensible first step in a complex multistage effort, it is easy to see how such self-reporting might lead to very self-serving responses from local school officials. It is difficult to disagree with the conclusion reached by Eric A. Hanushek and John F. Kain that "the absence of questions with any qualitative bite is particularly noticeable. There are many questions that relate to the presence of particular attributes, but few that relate to their quality."[37]

When viewed beside the most intellectually lasting educational research of the postwar years—including James S. Coleman's own innovative study of "adolescent society"—it is hard to shake the feeling that the authors of this report on the most urgent of issues, subjected to the tightest of deadlines and to the closest inspection by opposing political forces, could not go as deeply as the actual conditions in individual cities, districts, and classrooms warranted.

FREEDOM SCHOOL DAYS

"Freedom Summer" has an honored yet fleeting place in the popular memory of the civil rights years. It deserves to be recognized as a key moment in Cold War–era nation building on the American homefront. Beyond this, it is one of the most important chapters in the history of American education and pedagogical theory.[38]

In 1964 the students who went south to Mississippi to start Freedom Schools were engaged in the political work most essential to a thoroughgoing Second Reconstruction of the South, picking up where the nineteenth-century abolitionists had stopped. As one Stanford University volunteer with the American Friends Service Committee said, "In the long run, we want to make their entry into the schools easier . . . so that the kind of relationships that can be built up in the [desegregated] white school between the white and Negro children can be normal, easy, relaxed relationships. We're trying to produce the kind of integrated society that we hope for."[39]

Some consideration of the Freedom School movement is required because the southern chapter whose memory has from the beginning been so well tended is part of a larger, national story that was overlooked by the national press at the time. As Judith C. Hudson and Daniel Peter Hinman-Smith have documented, Freedom Schools also existed outside the South. School-centered civil rights protests led to student walkouts and the establishment of alternative Freedom Schools in several cities in the East and Midwest.[40]

One of the strengths of using the analytic tool of historical reenactment to evaluate the work of the Second Reconstruction is that it helps us to see the work of Freedom summer even more vividly. Howard Zinn began the process in 1964, when he explicitly cast the activists of SNCC as the "new abolitionists." In Zinn's account, they were, to borrow the language of Madison Avenue, the "new and improved" abolitionists. First, there were more of them: "In the most heated days of abolitionism, there were never that many dedicated people who turned their backs on ordinary pursuits and gave their lives to the movement."[41] And the majority of these new abolitionists "come from the ranks of the victims, not just because they are mostly Negroes, but because for the most part their fathers are janitors and laborers, their mothers maids and factory workers."[42] With this kind of leadership, the prospects of achieving a deeper social transformation of the nation were much improved.

Extending the reenactment metaphor to the white volunteers from the elite colleges and universities outside the South complicates things in useful ways. The northern volunteers, like their nineteenth-century predecessors, were, in the most formal sense, highly educated. Living in the South, sometimes with black families, deepened an understanding of poverty that had previously gone no further than reading Michael Harrington's *The Other America*.[43] Many of these volunteers lived with black families and at least began to see racism through the eyes of black Americans, including the reality of their own "whiteness." They also gained a more complex understanding of the political dynamics within their own country. They discovered that many blacks had an intimate knowledge of how the political system really worked and thus were more circumspect in their expectations of what activism could accomplish.[44]

These new abolitionists did share something very important with the abolitionists of old: an unusual degree of social advantage. As Doug McAdam points out, this cadre of freedom fighters, if they were not quite as economically comfortable as the abolitionists of old, were, by and large, the children of an old-money elite. These young Americans came from families whose median income was 50 percent above the nation's median family income. As especially fortunate and favored members of their generation, these abolitionists shared a self-confident zeal with their parents. As McAdam argues: "This self-assurance was reinforced by the popular version of American history that came to be widely shared in the Fifties and early Sixties. . . . We were a 'can-do' people, who accomplished whatever we set out to do. We had licked the Depression, turned the tide in World War II, and rebuilt Europe after the war. . . . Freedom Summer was an audacious undertaking consistent with [this] exaggerated sense of importance and potency shared by the privileged members of America's postwar generation."[45]

Keeping this sociological context in mind helps us to understand the words of advice and warning tendered by Vincent Harding to volunteers receiving training in Oxford, Ohio, before they departed for Mississippi: "Are you going as 'in' members of the society to pull the Outs in with you. . . . Are you going to bring the Negroes of Mississippi into the doubtful pleasures of middle-class existence or seek to build a new kind of existence in which words like 'middle class' may no longer be relevant. Are we trying to make liberal adjustments or basic change?"[46]

The architects of Freedom Summer had conceived that effort with a clear belief about what recruiting these particular white Americans as allies in Mississippi would bring to the tough and dangerous work ahead. Without their active assistance, the work being done by black activists would be invisible. Not only this, but these products of "influential parents" who now attended "good schools" stood a good chance of bringing "the rest of the country with them."[47] As we evaluate this strategic choice and its consequences, another fact should be kept in mind: the abolitionist teachers who went south after the Civil War worked, for more than a decade, under the watchful eye of an occupying federal army; the volunteers of Freedom Summer did not.[48]

This bringing together of two Americas, according to historian Claybourne Carson, led to "a complex interplay of resentment and compassion" as SNCC's black volunteers responded to the feelings of entitlement from among these specially recruited members of the white establishment, such as when one suggested that the group's time would be best spent focusing on more "educated" blacks.[49] Although the majority of the volunteer teachers seemed to take to heart the advice offered to them by Vincent Harding at the Oxford, Ohio, training camp, there were still some others who nonetheless entered the classroom with expectations and other "baggage" which, according to Mary Aikin Rothschild, made them "incapable of conversing with young black students on anything approaching an equal basis."[50]

NATION BUILDING WHEN THE NATION ISN'T NECESSARILY LOOKING: SEPTIMA CLARK'S SOUTH CAROLINA

In order to see how reenactment and innovation coexisted within the public stage created for the transmission of key values and strategies—the public school—we must go back to the school worlds in the South, those which preceded the Freedom Schools. A good starting point would be South Carolina at the turn of the twentieth century and the teaching life of Septima Clark. Her career as a teacher paid by the state ended in the 1950s, when she became a full-time civil rights activist. How does a teacher—a paid representative of the state—not only do her job but keep it as well? In what ways must she acknowledge and, to a certain extent, abide by the written and unwritten rules of a segregated society? To what extent can she, like the Freedom School teachers who came in her wake, provide some kind of basis for changing the rules of her society?

Beginning with the Port Royal Experiment during the Civil War, South Carolina has been sacred ground in the reconstruction of American society for two centuries and a reminder that the First and Second Reconstructions were closely connected despite a century's separation. South Carolina has a special significance to the present story because it is here where the record of the First Reconstruction can be uncovered and the parallels can be drawn.

For a half-century, Septima Clark taught in the public schools of Charleston and Johns Island, South Carolina. After she lost her job as a teacher in Charleston because of her active membership in the NAACP, she returned to Johns Island to help the Highlander Folk School organize citizenship schools there.[51] Clark began her teaching career in September of 1916, at the very young age of eighteen in the resource-starved two-room schoolhouse on the island just off the coast of her native Charleston. Clark and another teacher taught 132 students at the Promise Land School, located near two large farming plantations, for twenty-five and thirty-five dollars a month, respectively. Clark recalled: "The school was made of logs, and it had clay in between to keep the wind from coming in during the wintertime. It had shutters, but no window panes, no glass, no window sashes at all. Whenever the wind was blowing on one side, you had to keep those shutters closed. You opened up the other side so you could have some light. . . . There was a big chimley [*sic*] in the middle [of the room], and the girls would get grass to sweep the floor. . . . The boys cut wood and brought it in so you could heat in the wintertime. . . . A lot of people said the school was black to show black children were in there."[52]

Across the road was a "one-room school, white-washed white on the outside. . . . They had a bucket and a dipper. That teacher had a little bit more equipment in her house than we had in ours, although we had those one hundred and thirty-two children, and she had only three." That white teacher made eighty-five a month.[53] The recollections of participants in the Clarendon County, South Carolina, litigation that became part of *Brown v. Board* make clear that the material circumstances of the classroom Clark described were not unusual.[54]

As Clark's biographer, Katherine Mellen Charron, argued, teaching among the African American rural poor posed a whole new dimension of challenge. The utter absence of even the most basic material resources placed a premium on "creative genius" and "teacher improvisation."[55] Clark quickly learned how to make use of what was there to make teaching materials. Faced with an absence of blackboards or even rudimentary textbooks, Clark had to improvise. Before blackboards and chalk were provided, "we would bring from the city a dry cleaner's bag and write on that bag some things they could copy. For reading, we had to make up stories about things around them—the trees, foliage, the animals. They learned to read those words first."[56] As she got to know her students, they also began to teach her. One of the things she learned and came to admire about Johns Island people was their Gullah language, which was rooted deep in the island's past as a destination for slave ships coming from Africa. Over time, the islanders created Gullah by mixing English, French, and German with their African dialects.[57] Clark gradually integrated these words and the experiences they conveyed into her lesson plans: "I wrote their stories on dry cleaner bags, stories of their country right around them. . . . They told them to me and I wrote them on the . . . bags and tacked them on the wall."[58]

Clark was not prepared to meet the sea islanders, and she first encountered them as cultural strangers, "persons of the most primitive culture" who knew remarkably little of modern life.[59] Over time, Clark, however, was able to overcome what the historian Willie Lee Rose properly described as "a thin residue of accumulated habits and responses" that was deeply resistant to "the introduction of democratic manners."[60] It is important to see Clark as a kind of modified historical reenactor, a black woman retracing steps first taken by white New England women a little less than a century earlier. Like Clark in the early twentieth century, Esther Hill Hawks, a New England physician, came down to "Beaufort and adjacent isles" to help newly free slaves as part of the Port Royal Experiment. In her diary, Hawks writes that "the colored people have had their confidence so often abused that many of them are timid and suspicious."[61]

This suspicion was grounded in experience, rather than a generalized aversion to the new and the different, and from specific events that had been kept alive in memory. For example, as the Emancipation Proclamation appeared on the horizon, white Union soldiers had lied to these newly freed slaves about what it meant, dissuading them from attending political meetings with the lie that "General Saxton is going to get them all together and deliver them up to their old masters."[62]

In her fifty years as a teacher, Clark came to a key lesson about learning: it is a deeply reciprocal process, and genuine and respectful curiosity and day-to-day care about those one wishes to teach is an absolute prerequisite for success at this complex process of mutual discovery through trust. This wisdom enabled Clark to return to Johns Island in 1957 to contribute to a three-year effort by the Highlander Folk School to train its adult residents to clear the legal hurdles to voting.[63]

The cultural isolation from the world had come to the Sea Islands after the Civil War. Even if it did not leave the islanders culturally empty, it did accomplish its intended political purpose: a civic disengagement from the mainland that had not simply come with the territory. In her careful study of the citizenship-school experiment on the twentieth-century Sea Islands, educational historian Sandra Brennemen Oldendorf found, that during the First Reconstruction, voter turnout among the black residents had been 80 percent, compared to 60 percent among South Carolina whites. In the last decades of the nineteenth century, when the systematic disenfranchisement of black voters came to the South Carolina mainland, this purge of voters and suppression of political activism traveled to the Sea Islands as well.[64]

Clark's work as a teacher also illustrates how a more traditional school setting can be subtly reconstructed. During the 1944–45 academic year, as part of her master's research at Hampton University, Clark returned to these issues and drew upon these early lessons when she worked with thirty-four Columbia, South Carolina, sixth graders, many of whom were resistant to reading. First, she not only took them out to explore their surroundings, but she also made significant room for their interests and their world in the classroom. By featuring books on subjects to which children were drawn—whether they were the Robin Hood stories, biographies of George Washington Carver or adventurer Richard E. Byrd, or books on the children of North Africa—Clark found that a "genuine love of reading" was instilled even if these youngsters came from homes "that cared little or nothing for reading."[65]

Another part of her work was empowering students to teach each other in small groups, thereby building confidence and competence in all. Success in the classroom also led to positive results at home as the children's enthusiasm rubbed off onto their parents, many of whom regarded reading as merely another skill they had not mastered. When Clark found that successful teaching meant bringing the students into the process as active learners and, eventually, as teachers themselves, she discovered something crucial to the teachers of the Freedom School movement: Clark's experiment yielded more than an orderly classroom and good feelings; twenty-eight of thirty-four students gained between four months and two years in their reading level. For the academic year, these students registered a median gain of seven points on the school district's achievement tests in reading.[66]

Placing Clark's teaching life and her formal conclusions about teaching reading to sixth graders side by side with the compilations generated by the Annual Conference on Reading held at the University of Chicago in the 1940s and 1950s offers a sense of how teaching behind the lines of segregation might have distinctively shaped Clark's approach to education. Clark and these other expert teachers started with a focus on the physical and neurological processes that successful reading requires. They were also beginning to be aware that unexamined assumptions about the cultural emptiness of certain people stood in the way of genuine and lasting learning by both teacher and pupil. In understanding this final point, it must be said that Septima Clark was well ahead of the Chicago experts.[67]

In the many years since Clark's pioneering classroom work, the minimum cost to participate in the economic life of this nation has continued to increase. In the 1960s, as standardized tests became crucial mechanisms for sorting and selecting from a growing pool of people potentially qualified to advance academically, algebra became a gateway or a barrier to new opportunities. As we look back in order to see the present in higher definition, it is important to see that, as a teacher of reading, Clark pioneered the same techniques that civil rights activists Robert P. Moses and Charles E. Cobb Jr. have been using to open the doors of "higher math" to those to whom it has been presented as being beyond reach. In the hands of Moses, Cobb, and their thousands of allies around the United States, algebra, like reading and writing, is but another system of "abstract symbolic representations for underlying . . . concepts."[68] Like Clark, Moses and Cobb have found success by starting "with where the children are, experiences that they share [with others]. . . . We get them to reflect on these . . . then to form abstract conceptualizations out of their reflection, and then to apply the abstraction back to their experience."[69]

Between 1972 and 1982, as South Carolina's people struggled through another period of self-conscious political and social renewal to achieve a "New South," Septima Clark capped her own long years in public service as an elected member of Charleston's Board of Education, the very same body which had once dismissed her from the district's faculty because of her political activism. In this new role Clark was an honored and esteemed participant in and symbol of social change. And yet, her priorities were not broadly shared by her colleagues on the board. She succeeded most at reminding them that recent history demanded substantive inclusion—the admission of some new voices and ideas into the process of formulating the curriculum. However, even as she succeeded in getting at least some financial compensation from the Charleston district that had illegally dismissed her twenty years earlier, this was an equivocal and largely symbolic tribute to a noteworthy individual rather than a systemic resolution to a systematic injustice. Congressman James E. Clyburn, one of the many activists who entered public life under her tutelage, recalled the struggle to get Clark official restitution from the state of South Carolina: "The governor [John West] was on board, but we were never able to get a majority of the legislature to go along. We did get a modest lump sum payment. A few years later Representative Robert R. Wood got the legislature to revisit the issue and got several additional payments, but not full restitution."[70]

Underlying photo opportunities acknowledging past wrongs, some very familiar issues remained for this "New South" to address. Teacher pay in Charleston, and indeed throughout the South, remained the lowest in the nation. Garlands of recognition for Clark as a participant-symbol in social change—shaking hands with fellow southerner President Jimmy Carter and receiving high honors from the NAACP and the National Education Association—did not change certain facts of life: "Right now we have a school board made up of a number of businessmen. They are not very much concerned about the teachers, so I'm still in the minority." As her time in office came to an end, she was also an outspoken critic of President Ronald Reagan's cuts to federal education programs.[71]

SCHOOL-CENTERED NATION BUILDING IN MARCUS FOSTER'S PHILADELPHIA AND OAKLAND

As Davison M. Douglas's careful study of school segregation outside the South before *Brown v. Board* has made clear, school segregation—whether de jure or de facto—has a long national history.[72] Marcus A. Foster is best remembered today as the first African American to lead the public school system in Oakland, California. He took that difficult job at a time when Oakland was becoming infamous in the minds of some Americans as the home of the Black Panther Party for Self-Defense. We will arrive at that historical moment shortly, but we must begin in Philadelphia.

According to the *Philadelphia Tribune,* at the time of Foster's arrival in the spring of 1966, Simon Gratz High School had become the "mammoth five-story . . . private preserve of local gangs." Students were "being terrorized by hoodlums right under the noses of teachers and administrators."[73] In addition, the building was dilapidated and overcrowded. Repeated promises of a new gymnasium and other needed reinforcements had been broken. After entering the principal's office at midyear, and under some suspicion, Foster, with the backing of the district's central office, made full use of his power to utilize truant officers to remove troublemakers and bring frightened students back into school. Foster's arrival brought positive change. In early 1968 *Tribune* reporter William C. Green covered the emerging consensus that "Gratz has advanced to such a degree that the school is charting a course for others to follow." Of the man in the principal's office, Green wrote, "Principal Foster has . . . the respect of the faculty and the student body and has shown his concern . . . in deeds rather than words."[74]

Constructive change, however, took time, and sometimes there were steps backward in the midst of forward movement. In the fall of 1967, a female twelfth-grade Gratz student was trampled "as hundreds of students raced wildly through the corridors shouting Black Nationalist slogans and setting fires [to] trash cans."[75] Things got so bad that some parents kept their children out of school. "I'd rather see the truant officer than the undertaker," one parent told the *Philadelphia Tribune*.[76] On October 27, fourteen hundred Gratz students boycotted classes to protest many serious issues: a school board long unresponsive to student complaints about inadequate and unsanitary facilities and the lack of African American history in the curriculum, the presence of military recruiters on the Gratz campus, the requirement to salute the flag, and district prohibition on African-themed clothing.[77] Foster agreed that the wearing of African clothing could be permitted; he also insisted on the salute of the flag unless a student was excused by his or her minister.[78] Foster emphatically endorsed an African American history curriculum.[79] The armed forces remained on campus, and the U.S. Naval Air Engineering Center joined the Data Preparation Corporation as part of a program to train Gratz students for jobs in emerging technologies.[80]

Foster's toughest challenge was not managing student protest over the war in Vietnam, the curriculum, or the dress code, but securing the school's right to expand onto nearby land. Although there were two plots of land adjacent to the school available for use, the two additional plots needed for the expansion were occupied by fourteen white middle-class families. "The Gratz issue was a hot potato," Foster admitted. "An all-black school was trying to put fourteen white homeowners off their land. It was almost unthinkable. True, the city and the two local universities had been relocating thousands of black people for years. But now the tables were being turned. It was one thing to have white universities moving poor black people and something else to have poor black people moving middle-class white people."[81]

The community campaign succeeded because it came after years of going through the "proper channels." Philadelphia's political establishment knew the need well. One of the consequences of the campaign that Foster began was that it created pressure across the establishment. On the fateful evening, with riot police surrounding the building, 450 community members filled the chambers as the school board voted seven to one to exercise eminent domain over the homes to make way for the expansion.[82] During the meeting there was no shortage of people to remind the board that, "if those fourteen white homes were Negro homes, they'd just tell you to move and that would be it."[83]

The lesson for Foster of the Philadelphia years was "*everybody is part of the system,* even those who wish to change it" (emphasis in the original). "The immediate advantage of this assumption," according to Foster, "is that it legitimates all the forces present. Our attention, thus, can focus on problems, not villains."[84] The symbol of such a learning environment is not a ballot box or the little handheld devices used in focus groups but an open door that any constituent—student, teacher, or parent—can walk through, and a sustained hearing that can be held if they are not always an agreement. The bottom line for Foster was the creation of an ordered environment where problems could be resolved and tangible results achieved.

Honoring this success must include an acknowledgment of its personal cost. Foster paid a high price for his skillful diplomacy. In October 1967 Foster suffered a heart attack and was hospitalized. Even after this dramatic setback, Foster worked from his hospital bed to help settle a dispute between a group of Gratz students and a local business owner.[85] Less than two years later, in the spring of 1969, Foster was again ordered to a hospital bed for two weeks to recover from "strain from overwork."[86]

Foster's record in Philadelphia brought him to the attention of Oakland's leaders. As a key player in Oakland's ultimately successful recruiting effort told the *Oakland Tribune,* the search committee's research confirmed that Foster was "considered to be one of the top men in the east by anybody with any knowledge of urban education and its problems."[87]

When Marcus Foster went to Oakland, he was moving from one historic city to another. Though often overshadowed in the nation's political and cultural life by events and personalities in New York City, Philadelphia was the birthplace of the American constitutional order. Across the continent, Oakland, California, was another shadow city beside its neighbor across the bay, San Francisco. This changed to a degree in the middle 1960s, as Oakland became internationally known as the headquarters of the Black Panther Party for Self-Defense. In addition, the championship performance of its major league football and baseball franchises, the Oakland Raiders and the Oakland A's, provided townspeople with an additional, and less controversial, source of pride and national visibility.[88]

Foster in Oakland

Leaving Philadelphia was a difficult decision for Foster. He had worked for the Philadelphia district for his entire professional career. Foster was drawn to Oakland because it was "a microcosm of larger cities where it's difficult to get handles on problems." Problems that seemed overwhelming in a school system of 291,000 students might actually get more direct and sustained attention in Oakland, a more geographically compact district of 70,000 students.[89] Certainly Foster's tense yet successful tenure at Gratz High School prepared him well to meet the political challenges that seemed to abound in Oakland—especially navigating the conflicting demands of students now immersed in a more explicitly politicized youth culture promoting new conceptions of rights and responsibilities.

Foster worked hard to convince local activists accustomed to battling a white establishment, which they viewed with suspicion, that he was not a racial "show piece for a tax election," that he intended to stay and become a fully vested member of Oakland's slowly emerging new political order.[90] From his first days on the job, Foster embraced his role as public advocate in chief for the Oakland public schools. In 1972 Foster led two thousand teachers, parents, and students on an unprecedented trip to Sacramento to successfully lobby the legislature for increased funding for urban school districts.

Both John P. Spencer's excellent intellectual biography and press accounts from the time put Foster at the center of this intense public campaign. Although the available public record does not permit us to measure Foster's influence more precisely, it is clear that the Alameda County delegation to the state legislature saw him as one of their strongest assets in meetings with other legislators and with a Reagan administration on record as opposing new funding.[91] Within the district itself, much of what had worked in Philadelphia also worked in Oakland. Committees of parents were brought in to mediate disciplinary issues, local churches became important centers of after-school learning, and business leaders worked effectively to train students for entry-level jobs.[92]

It is, however, equally clear that Foster may have been unprepared for the amount of time he would need to devote to keeping the most basic and necessary state funding in place as the number of students attending the Oakland public schools continued to fall. In his expectations of what he could accomplish as superintendant, Foster may have relied a little too heavily on his previous experience as a school principal. Foster was confident that, as superintendant, he would now be able to "deal from the top without filtering through others."[93]

It is certainly true that, as a lifelong educator, Marcus Foster was no stranger to politics—in the educational bureaucracy, in the schools, and in their neighborhoods. Indeed, his accomplishments to that date are strong evidence that he already understood what many academic experts were only beginning to appreciate in the 1970s: schools were themselves "miniature political systems which share major characteristics with more obvious and familiar political systems."[94] As the leader of a citywide institution, he was still responsible for helping teachers and students work "in a kind of isolation from the pressures and anxieties of real life," where one could experiment "without serious repercussions" and "have the experience of setting up their ideas against those of an adult."[95] Now Foster had to spend more of his time than ever before working directly with elected officials, congressional committees, union leaders, and the broader electorate without the institutional intermediaries that had been there when he had been a principal or an assistant superintendant in Philadelphia.

The politics of paying for the public's schools have never been easily mastered. Perhaps the most important lesson that Americans and their elected leaders learned in the fifty-year effort to meet the legal imperative to desegregate public education was this: at that most immediately accessible and intimate touch point of the American political system, the school board and bond elections, transfers of resources (which are divisive in national politics) can get especially ferocious.

Though Marcus Foster was a self-identified integrationist, accomplishing this mission was not his most important challenge.[96] It was Foster's most pressing responsibility, one that he shared with local officials throughout the country, to spend much of his time trying to preserve the monies his district already had but was in danger of losing because of declining enrollments. It did not matter that the money required to meet fixed costs was rising rapidly or that many more students who now entered the public school system urgently needed a whole range of expensive academic and social interventions.[97] In 1970, Oakland, like many other American cities, was entering a third decade in which it would lose its population as well the industrial base of its economy.[98]

Like the leaders of the Detroit school system, Foster faced an electorate who had been demonstrating their outright resistance to approving new school bonds going back to the middle 1950s. As recently as 1969, two-thirds of Oakland's voters had rejected a new bond. The district tried again in June of 1970 and, in a vote taken only a few weeks after Foster's arrival, a majority (but not the required super majority of two-thirds) voted yes. Not until 1973 was there a super-majority, and even here it must be noted that the lead issue in presenting the bond on the ballot was that it was intended to make the schools earthquake safe, making it somewhat unclear how much of this victory can be seen as a voter approval of Foster's leadership.[99]

During his years in Oakland, Foster provided compelling proof that "people from the Oakland hills to the Oakland flatlands have one thing in common—concern for what happens to children."[100] In Oakland, as in Philadelphia, Foster brought the community into the school: 2,400 volunteers and 130 local businesses were recruited to "work inside the school to contribute in a variety of ways from curriculum planning, conflict resolution to job training." And yet the power of these new forces to bring new energy was blunted by the enormity of the district's overall fiscal crisis. In the fiscal year 1971–72, Foster's administration incurred a $3.5 million deficit in meeting the requirements of an already lean budget of $68 million. In these conditions, the new resources tapped by Foster became instead "the only thing that has kept us afloat and kept us in some kind of posture where we can meet these needs."[101] Foster told the U.S. Congress in 1971, "The major reasons for this fiscal crisis are the increased resistance of local property owners to add to their already heavy tax burden, the reluctance of state legislatures to increase taxes for school spending, and the minimal contribution of the federal government to our general education programs."[102]

Foster had to cut 200 teachers from the district's faculty, raising the student/teacher ratio in the Oakland schools from an already high 28.6 to 1 to 31 to 1. In response, the Oakland branch of the American Federation of Teachers, soon joined by a Black Panther Party making a serious bid for political legitimacy, chided Foster that "school administrators who coined the slogan 'it's for the kids' must live up to their rhetoric."[103] Judged by the public rhetoric invoked on both sides over the next two years, the rancor between these two opposing forces would only grow. In 1973, when another strike seemed imminent, Foster branded the threat of a walkout as "illegal harassment" that would be taken into the courts for certain vindication. Such language earned for Foster the title of "unchallenged demagogue" for the Oakland school administration from the Black Panther Party.[104]

If the de jure segregation in the South Carolina of Septima Clark's day was expressed in a particular kind of enforced scarcity on essential resources, this condition would remain in force in the school systems of later generations. To these problems, a new threat must be added: the infiltration of the schools by a growing market in illegal drugs. Of all the critical problems Foster confronted at Gratz, illegal drug use did not rise to the level of being detected and discussed in the local press. In Oakland, however, it was a rapidly growing source of pressure upon the school system. This pressure was so powerful that policing it became virtually the only source of substantial new public revenue brought into the schools during Foster's tenure.[105] While the police and Foster's school administrators worked closely together to identify and apprehend drug dealers, the greater part of the problem was how to address the student who was becoming an addict. Far more important to Foster than increasing a police presence on campus was utilizing the savvy assistants already in the schools "who are sophisticated themselves in the matter of drug abuse" and "are alert for the . . . older youth out of school . . . who come from off campus . . . to conduct illegal activities." While these trusted community members would coordinate with the police where necessary, their primary job was to be "supportive of the student" needing help.[106]

The struggle to extend existing resources easily overshadowed Foster's new initiatives and accomplishments. The Oakland district had successfully assumed responsibility for Head Start from a weak community action agency. Major philanthropies had stepped forward to support greater community participation. Foster was acknowledged by local legislatures to be an effective lobbyist for Oakland schools. Greater parental involvement had contributed to a 21 percent decline in the dropout rate.[107] Nonetheless, by the beginning of his fourth full academic year on the job, Foster felt compelled to confess that "innovation has not turned things around. . . . We need a more fundamental approach to meet the needs of our system."[108]

Marcus Foster's life came to an end in the early evening of November 6, 1973, when he and his deputy, Robert Blackburn, were shot as they walked to Blackburn's car after a school board meeting. Within a few days, a group calling itself the Symbionese Liberation Army would claim responsibility for the murder, citing Foster's support of a greater police presence within Oakland schools. In January of 1974, two of its members were arrested for the crime during a routine traffic stop, which turned suddenly violent. One month later the SLA would commit another crime—the kidnapping of newspaper heiress Patricia Hearst—which would earn the group a larger footnote in recent American political history.[109]

For any community, the public assassination of a leader is a traumatic event. A resolution passed by the school board identified November 6 as "the saddest day in the history of Oakland and the Oakland public schools." The impact of this particular blow was further magnified by Oakland's emergence since the mid-sixties as a center of especially consequential political conflict and experimentation. Thus, the Foster killing, though a local event, was easily linked to the national trauma of recent years. Congressman Ron Dellums, the leader of Oakland's emerging and more strongly left-leaning political establishment, did not exaggerate when he said, "Not since the assassination of Martin Luther King have I been so jolted by a senseless and inhumane act"; the intense merging of local and national politics in Oakland are also made painfully plain in school board member Anne Cornielle's instant reaction that "it was like when Kennedy was assassinated."[110] Though she was most likely alluding to President Kennedy's assassination almost exactly ten years earlier, it says something terribly sad and significant that those words could equally well have been referring to two separate killings of a Kennedy, one in 1963 and the other in 1968.

There is however perhaps no stronger testament to how the local and the national had become so fused in California politics than that Governor Ronald Reagan, a conservative Republican preparing to leave the governorship to begin the last and most important chapter of his political career, was moved to offer both condolences for Foster's murder and ten thousand dollars in state funds to add to the forty thousand dollars in public and private donations raised as a reward for information leading to the capture of Foster's killers. As Reagan said at the time:

> I am shocked and saddened over this vicious attack and the resulting tragedy.
>
> Marcus Foster was an outstanding man in the midst of a brilliant career. I am confident that if this tragedy had not occurred, he would have received national recognition as one of our country's leading educators. He was a "no-nonsense" leader whose main purpose was to improve the quality of education for all children. His loss will be felt by present and future students in Oakland, by California and the entire educational community.
>
> Mrs. Reagan and I extend our sincere sympathies to his wife and children. We join all Californians in mourning his death.[111]

The enactment of the "No Child Left Behind Act" in 2001 has changed the context in which Americans debate public education. The often-pernicious consequences of tying so many educational outcomes and other resources to student performance on standardized tests are now front and center. This has moved another disturbing trend further into the background. Of all the challenges that are routinely presented by the American political system, the most difficult one has always been convincing local taxpayers to increase their support of local schools. In Philadelphia and in Oakland, Marcus Foster sought to address the resource scarcity imposed on parts of these communities by bringing the private sector into a partnership. In the last generation, what was once an innovation has become a standard procedure. Today, parents in school districts across this country must often provide basic supplies to their local schools. So too today do businesses—large and small—advertise the dollars they donate to local schools. And, in the end, monies that were once envisioned as supplemental and enriching have become essential and irreplaceable in a system whose costs continue to grow. We have done little more than manage what seems to be a chronic and permanent lack of political and institutional development equal to meeting this crucial national need.

THE COMMONS OF THE SCHOOL

Septima Clark and Marcus Foster were adults who not only cared about children in the abstract sense that the American polity ritualistically requires, but they also possessed a vigorous and fully developed sense that schools, if they are to teach equal participation in civic work, must most of all be organized around the capacity of children to learn and interact as well as "sit still" and react to adult initiatives. To tell a more student-centered story about the public school as the first "commons" of this particular nation, we move to Topeka, Kansas, and an especially valuable and rare set of historical sources: student newspapers and yearbooks.[112]

In 1854, Kansas was the center of a deepening popular struggle over whether slavery could spread westward. This territory came to be known as "Bleeding Kansas," the living symbol of a polity speeding toward disunion. Exactly one hundred years later, in *Brown v. Board of Education,* the Supreme Court called the nation to the unfinished work from that Civil War. Although Topeka's high school was never considered officially segregated, and thus never the center of a formal desegregation process (*Brown* had challenged segregation in the elementary schools), the challenge of desegregation came, nonetheless, in the aftermath of the assassination of Martin Luther King Jr. in 1968. This issue emerged at a time when student leaders were already active on other issues.[113]

Between 1950 and 1980, the political culture of students at Topeka High followed a path generally familiar to any student of postwar American history. By 1950, as the armed forces and major sports leagues were beginning to desegregate, Topeka High's separate black basketball team was discontinued, as were the school's racially separate social events.[114] From the 1950s to the mid-1960s, the idea that Americans were the representatives of "democracy and peace" in a world far too dominated by "servitude and unrest" was especially prominent.[115] As the threat of a general war receded in the 1960s, the debate over the quality of democracy at home became more central. In the national polity, this meant an explicit debate over racial segregation and the need to ensure equal rights and greater cultural understanding and respect for African Americans. Within the polity of Topeka High, there was a more fractious climate, but racial issues were not yet at its center.

Beginning in the late 1950s and continuing into the 1970s, there appeared two other indications of a changed atmosphere at the school: first, there was the more regular and more pointed coverage of the student government in the school newspaper, the *Topeka High World*; and, second, there was extensive coverage of disturbing changes in student conduct, particularly cheating, "rowdyism," and even outright rudeness at school assemblies and elsewhere.[116] At least on the issue of cheating and its connection to a decline in moral standards, these debates between students resonated with themes also found in the national debate over the meaning of the *Quiz Show* scandals of the late 1950s, not to mention the soul searching over national decline provoked by the Soviet launch of a Sputnik satellite.

As in the larger polity, concern with a rising tide of discontent continued in the Topeka High polity well into the 1970s. In these years, student leaders demanded that student government actually have some power to govern the school, especially where student discipline was at issue. "The main reason we have student government is not for experience," one editorialist penned in the late spring of 1964. Circumstances called for the "WORKING of a government" to adjudicate disputes and administer "climate control" between students and faculty.[117] To the consternation of some faculty, the student paper was also giving more space to the coverage of national politics, leading one teacher to publically charge that the paper was attempting to sway student opinion in the Johnson-Goldwater contest of 1964.[118]

Greater political assertiveness by students was not the only reason for a change in the rhythm of public life on campus. Another factor to consider is the introduction of more social science courses and new ways of engaging students in civic affairs. The 1963 edition of the Topeka High annual notes that a new course in economics was being taught to "overflow classes," while students of American government were now going out into the community to study urban renewal and the "inflammable city manager situation."[119]

By the late 1960s, African Americans were an estimated 20 percent of the slightly more than two-thousand-member student body.[120] There was scant attention to racial issues in the *World* until the spring of 1965, when the violence in Selma, Alabama, made tangible the need for a federal voting rights act, and then again in 1968, when King was slain. Even an issue as important as *Brown* received no editorial attention when it came down in May 1954 (though this may be because it came so close to the end of the school year). The Little Rock crisis three years later registered only briefly in the paper's pages. African American students are not seen regularly participating in campus club life in either the *World* or the yearbook, the *Sunflower,* except as athletes, until the late 1960s.[121]

King's assassination in 1968 provoked a desegregation process in the sense that patterns of racial separation were brought to light and challenged. For some African American students, the failure of the Topeka High student body to elect a black cheerleader spoke to a broader degree of insensitivity. Why was the election held on the day of Martin Luther King's funeral (a day on which most African American students had chosen to stay home out of respect for the martyred civil rights leader)? This event caused many to reconsider other election procedures: why did students need to register to vote when they were already registered as students? Why limit voting to a small window of time before the school day began?[122] The Topeka High student body also reacted by electing African Americans to student body offices for the first time. Of greater importance to the students interviewed by the research team led by sociologist Frank Petroni, however, were the efforts to desegregate the cheer squad and select African Americans to serve as royalty at the all-school party.[123]

In the fall of 1968, black students established their own student organization, but the *World*'s coverage of the group's second meeting quoted no students, only the faculty advisor (the vice-principal of Division D) and another adult, both of whom offered reassurance about what "Black Power" meant: "Black power, yes, but Black pride is more important to me."[124] Within a few short years, a faculty report summarized in the *World* spoke candidly about the problems that came with a more open expression of grievances: "Whites have a conditioned fear of blacks. Teachers are afraid of troublemakers and don't discipline blacks because of fear of the student and/or fear that they will not receive backing from the administration."[125]

The more openly contentious atmosphere on campus also spurred further debate on how the school's governance should be organized. In the work to come, student leaders were part of a national trend of greater political activism among high school students.[126] The process at Topeka reached a milestone in the 1972–73 academic year, when students and faculty instituted an ambitious structure of shared student-faculty governance. There is little in the published record about that experiment, but one of the arguments for the new governmental system was growing student apathy; yet, as the experiment proceeded—at one point involving as many as eleven committees covering virtually every aspect of school life, from attendance to the problems of the "transitional student"—this same apathy was also identified as a barrier to its success.[127] By 1979 the more traditional student government had returned without any published commentary on why the experiment had ended.[128] It would be a mistake to identify this experiment as a brief efflorescence that ultimately demonstrated the shallowness of student commitment. After all, students at Topeka High had been engaged in a self-conscious process of political reconstruction since at least 1964.

What of the specifically racial issues raised by King's death within in the Topeka High community? When they interviewed students about race relations within the school, sociologists Frank Petroni, Ernest A. Hirsch, and C. Lillian Petroni found certain disturbing consistencies across a fairly well-elaborated social system in which economic class also played a decisive role. Some members of the "black elite" were unsparing in their criticism of black students from working-class families as "trashy niggers." Such disclosures surprised Frank Petroni and his colleagues. "Few white persons carrying on a serious interracial discussion . . . would permit themselves to speak like this. In a sense, some elite Negroes seem to manifest as much, if not more, racial discrimination as do whites."[129]

Among the white majority of "Plains High" (the name given to the school in the final study), formal ideology did not predict actual conduct.[130] According to members of the black and white elite, "black trash" and "white trash" were apt to have the most interaction (according to a black student, "The white trash look up to the Negro for that soul stuff"). As in the general society, income and the degree of racial contact were closely related, with interracial contact decreasing as income rose. Students on the college prep track were likely to have the least interaction with black students because so few black students were in their classes, yet these students also often articulated the most liberal positions on race.[131]

These interviews with students reveal that they shared much with the adults living in the same society, from the most extreme racism of "Black Power means Niggers" to eloquent and abstract testimonies from whites about the need for Black Power and the need to end institutional racism. The "hippies," who expressed a great deal of sympathy for ideas of Black Power ("having the same kind of power white people have"), associated most with members of the black elite, even though the hippies disdained these particular black students as inauthentic. When asked why they do not associate with more "authentic" blacks in the school, these students responded that "they're not in my crowd."[132]

In the 1970s racial friction between working-class whites and working-class blacks was made especially visible by the struggle over busing in Boston. Also building in this era, but not fully visible until the Supreme Court's *Bakke* decision in 1978, was tension within a more affluent group of white Americans over what a Second Reconstruction might require in terms of affirmative action to ensure access to the most selective public and private colleges and universities. The Petroni study offers a brief glimpse of the dividing lines that would harden and become more visible in the 1980s and 1990s. According to some of the most socially and politically progressive students, some of the more militant and outspoken black students "would have to learn that they don't deserve special privileges" and that "black rage" could not be used to legitimate or excuse disruptive behavior.[133]

Petroni and his colleagues' findings confirmed that these students shared much with their parents and, indeed, with the rest of the adult world they were about to enter. Topeka High students were "no different from [their] parents, teachers and principals who, if asked, also would locate the problem of race relations in 'others.'"[134] These observers concluded that Topeka High was no more "integrated" than it had been in 1950. "While the barriers of a formal Jim Crow system have been removed, Negroes and whites still maintain their separation. They do not recognize that the *formal* system of segregation has been replaced by an informal pattern, which is almost as divisive as the one that existed two decades ago."[135]

Across the dividing lines of race and class, members of the Topeka High polity, like many other Americans, held to a "shallow conception of integration" that was satisfied with only the mere juxtaposition of blacks and whites "in the same area," not by whether they formed any deeper relationships or understandings.[136] There is a clear parallel between this conclusion and the atmosphere found at the North Carolina elementary school noted earlier, which was undergoing desegregation in the same period. Although regionally distinctive histories and traditions are essential to understanding American race relations, the distance between blacks and whites has been a *national* fact of life.

As the 1970s proceeded, the conversation about race continued, joined by a new pressure from students of both genders to work toward gender equality, especially in the support of women's sports.[137] New challenges, made more difficult by a weaker economy and the migration out of the city to surrounding suburbs, caused Topeka High's leadership to take the initiative in new key areas. In early 1975, the *World* devoted two full and generously illustrated pages to the work of the counseling staff. Featuring shots of individual students meeting with counselors, the article reminded students that counselors were available not only to help with future academic and vocational plans but also with the more immediate problems that sometimes come with adolescence and don't necessarily originate at school. As one counselor told the *World,* "It's a very scary thing for a teenager [to talk about personal problems]. It takes a lot of courage to come to a counselor and talk. . . . We are here to help students figure out personal problems."[138] A new child development lab challenged the notion that child care is the responsibility only of women as it trained students to help with child care in local schools and programs such as Head Start.[139]

THE SCHOOL AND SOCIETY

Whether a person chooses to understand society as advanced, developing, or underdeveloped, school is the institution where its constituents and constituent parts come together in an effort to create a shared and integrated vision of one's relationship to a larger world. In its conflicts and agreements, the school is necessarily an extension of the political and social world around it. Even when parents opt their children out of this public process by homeschooling or pursuing some other extra-public option, they cannot escape the fact that they are acting in direct response—and often in a very forceful dissent—to important parts of the outer commons.

To take seriously the idea that all nations and peoples remain in some sense and in some way "underdeveloped"—that fundamental conflicts between the demands of the "whole" and the conflicting demands of its parts will always be present politically, if not always actively—means acceptance as natural and proper some irresolution in the final result of composing these differences. In the middle of the Second World War, looking forward to the coming chapter of American nation building, Robert Redfield offered the following advice to parents of children attending the University of Chicago's Laboratory School: "I do not know whether the schools can make a society reorganize itself. I doubt if the schools can create a coherent vision in a society that lacks such a vision. It seems to me that the schools will continue to include people with many different visions of the desirable society and with different kinds of convictions and lack of convictions. . . . The problem of the moral order is . . . not exclusively that of the schools but involves all our institutions. Even the home still has something to do with it. . . . Father and mother are home with the children, but also present are Aunt Jemima, Captain Midnight and Jack Armstrong, the All-American Boy."[140]

This is solid wisdom indeed, and applying a full measure of its value to understanding the modern United States requires keeping the metaphors of the school and of schooling close at hand when considering the public world and political culture in which the respective creators of the *Children of Crisis* series, *Fat Albert and the Cosby Kids,* and *Sesame Street* each sought to carry forward the work of public education.

3

ROBERT COLES AS DOMESTIC GOODWILL AMBASSADOR OF THE SECOND RECONSTRUCTION

> There is no keeping up with history, but I hope the record set forth here will be of some worth to future historians who find themselves interested in how a few Americans lived through a critical time in their lives and this country's development as a democracy.
>
> —ROBERT COLES, *Children of Crisis: A Study of Courage and Fear* (1967)

In 1960, Robert Coles, a Harvard-trained physician and psychiatrist newly married to fellow New Englander Jane Hallowell, returned to the South. Only a few years earlier, as a captain in the U.S. Air Force, he had been stationed, not by choice, at Keesler Air Force Base in Biloxi, Mississippi, where he had been an administrator at a neuropsychiatric hospital. This time, Robert and Jane Coles, with the moral and financial support of their families, returned as a team to study the lives of children at the center of a region undergoing desegregation.[1] The result of that second journey south was volume 1 of the *Children of Crisis* series, published in five volumes between 1967 and 1977.[2] The publication of volumes 2 and 3 were marked in 1972 by a cover story on Coles in *Time* magazine under the title "America's Forgotten Children."[3]

Ruth Mehrtens Galvin, editor of *Time*'s Behavior section, researcher Virginia Adams, and reporter Nancy Newman honored Coles as "the most influential living psychiatrist in the [United States]," not because of a breakthrough in theory but for a widely admired public experiment in which his subjects were also his intellectual collaborators. Coles was worthy of this special public attention because he was a genuine expert who was also deeply suspicious of the dogmas that can be induced by too reflexively observing the otherwise legitimate routines required to become an expert. Most of all, Coles was recognized for his work with Americans testing their citizenship on the front lines of the nation's struggles with poverty and racism. To quote *Time,* "By rising above the set prejudices of both liberals and conservatives, Coles helps depolarize a divided society. He has performed one of the most difficult and important feats of all: to criticize America and yet to love it, to lament the nation's weaknesses . . . while continuing to cherish its strengths. *Most important, he avoids the sterile dogma of social science and speaks, unashamedly, from the heart*" (emphasis added).[4]

In his life as a participant-observer of American lives, the economically comfortable, Harvard-educated Coles straddled the boundaries of class and culture. Whether Coles was working in New Mexico or Atlanta, he and his family would always settle in "a working-class neighborhood . . . [and] would always try to get away, try to be with ordinary people as neighbors."[5] In this carefully considered synthesis of life and work, Coles endeavored to act as "an intermediary of sorts—someone who tries to hear and then prompts others to listen."[6] These skills as a diplomat and a go-between served Coles well not only in his work with families enduring various kinds of hardship but also in walking through the ideological minefield created during the 1960s, when debates within social science about the African American family structure and the nature of poverty and the poor spilled out into the larger political culture.

Coles contributed to the Age of *Brown*—and its invitation to commencing a program of internal nation building beyond the construction of roads and bridges—as a practitioner of cultural exchange within the United States. "Cultural exchange" was an approach to public diplomacy which sought to construct bridges of mutual understanding between peoples of different lands and cultures. This idea was given its most famous and enduring expression in American foreign policy by the Fulbright Fellowship program, which has flourished since the Second World War. It was hoped that the exchange of artists and scholars between the United States and other nations would accomplish what professional diplomats could not:

enhance human understanding through direct personal contacts. There were, of course, other motivations at work: when the Fulbright program sent a Lincoln scholar or the State Department sent African American jazz musicians abroad, it was to the capitals of nonaligned nations in the developing world. This was an exercise of American soft power in a larger ideological struggle. As genuinely idealistic as some of the motivations for exchange indeed were, there is no getting around the fact that this was not an encounter of geopolitical equals. Americans visited other countries with strong dollars in their pockets and were, regardless of their precise intellectual mission, fortified by the conviction that they were visitors from the most powerful center of that universe. Visitors who came to the United States were either from once-great imperial nations now demoted to more peripheral roles in world affairs or new nations struggling to find their way in a postcolonial world. Either way, "center" and "periphery" remained stable conceptual points applied to a changing map.

In a similar way, the Coles cultural exchange program was fraught with potential problems. He was the man with the resources—education (especially medical expertise), money, and contacts. His subjects possessed few, if any, of these resources to exchange. Coles was acutely aware of this as he wrote about the lives of the hard-pressed and the downright poor. Beyond providing direct assistance to individual families, Coles sought to even out the exchange by turning over a larger and larger part of each volume of the *Children of Crisis* series to the direct testimony of these untrained individuals; they share the interpretive stage with him to such an extent that Coles sometimes seems to disappear from the study. Coles's subjects became his collaborators, giving evidence that many people without a formal education nonetheless understood their situations quite well—to an advanced degree, in fact—and would be up to the challenge of playing a larger part in society if given the opportunity.

"WHITE KNIGHT"

When the Coleses embarked on their southern research in 1960, they had relatively little knowledge of the complexity of the work they were undertaking. In 1960 a black social scientist could not have conducted this research. Psychologist Kenneth B. Clark, who had conducted his famous doll research in the South and Border South, explained to Coles how the continuing fact of segregation might hinder his work and cloud his findings: "If you were a Negro and poor, you'd be hearing different words from those . . . children, writing up a different research project; and you sure wouldn't be thinking of (not in your wildest dreams!) doing interviews with white children and their parents—or with the schoolteachers. . . . I couldn't do [your] project either—even in Negro homes. . . . I'm a Northerner and I've lived a comfortable protected life; it would be hard for me to leave it for that world of danger and violence."[7]

Looking back upon these years from the distance of the 1990s, Coles candidly concluded that being white gave him an advantage as a social investigator. In a society in which white privilege was normative, whiteness coupled with education and social standing had "served to protect me. . . . I was a white knight who needed have no fear, and who thought . . . he could go anywhere and talk to anyone."[8] Such confidence, Coles argued, however admirable, is also a privilege, an entitlement that comes with a certain kind of life that, to begin with, was lived on the white side of the color line. Coles confessed that "I cringe today at my naïveté and my self-assurance, and maybe my unknowing . . . arrogance—even as I doubt that without that psychological, never mind racial and social background, I could have gotten even to first base on either side of those railroad tracks I visited in those beleaguered Southern cities of the early 1960s."[9]

The first observation that Coles offered readers of *Children of Crisis: A Study of Courage and Fear* was that, on his first visit to the South as an Air Force officer, he had been unaware of the way the segregated social system supported him. He wrote, "I recall how easily I slipped into its very distinctive life and how pleasant I found that life to be as a white, middle-class professional man, and so I fit easily into . . . Southern society. Only gradually did I begin to notice the injustice at hand, and as a consequence take up my particular effort against it."[10]

Coles concentrated here on children as focal points in a larger community. In this connection, it is important to remember some other forces at work in American society. The combination of the Baby Boom and the impact of television, newsmagazines, and paperback books spread new knowledge about child health and child development into every part of American society, including "cabins and tenements far removed from our national life."[11] Although children received attention from Coles as principal actors and symbols, Coles was equally attentive to the lives and ideas of their parents and teachers. What resulted was an unusually detailed time-lapse photograph of how human beings take in, live with, and interpret the culture around them.

Coles's early reckonings with the theory of what racism actually did to people was informed by psychoanalysts Abram Kardiner and Lionel Ovesey's *Mark of Oppression,* which emphasized the damage caused to the Negro personality by white racism. Coles's eagerness to apply the latest theoretical knowledge to interpreting the findings of his field research created a problem that was eloquently defined by his wife and professional collaborator, Jane Coles. Early in their work together, she criticized her husband for being too eager to "characterize the people we see! Why don't you let them *be?* Why don't you pay attention to each person in each family that we visit, and stop trying to lump them together?"[12] From the anthropologists Allison Davis and John Dollard, and especially Oscar Lewis, Coles had learned the merit of letting "the people speak without interruption," a mode of presentation that would characterize future volumes in the *Children of Crisis* series.[13] Coles developed a warm professional friendship with Lewis and credits Lewis with introducing him to the tape recorder as a research tool.[14]

Although Coles's chosen medium for examining how children blend their external and internal worlds was children's drawings, Kenneth and Mamie Clark's emblematic doll studies had a special importance beyond Coles's personal relationship with Kenneth Clark. In a sense, Coles elaborated a line of inquiry the Clarks were very closely associated with: Coles measured how core social values are reflected in children's choices about how to represent the world they see and experience. Coles's fieldwork also partially confirms the Clarks' findings that children have generally developed extremely negative associations with the colors brown and black. At the same time, a close comparison of Coles's and the Clarks' work highlights important differences. The Clarks' work with children focused rather narrowly on reactions that are manifest as the children are asked to relate themselves (through the act of choosing one doll over another, for instance) to the outside world. From this, the Clarks assumed, by describing the reactions (or lack thereof), that an internalization of negative social and cultural messages had occurred. The Clarks did not present each child's life history, nor did they discuss the children's parents. The Clarks were concerned with documenting something significant but narrower in scope: that the children had received negative social and cultural messages and, at the very least, understood these negative messages. Coles, on the other hand, tried to assess what the child actually does with those messages—the particular, individual, and unique meanings that he or she applies to them—over the course of a childhood.

When he studied the drawings of the many children he and Jane Coles visited over hundreds of hours, Coles looked for clues as to how children made sense of the culture around them. The children's drawings were full of "energetic symbolization" about the world and its meanings and messages.[15] It took six months, for instance, for the six-year-old Ruby Bridges to use her brown or black crayons to represent anything other than dirt. In the work children drew for Coles, size was as important as color as a way of representing the differences in status and power created by segregation. According to Coles, Ruby's representations of white people were "larger and more life-like. Negroes were smaller, their bodies less intact."[16] In Ruby's drawings, however, African Americans were given larger ears, perhaps because they needed them to compensate for their lack of power in other areas.[17]

If capturing human feelings and experiences requires listening to many different voices telling many different stories, Coles also understood that one color or one human feature can hold more than one symbolic meaning.[18] Coles's analysis of the drawings by African American children led to a negative conclusion about the symbolic meaning of brown and black: "Every Negro child I know has had to take notice in some way of what skin color signifies in our society. If they do not easily . . . talk about it, their drawings surely indicate that the subject is on their minds. Like Ruby, they have trouble using brown and black crayons."[19] At the same time, when Ruby drew her grandfather in his pastoral setting, Coles noted that "brown and black were used appropriately and freely" under the cloak of protection offered by the memory of her grandfather, including to represent a very large brown man, very much intact ("Momma . . . says her daddy is the strongest man you can find," Ruby had said). For Ruby, her grandfather's Delta farm was a refuge where it was safe to be yourself ("If things gets real bad we can always go there").[20]

Coles's long exposure to black children and their families enabled him to see a fuller picture of how strength and weakness often coexist in one person or one family. Coles agreed with the findings of the famous "Moynihan Report," written by his friend and colleague sociologist Daniel Patrick Moynihan in 1965, on the special problems facing the black family. At the same time, Coles found Moynihan's presentation problematic and the controversy generated by the report unproductive. To sociologist David Riesman, Coles expressed frustration at how the lines of debate over the report had become drawn—"Why we have to come out for or against something is perhaps a more important problem or issue. . . . I think I know what [Pat] was trying to do, and I am for it, but I also think that some of things that he says have to be much more carefully thought about than he has yet done."[21] At the same time, Coles found Moynihan's awareness that the dynamics of class were compounding the injustices of race an important contribution. Finally, Moynihan's sincerity of motive (perhaps highlighted for Coles by the rhetorical overkill of some of the attacks on his friend) ultimately caused Coles to call Moynihan "just about the most courageous man in America today" for his outspokenness.[22]

In the *Children of Crisis* series, Coles provided an alternate model for addressing both the damage and the endurance embedded in the lives of many African Americans. "Fear, hate, hunger and utter segregation from the rest of the community establish an atmosphere that inevitably affects the child and the parent every day and profoundly." At the same time, Coles made clear that the damage to children resides not in some flaw deep in the African American family (Coles found that "in the first years of infancy and early childhood," African American families, though hard-pressed, often successfully provide comfort and protection), "but in those later years . . . the world's restrictions become decisive antagonists to the boy or girl" who must "come to terms with the distinct fact of the Negro's powerlessness in American society."[23]

Moynihan had intended his report to provoke not only debate, but also a more enlightened national policy to protect and preserve families under stress. Unfortunately, this became, in Moynihan's own words, "a moment lost." His words were widely interpreted within the civil rights community as a sensationalist effort to blame the victims of a long national history of institutional racism for their current plight. Moynihan, of course, was partly responsible for this misunderstanding of his report.[24]

Moynihan was far more a politician ambitious for political advancement than a social scientist seeking to make his name by provocatively breaking new ground in a controversial area. Moynihan was neither a racist nor an empty opportunist with no genuine commitment to the issues he championed, including the black family. Among politicians, Moynihan does not seem uniquely grasping or opportunistic, but he was, at thirty-eight, a young man in a hurry, and his report was vague and sloppy because it was hurriedly written in part, perhaps, to coincide with his entry into New York City electoral politics as a favorite candidate of the Johnson White House for a major citywide office. Moynihan, who was about to resign as assistant secretary of labor, leaked the report to journalist Robert Novak (the first person to refer in print to the document as the "Moynihan Report") barely one month before primary day in Moynihan's only unsuccessful campaign, to become the Democratic nominee for city council president (a position filled by a citywide vote).[25] This part of the political puzzle has been missing from historical accounts because the report seems to have played very little role in the campaign or in Moynihan's defeat. The famous controversy took time to build, arriving in 1966 and continuing well into 1967.

There were some larger and less personal factors in the failure of the debate to generate a positive policy result: even at the high point of the Great Society, it is far from clear that a large-scale social program of family allowances (coming on top of Medicare) could have been enacted. Left unaddressed (then and later) was the overarching fact that, beginning in the 1960s, American working and wage earning were taking place in an increasingly diffused and competitive global economy in which the United States was but one of many highly developed economies. For African Americans, this was a development with special implications. As Earl Lewis has argued, the economic and political shackles formally imposed by segregation were coming off just as the general price of entry into the American middle class was rising steeply.[26]

Potentially powerful historical moments don't occur very often, and they can be easily lost. In this case, Moynihan and some of his more inflammatory critics must share responsibility for their debate making it more difficult to discuss the connections between a changing economy and the stability of American families, as well as those connections between historical exclusion based on race and continuing exclusion rooted in a changing economy.

BEHIND THE WHITE LINE

In spite of the completeness of his preparation, Coles was unable to surmount some barriers to research by segregation. Coles's picture of white southerners in crisis because they oppose desegregation efforts is not quite as complete as that of the black southerners. Looking back, in 1971 Coles, in perhaps his single most important essay on his fieldwork, "The Observer and the Observed," discussed how he wrestled with his own reaction to what he heard and how he conformed to the stereotype held by his white listener of the coldly and silently judgmental professor whose mind was busy filing away this man as a social type. Jane Coles prodded him to look again, this time more closely to see experiences and attitudes that Coles had in common with his interlocutors.

> "He and his wife are so predictable," I once said to my wife as we were leaving the house—after they had been thoroughly kind to us, fed us . . . delicious fried chicken and okra and cooked tomatoes and mashed potatoes and home-baked bread and pecan pie topped with ice cream. If I was annoyed, my wife was annoyed with me. She sensed my irritation and impatience and at times outrage. She too felt dismayed and saddened by what she heard. But she also felt something else: she felt that in such a home we were in the presence of more than odd or idiosyncratic or unusual people. . . . For my wife, "they" were in many respects "us"—if not all of us, then most of "us." . . . She simply would not stop pointing out that if there were differences between us and some of the white hecklers we had met on the street, some of the white people we were getting to know, there were also many things we shared . . . as white people, as Americans, as men and women alive in the second half of the twentieth century. Nor would she allow me to get away with saying that my job was to find out how the black children were getting along.[27]

In later books—especially *The Buses Rolled* and *The Middle Americans*[28]—Coles gave equal attention to those being pushed to make a change that they deeply oppose; the racism is there, tangled up in complicated ways with other emotions that cannot be summarily discounted as window dressing for racism.[29] As for the representation of white families mobilized against segregation in volume one of *Children of Crisis,* Jane Coles's victory was, at that point, only partial. Perhaps the only segregationist counterpart to Ruby Bridges in the series is Jimmy, Ruby's white classmate, who was clearly an ideological racist, although a sometimes inconsistent one. That he was a classmate at all is the fly in the ointment: Jimmy's parents may not have had the financial means to send their child to a private school, to buy their way out of desegregation and perhaps out of meeting the Coleses' research team. They withdrew him when the protests began and returned him once they had subsided. Beyond this, nothing is known about Jimmy's parents or family life.[30] There are, in addition to Jimmy, bitterly segregationist youths and parents represented in the *Children of Crisis* series, but there is no comparable family picture.

Much has been made of how racism and hate are reflected in the disfigured and distorted perceptions that African Americans, in some circumstances, seemed to hold of themselves. By contrast, there seems little appreciation that racism can distort the perceptions held by both parties, including the one with the upper hand. Though segregation may have kept them apart until now, Jimmy and Ruby's drawings also show a shared distorted perception of brown people. When Jimmy, an exacting reproducer of details in other contexts, drew Ruby, Coles declared that "it is almost as if he had suddenly embraced surrealism." For Jimmy, brown was the key symbolic detail for understanding people thus colored: "Either they were in some fashion related to animals, or the color of their skin proved that, if they were human, they were dirty human beings—and dangerous too."[31]

Under questioning from Coles, Jimmy explained that "she's funny. She's not like us, so I can't draw her like my friends. Besides," he added in a moment of gifted observation, "she hides a lot from us."[32] Over the course of Jimmy's going to school with Ruby, his drawings changed, reflecting an emergent and at least a partially new consciousness. Jimmy's drawings became a time-lapse photograph of one individual's internal response to a changing outside world: "In time [Jimmy] regularly came to see [Ruby] as an individual. Amorphous spots and smudges of brown slowly took form and structure. . . . Eventually she gained eyes and well-formed ears."[33]

The segregationist Coles focused on in volume 1 is an adult identified as Mrs. Patterson. Mrs. Patterson did not have the means to send a child to private school in order to avoid desegregation. Her economic poverty became matched by an exhaustion and poverty of the spirit. At that point in her life, this drastic change in the social order was beyond her emotional means to accept. "I have enough to do," she told Coles, "just to keep us alive without niggers coming around. They're lower than a dog in behavior. At least he knows his place and I can keep him clean. You can't do that with them. They're dirty. Have you ever seen the food they eat? They eat pig food and they eat it just like pigs, too."[34]

According to Coles, Mrs. Patterson, the virtually single mother of five children between the ages of four and seventeen, was fighting a losing battle of attrition with some dire circumstances. Coles wrote, "She is struggling to manage herself in the face of poverty, ignorance, social isolation . . . and virtual abandonment by her occasionally employed husband."[35] This language and the imagery they bring to mind are another summons to remember the lost opportunity represented by skewed discussion of the Negro family in the mid- and late 1960s. Poverty, ignorance, and social isolation are not the flaws of one person, people, or race but conditions confronted by many people in many circumstances. As one child told Coles, "The rich folks decide how the poor folks live."[36] This sense of class resentment was shared by many whites, even some like the New Orleans fireman's wife, who challenged Coles: "You want to know how my children like going to school with the colored? Why don't you talk to the people in the federal government or the rich people in the Garden District? Ask them what they think they have done to us. You can't really know about plain working people like us, unless you go find out about the big shots. It's their decisions that make us live the way we do."[37]

A SOCIAL SCIENTIST ENTERS HIS POLITICAL CULTURE

Coles's education in the practical politics of translating research findings into an improved society formally began in 1965, the first year of the Great Society's War on Poverty. Coles spoke on behalf of the Child Development Group of Mississippi (CDGM), which was trying to bring Project Head Start, begun by the Office of Economic Opportunity (OEO), to Mississippi.

He was, by now, a heavily credentialed expert with considerable fieldwork behind him. Though Coles had many recommendations to improve CDGM programs, these were quite minor when placed against all that was being done correctly. As he observed: "In my ten years of work in child psychiatry, I have yet to see a program like this one, in the sense that against almost impossible odds children have been taught and also receive the benefits of medical care in a manner and with a thoroughness that is truly extraordinary. . . . this program is actually reaching the poor children and doing so in a way that that makes any doctor feel truly impressed."[38]

The struggle over the CDGM deserves to be remembered as another defining moment in the nation building of the 1950s and 1960s. U.S. Senators John Stennis, James Eastland, and other members of Mississippi establishment had good reason to fear the CDGM. Like the Freedom Summer of 1964, the CDGM was an initiative from within Mississippi that had powerful out-of-state allies. Expertise and money were coming from outside Mississippi to meet the expressed need and desire of some Mississippi parents to "give our children something to think about and talk about." Many of these parents developed lesson plans influenced by the Montessori method, which encouraged learning through unfettered exploration—"free choice time," during which each child would be encouraged "to think for himself."[39]

What could be more conducive to a potential reconstruction of Mississippi, to its evolution into a more open national society? Not only this but a unique ingredient of Project Head Start was its reliance on the parents of the program's children themselves. In addition to providing nutrition and early learning to children, Head Start was also an employment and training program for parents, especially mothers. With the guidance of Montessori teacher Lena Gitter (an out-of-state volunteer), Head Start mothers not only earned some income but also gained hands-on experience turning muffin tins, string, and dried beans into a "sorting game to teach children distinctions of size and color."[40]

Senators Stennis and Eastland and Governor Paul Johnson correctly saw little effective difference between the work of the CDGM and the work of the Freedom Summer movement. Whether it was a "Freedom School" staffed by many out-of-state volunteers or a network of CDGM Head Start centers receiving millions of dollars in federal funds, in each case the fundamental goal was, in the words of political theorist Danielle S. Allen, "to cultivate new habits of citizenship," stressing agency over mere silent acceptance.[41] What these leaders refused to understand was that, in each case, these initiatives were Mississippi born and bred and brought together by new historical circumstances.

It is a measure of Coles's solid reputation in Washington, D.C., and in the South "as an involved Movement person," even before his first book appeared in 1967, that the Washington OEO recruited him to go down to Mississippi to appraise the CDGM's medical programs (which earned his strong endorsement).[42] The fact that Coles came as an emissary from Washington caused many within the CDGM to view him with a new skepticism; others allied with the CDGM saw in him a leader who might be strong enough to defend the group against a once-enthusiastic federal patron now seemingly looking for a way to satisfy the CDGM's powerful congressional foes. According to federal poverty warrior and ardent CDGM advocate Polly Greenberg's account, Coles conducted a rigorous review of the CDGM's medical programs, which included examining several children and reporting back to the OEO, in writing, on their condition. He seemed reticent to comment on the larger intrigues at work. "He had been told to get the health picture," Greenberg wrote, "and he had set out to do just that," while avoiding what may have been the OEO's real plan, which was to install Coles as the CDGM's new director.[43]

In the end, the CDGM succeeded in staving off its immediate demise at the hands of Stennis, Eastland, and Johnson. Allies in the labor movement and beyond responded to the CDGM's call for help to prevent a timid OEO from "secretly set[ting] up a new board of directors made up of white businessmen, plantation owners and a few Negroes and taking the CDGM out of the hands of poor people."[44] Ultimately, however, the CDGM was supplanted by a program with direct ties to the Governor's Office. This was the result of congressional modifications of the OEO's "community action" programs to ensure greater control by mayors and governors. The whole experience left Coles very uncomfortable with how he had played the hand the OEO had dealt him and wishing he had been more outspoken against federal efforts to wrest control of the CDGM from its founders.[45]

The fight over the CDGM's legitimacy as a recipient of federal antipoverty funds was itself but a few pages in a larger chapter of social upheaval tied to the intensifying mechanization of agriculture and the extension of the minimum wage to agricultural workers. As civil rights activism also intensified, the process of mechanization and the extension of the minimum wage were used as a pretext for planters to economically disenfranchise hundreds of thousands of unskilled workers whose families were left, in many cases, without a cash income sufficient to qualify for food stamps and other forms of commodity assistance.[46] By the spring and summer of 1967, a new crisis—a hunger crisis—was being superimposed upon the existing political conflict over whether "outsiders" had hijacked the community-action element of the federal War on Poverty to bring an unwise and unwanted social and political revolution to Mississippi. This crisis brought Coles back up to Capitol Hill, with his friends and allies from the struggle to keep the Child Development Group of Mississippi alive and independent. Among this group was Marian Wright Edelman, the brilliant Mississippi-born and Yale-educated civil rights attorney for whom the CDGM struggle would be the first public chapter in a long career of social activism extending into the present. As Wright told a U.S. Senate subcommittee investigating the situation in Mississippi,

> After two civil rights bills and the third year of the poverty bill's operation, the situation of the Negro [in Mississippi] is that he's poorer than he was; he has less housing; he's as badly educated; he's almost in despair. We now face a major crisis in the Mississippi Delta. . . . there has been a gradual trend toward . . . mechanization. . . . Those people who have only the skills of chopping and picking cotton have absolutely nothing to do. . . . Now, what are we going to do with these people. . . . Here you have a number of people who have never had any skills, who are basically illiterate . . . who have little housing—absolutely no place to go, no jobs and no hopes of getting any. . . . We are still finding a tremendously bad pattern of racial discrimination and maladministration of the welfare program. . . . the welfare program is . . . being used to punish people who [have] participated in civil rights activities or have participated in community action programs of the more radical nature than those controlled by the State.[47]

Coles, representing a delegation of physicians conducting an investigation of malnutrition and outright starvation on behalf of the Field Foundation, agreed: "Let me summarize what we have seen: Evidence of vitamin and mineral deficiencies; serious untreated skin infections and ulcerations; eye and ear diseases; unattended bone diseases . . . prevalence of bacteria and parasitic diseases . . . diseases of the lungs and heart requiring surgery which have gone undiagnosed [and] untreated; epidemic and neurological disorders receiving no care; kidney ailments that in other children would require hospitalization. Finally, in girls and boys in every county we visited, evidence of severe malnutrition with injuries in the body tissues, muscles, bones and skin."[48]

Although Coles could confirm Wright's charge that raw "political factors . . . determine to a very significant degree the eligibility of families" for various kinds of aid, this was not his most significant contribution to this public record; rather, it was in his psychological and psychiatric interpretation of what starvation does to the mind and imagination. In a testimony delivered in July 1967, Coles described his work on volume 2 of *Children of Crisis,* "in which I am describing in detail what it means to a child when his parents are sick more or less all the time and are hungry more or less regularly. . . . They become tired, petulant, suspicious and finally apathetic. . . . From all that one can learn . . . the aches and sores of the body become for a child of four or five more than a concrete physical fact of life; [they] bring to the child's mind reflections of his worth and [the] judgment upon him and his family [by] the outside world, which he not only feels but [by which] he judges himself. They ask themselves and others what they have done to deserve the pain they seem to feel."[49]

Coles's fieldwork led him to the conclusion that it was not adversity that caused this spirit of resentful surrender but the lack of basic nutritional necessities. Adversity weakens the individual only when it is experienced without the love and support of others. And the absence of constructive challenge in the life of a person surrounded by material comfort alone might well lead to a variant of the sullen resentment experienced by those without basic nutritional, medical, and psychological support. In an appearance before another committee in late 1966, Coles reminded the assembled senators of the strength he had observed in Ruby Bridges as she walked through the angry New Orleans mob:

> If you will remember the little girl who went through the mobs in New Orleans to go into a school: for a while she was all by herself in that building, and then one by one, one or two little [white] children came back. Now she is becoming a teenager. She is a girl of great personal strength and dignity.

I came to see her, looking for the trouble that I confidently expected to find. I expected her to be filled with trouble, and in a sense I had to change my whole way of looking at people, because she had not only survived, but she has endured and persisted. . . . How is it that other children—some from bleak homes, but some from very comfortable ones—fail to develop much beyond sullen, apathetic or enormously angry men and women, even though they never face the stress of mobs? Could it be that children are hurt not by stress but by boredom, by a sense of uselessness, futility, stress that leads nowhere?[50]

The publication of volume 1 opened a new Washington-centered phase in Coles's work within the political system. In addition to publishing essays in leading journals, Coles regularly testified before Congress between 1966 and 1973, a period characterized by both social breakthrough and backlash. Between 1966 and 1968, Coles also developed a particularly close friendship with Senator Robert F. Kennedy and Peter Edelman, a key legislative aide (who married Marian Wright in 1968). That friendship, Peter Edelman remembered, began with a colloquy between the two men about how black children experienced the discovery of being black and poor in a country that many celebrated as being white and rich.[51]

KENNEDY: First, talking about the Negro, what is it that you think would be the best thing that could happen for the Negro child growing up in the ghettos of the United States today?

COLES: I have the feeling . . . that the young Negro children of the slums . . . I can prove it from what they say and what they draw, are waiting to learn that the rigid biblical morality that they have . . . will pay off. I think that what they need is evidence from the rest of us that this is true, and I think that there are many, many hundreds of thousands of white parents and young people in this country who don't know how to do this, but want to do it. . . . I think that if . . . the teachers, the young doctors . . . the young lawyers who are craving some way of doing this [could] be enabled to go into the ghettos, the children could see them and learn from them, then I think these children would learn their own worth. And they would teach and help their "helpers" too.

KENNEDY: What is it that you think would be the most valuable thing that they could receive?

COLES: I don't think there is any one answer, but one answer is a *presence* . . . of *opportunity,* which I know has become such a downtrodden cliché now. What I see in these children is unnerving because they tell me that they . . . simply don't believe that the various statements that they hear about what is going to be done about the ghetto mean anything and what they confront the observer with is their conviction that the rest of the nation is full of hypocrisy.

KENNEDY: That is what my judgment would be. Nevertheless, going into some of these areas and looking at the faces of the children between the ages of six and twelve and then comparing [them] to the faces of children . . . from very wealthy homes . . . my strong impression is that the ones who come from these ghetto areas are much, much happier. . . . Do you think that is true or not?

COLES: These children have vitality and energy, and a kind of awareness that . . . we would consider the essence of sophistication. . . . How do you tell the contented American middle class, that craves every new kind of child training . . . that their children need suffering and stress?

KENNEDY: I was just wondering if you think it is possible . . . that the school system in the ghetto . . . might be made effective?

COLES: Well, I have seen school systems . . . that have ignored the regular school systems of this country. [In] the Freedom Schools of the North and the South, there is in existence an entire underground of schools of students who are teaching . . . children. They are doing a marvelous job. . . . However, the problem that afflicts both these children and their teachers is that the teachers cannot give them jobs when they get to be about fifteen or sixteen, and now many of the students who are conducting these schools now say they are also being called hypocrites. . . . It hasn't paid off. . . . I wish the people could see the early childhood of some of these children, the particular closeness they feel toward their parents, the way their parents try to protect them from what is going on outside. Then the child goes out into the street, becomes very active . . . energetic, exploratory, full of all kinds of things. [By age twenty] they live on in a kind of cynical and angry fashion . . . So the sense of betrayal following this extremely moral attempt to live up to society is an astonishing . . . and a very horrifying thing to watch.[52]

This colloquy between Kennedy and Coles is especially significant because it seems to have had a great impact on Kennedy. Several months later, in March 1967, Senator Kennedy, in a speech to the Child Study Association, directly referenced Coles's research and testimony no fewer than three times. Kennedy seemed especially in awe of the children's plasticity and dynamism, which fueled his hope that casting a special light on the child might provide a new political momentum for positive change in a world whose youth sometimes seemed to be turning from SDS (Students for a Democratic Society) to LSD. Dr. Coles's first lesson to Senator Kennedy came directly from *Children of Crisis: A Study of Courage and Fear.* Kennedy was struck not only by the courage of Ruby Bridges but also by the prospect of something not directly demonstrated in the book itself: that her friend Jimmy's revised drawings of Ruby as a more fully developed human being might actually also have a long-term influence on Jimmy's parents.[53]

Senator Kennedy was also taken with Coles's observation that black children from very impoverished families nonetheless "have a vitality and an energy, and a sly vigorous awareness that their more comfortable white contemporaries often do not have." And yet a life lived without many necessities in an otherwise wealthy world develops these children into "bitter, frustrated, withdrawn, hostile teenagers."[54] Finally, Kennedy directly quoted Coles's Senate testimony that the attitudes and behaviors of teachers and administrators in "ghetto schools" have the cumulative impact of killing that spirit as "inappropriate" and even because it may be "too much for us."[55]

As a scene in the larger historical drama of the Great Society years, this colloquy also provides a full view of the beginnings of a dialogue about the social and political price of pursuing the Second Reconstruction. Fundamental questions were honestly grappled with: How will the youngest African Americans be brought into the entire system, not just its political institutions? What would the economic costs be? What demands should be made upon traditional institutions, especially schools? What might be the role of the new institutions of the movement (such as Freedom Schools) in a reconstructed order? What should be the places and the roles of various parts of "white America" in the society to come? Could the somewhat unsteady American welfare state be extended and broadened to close the serious gaps in wealth that exist among the allegedly free and equal whites? How could the need for challenge be sold to those without it?

The exchange between Kennedy and Coles is one of several starting points for a conversation that took place in various forms over the next decade. The Reagan election of 1980, even if it did not fulfill all the hopes of its partisans for a smaller government not obliged to consider any of these questions, did, over the long term, tilt the debate decisively against the kind of change that Kennedy, Coles, and their allies wished to pursue.

Coles's work with Kennedy marked him in lasting ways. According to Coles, it was Kennedy who urged him to broaden his in-depth research of the poor to include Chicano, Native American, and Eskimo children.[56] In his devotion to listening to all voices, in his passion for understanding those who chose George Wallace over Hubert Humphrey or George McGovern when they voted (if they voted at all), Coles was performing the bridge-building work in social science that Kennedy attempted in electoral politics.[57]

As a recognized force, especially in the liberal neighborhoods of the American establishment, Coles used his political contacts to raise the visibility of his research. Emerging national liberal leaders (and future presidential candidates) Walter F. Mondale, McGovern, and Edward M. Kennedy sought his expertise and lent him political credibility by providing introductions to very short distillations of his fieldwork.[58] In content, these additional books were lavishly illustrated reminders not only of the cultural ambiance of the 1930s in order to highlight a continuity of needs thirty years later but also of the racism that continued to configure political necessity in such a way that even FDR, in his turn, decided it would be best to look the other way until the political realities improved.

Of his friendships with political leaders in this period, the most important, after Kennedy, was with U.S. Senator Walter Mondale. Their correspondence extended from 1967 until 1976, when Mondale was elected vice-president. What began as a correspondence between Senator Mondale and Dr. Coles in March 1967 became an exchange between Fritz and Bob by August 1969 and continued in that tone through 1976. In his work as an occasional essayist for the *New Republic,* Coles lauded Mondale's frank advocacy for the poor and the powerless. He followed the publication of his profile, "Mondale of Minnesota: Champion of Powerless People," in the December 25, 1971, issue,[59] with a warm letter looking to the role he hoped Mondale would play in the 1972 election campaign: "If I were Edmund Muskie and had just received the nomination of the Democratic Party for the presidency, I would turn to you and ask you to be a running mate. The both of you could go to the working people of this country, the factory workers, the blue-collar workers and white-collar workers, the small farmers, and raise hell with the way a whole range of things are being done in Washington. There's plenty of populism left in the people of this country, and it is simply there waiting to be approached sensibly and forthrightly."[60]

Sometimes the necessities of research complicated political involvement. Although Coles accepted an invitation to advise the McGovern campaign in 1972, he did fear that too high profile a role would complicate his fieldwork among working-class whites in Boston.[61]

From the public platform created by *Children of Crisis,* Coles sought to engage with the public by challenging enduring stereotypes about the poor and drawing a stark contrast between a generous and Olympian rhetoric about the generosity of its government and the miserliness of the daily operational practice. Two years after the passage of the Voting Rights Act, in an essay for the *New York Times Magazine* timed with the publication of the first volume of *Children of Crisis,* Coles opposed the tyranny of certain all-American dictators and championed the right of even the very poorest Americans to live and be treated as citizens: "In Alabama and Mississippi and elsewhere in the South, poor people of both races remain hopelessly divided by years of hate and fear. They are still the victims and the oppressors still the jailers who beat the 'uppity ones,' still the governors and would-be governors who rant and rave, and worst of all, people by the many thousands who are lucky to earn $800 or $900 in a year. School libraries, the vote—they are . . . irrelevant in the lives of migrant farm workers, tenant farmers or sharecroppers, all of whom live as citizens of this rich, strong and God-fearing Republic."[62]

The same article offered a child's-eye view of social change from an African American boy drawing a brown school bus (with a face for an engine and eyes for headlights): "Children are like dreamers: they remember everything and say or draw the most explicitly symbolic things. I have no doubt that, in this instance, a Negro boy was showing me what older Negroes in both the South and the North keep telling me: the past was the past. The bus was carrying him away from ladders, trees and death. . . . he was moving toward the sun, toward something that would promise life and freedom. . . . 'The bus can go real fast [the boy tells Coles], so if anyone gives us trouble, we can show him.'"[63]

Barely a week after Neil Armstrong and Edwin Aldrin had landed on the lunar surface in July of 1969, Coles went before Congress and linked that symbol of his nation's First World status to the fate of Americans still trapped in economically poor and politically powerless communities throughout the country: "They live fifty miles from Cape Kennedy. No billions have been spent on them and they are not going any place, including the moon. They are just living where they are, though. They do a lot of traveling up and down the Eastern seaboard. They are predominantly children."[64]

In the same hearing, Coles spoke directly to another enduring stereotype of American political culture: the idea that people are poor by choice or out of laziness. "No group of people I have worked with . . . tried harder to work . . . in exchange for the desire to work . . . these workers are kept apart like no others . . . are denied even halfway decent wages, asked to live homeless and vagabond lives, lives of virtual peonage."[65] Coles's testimony was part of a larger effort to create a more coherent and thickly woven safety net to insure that no American went hungry. The tangible product of this work was achieved in the mid-1970s, with the expansion of the federal Food Stamp and School Lunch programs.[66]

Like so many liberals of the time, Coles wanted to understand the problems faced by white Americans who, in politics and social background, were so different from himself. Specifically, how could white middle- and working-class voters be brought within a coalition supporting not only measures to secure equal opportunity for minorities but also a program that would give economic security to all? Searching for answers to these kinds of questions was at the heart of Coles's fieldwork; and it drew the respectful interest of the Nixon administration as he worked on *The Middle Americans*.[67] It also drew him toward political figures like Mondale, who, he hoped, would have the political skills and opportunity to build a new kind of New Deal coalition. The steps toward that goal were taken, he believed, by answering key questions such as, why did such a large majority of whites oppose busing? Was it just racism and a knee-jerk resistance to having a difficult life unsettled further? Or did this silent majority have something more to tell us? When the desegregation challenge moved North, Coles moved with it. In 1968 and 1969, Coles observed busing from the ground up in thirteen cities outside the South.[68]

As part of this work, Coles documented how closely the protest against busing and other symbols of social change during the Second Reconstruction blended with surrounding grievances about a new sense of powerlessness and economic insecurity. Consider the words of a white Boston mother who opposed crosstown busing:

> I'm not against any individual child. I am *not* a racist. . . . I just won't have my child bused to some god-awful slum school, and I don't want children from God knows where coming over here. We put our last cent into this home. We both work to keep up with the mortgage and the expenses. We're not rich; we can't afford to be generous at someone else's expense. We just want to live peacefully out here. . . . We want to be able to go out of our house without carrying a gun or holding on to a German police dog. We want to see them off to school, and not sit for the rest of the day wondering, Are they safe, will there be a big fight, and are they afraid even to walk home if they miss the bus? That's why I'm opposed to bringing kids from one kind of section to another; it's going against what's natural for both groups of people. And if they try to take *our* children across the city, just because some college professors and professional agitators . . . say they should go, we'll have a civil war right up here in the North! Anyway, no one asks us about anything, so I guess we have to learn how to band together and take care of ourselves.[69]

Coles follows this passage with a tough analysis of where perhaps he and his allies in the civil rights movement had missed something important:

> For her and people like her all over the country school desegregation entails not only social and economic threats but a kind of political affront: others begin to flex their muscles and make their point, whereas "ordinary working people . . . have to sit back and take it, always take it." Taking it, she registers surprise, annoyance, resentment, confusion, fear, anger—and, not least, a sense of powerlessness, conveyed sometimes in the briefest but most plaintive of questions: "Why us?" And, for a while, many of us involved in

> one way or another with the civil rights movement had little interest in answering such a question. She was a "racist" or a "covert racist"—that is, if we even thought about her at all. Chances are we didn't, at least not in the beginning. . . . There were, in our minds, the blacks, a terribly hurt and denied people, and us, their allies.[70]

Placing the quotes by Coles and his subjects in this section side by side gives a clear sense of the sociopolitical challenge that liberals of the Great Society/Second Reconstruction period sought to master: building a strong coalition of the powerless, the migrant worker, the lower-middle-class and middle-class white men and women, pressed hard by rising property taxes and increasing uncertainty about the future, and newly enfranchised and energized blacks.

For black parents, the risks and fears were also great, but they were mixed with the hope that present difficulties might bring substantial future dividends in educational opportunity. Coles captured the difficult calculation of the cost-benefit analysis of social change in the following quotation: "'I try to tell my daughter every morning . . . that when she gets on a bus, she's building a future for herself, and when she enters that school, she's doing more building, and when she leaves in the afternoon, she's put in a day of building, besides learning her numbers and her letters.' The child got the message. She seemed too serious, too intent on that building her mother kept on mentioning."[71]

Some blacks worried about the special costs their children had to pay in the desegregation experiment. As one woman in Berkeley, California, shared, "We worry about the Negro children; is it too much for them to be at school with boys and girls who have so much more, are far better prepared?" These new fears coexisted with older ones about the consequences of becoming *too* conscious of race: "'What does that white teacher mean asking me to do that? Why did the white girl say what she did to me?' Oh, I've spent a lifetime with those questions. . . . I hope and pray . . . that this new busing program will help *this generation* of Negro children grow up differently."[72]

Most important in determining a parent and child's attitude toward busing was where they believed themselves to be headed as a result. When he rode the school buses of Berkeley for one week in the fall of 1968, Coles found a community very much like the many others he would visit, where tension, anxiety, and guarded optimism were all close neighbors. The Berkeley differences that did exist had to do with a process initiated by the school district. Community members were actively brought into decision making at every point, emphasizing class as well as race issues in a way that Coles deeply admired. In addition, the busing plan was a two-way process, which required sacrifice by both whites and blacks and by rich and poor.[73]

The approach in Berkeley stood in positive contrast to the later approach in Boston. In the fall of 1974, when busing came to Boston by the order of a federal court, Coles took issue with the approach. In an interview with *Boston Globe* columnist Mike Barnicle, Coles charged that the busing program was "a scandal . . . I do not think that busing should be imposed on working- class people exclusively. It should cross these lines and people in the suburbs should share [in] it."[74]

The fact that Coles believed himself to be speaking about the struggles of "working class people who happen to be white and working class people who happen to black . . . both of whom are very hard-pressed; neither of whom has much leverage on anything" was lost on many admirers of Coles, people who had counted him as an ally in pursuit of fundamental social reform. In the transcript which took up most of page 23 of the *Boston Globe* on October 15, 1974, Coles attempted to explain the "contradictory and conflicting emotions" felt by white policemen, firemen, teachers, and others who found themselves trying to serve their South Boston community in a time of crisis: "It's nerve-wracking. They feel constantly misunderstood. These are people who are being called pigs now by their own. They have been called fascists by the liberal and radical ideologues; ignorant and uncouth on general principle by all the suburban people who come into the city and now their own community feels that they have betrayed them."[75]

Whatever the merits of that particular analysis of South Boston's people, there is a glaring absence of any discussion of what black students and their parents were experiencing, especially the violence targeted at blacks, an omission especially startling when set beside Coles's own writings on desegregation in these years. *Post* columnist Hubie Jones (also a professor of urban planning at MIT) feared that Coles's comments would "divert public attention from the central issue, which is racism," and "create sympathy for persons engaging in violence."[76]

In a way that has been overlooked, Coles's comments are entirely of a piece and consistent with his work during the Second Reconstruction, especially in the years right after the assassinations of Martin Luther King Jr. and Robert F. Kennedy. Like the liberal politicians with whom he made common cause in the early and middle 1970s, Coles was engaged in trying to find ways of reaching out to the white ethnic working class who shared many hardships with black Americans. As C. Vann Woodward, Lawrence Goodwin, Steven Hahn, Nell Irvin Painter, and Michael Kazin have each memorably demonstrated, this has been a lasting challenge for those dedicated to the creation of a multiracial social democracy in the United States.[77]

After the death of Robert Kennedy, his electoral performance in the 1968 Democratic presidential primaries (especially his winning plurality in the Indiana primary) acquired a significance that was not fully justified either by Kennedy's 42 percent of the vote there nor his victories in later primaries; the Indiana victory was taken as evidence that Robert Kennedy—and perhaps only Robert Kennedy—could do what Democrats must do to win now that the post–New Deal era had finally arrived: build a coalition of the alienated and economically disenfranchised working class: white, black, brown, and red.[78] Coles devoted himself after 1968 to rediscovering all parts and constituencies of this historically elusive "other America."

GOODWILL DIPLOMAT

For those taken aback by Coles's comments on busing in Boston, the next few years held further surprises as his continued travels throughout the country gave him a deep understanding of the conservative populism that elected and reelected Ronald Reagan as president of the United States. Writing in April 1980 in the pages of the *New Republic,* Coles told of recent visits to the sites of his research during the 1960s and early 1970s. In the suburbs of Boston, the American South, and the working-class Chicano neighborhoods of Albuquerque, Coles observed the "politics of scarcity and fear at work: racial slurs directed at blacks for being demanding or 'lazy,'" and at Indians for "not being really being part of this country."[79]

To these Americans, Reagan possessed Jimmy Carter's honesty in combination with a toughness seen to be lacking in an overwhelmed incumbent. For his part, Carter was not the "fighting populist" in the mold of Harry Truman. Unlike Truman, who stood his ground even when public opinion was against him, Carter moved to where short-term political necessity directed him, a strategy that caused him, by the latter days of his term, to imitate rather than credibly distinguish himself from Reagan.[80] Consequently, Coles urged his readers not to underestimate the drawing power of Reagan, who, after all, had served as the governor of the nation's largest state for eight years without bringing disaster to the state's government.[81]

The economic and political disappointments of the previous decade and Reagan's own record of accomplishment through negotiation as governor of California made it difficult to marginalize the Republican candidate as an out-of-touch extremist. In the sixteen years since Lyndon Johnson defeated Barry Goldwater, "the people [have been] 'educated' from so many quarters, for so many recent years to believe that liberalism is bankrupt, that any sudden attempt to paint Reagan into a reactionary corner may not be so easily managed."[82]

Working as a goodwill ambassador to a variety of "other Americans," Coles assigned to himself the teaching task of helping a public greatly concerned with external threats to look inward. As part of the process of interaction and exchange, these various people taught Coles to be wary of generalization in the name of advancing a theoretical good. Coles was someone who consciously and conscientiously straddled various "worlds" within American society so that the whole might be seen more clearly.

Although he was no longer in demand as a congressional witness, Coles remained in touch with many of the people he had become acquainted with in his fieldwork for the *Children of Crisis* series. In 1960 he had gotten to know Ruby Bridges and her family when the girl first "stepped into history's shadow" at the age of six to be the sole and solitary representative of her race and William Frantz Elementary School (an event made indelible by Norman Rockwell's painting *The Problem We All Live With*), and he stayed the course with her and with her family over the next forty years, even serving as an advisor to Ruby Bridges Hall, when, in 1995, she moved cautiously to become a public figure on her own terms, at the helm of the Ruby Bridges Foundation.[83]

In recognition of his four decades of fieldwork and writing, Coles received numerous honors, beginning with a Pulitzer Prize in 1973 for volumes 2 and 3 of the *Children of Crisis* series. In 1981 the MacArthur Foundation included him among the first class of scholars to receive what have become colloquially known as "genius grants." Ten years later, and not quite twenty-four years after the first volume of *Children of Crisis* was published in 1967, Coles's *The Spiritual Life of Children* entered the *New York Times* best-seller list at number twelve, followed almost exactly six years later by *The Moral Intelligence of Children.*[84] In 1998 President Bill Clinton awarded Coles the highest civilian honor, the Presidential Medal of Freedom. Two years later, Clinton awarded Ruby Bridges Hall the Presidential Citizens Medal. In 2001, before the 9/11 attacks, Bill Clinton's successor, George W. Bush, honored Coles with a National Humanities Medal.

Robert Coles's family resources enabled him to set himself up as an independent, on-the-ground expert witness to both the hope and the trauma of his nation's return to the work of social reconstruction in the late middle years of the twentieth century. And it is in this capacity, as an independent expert witness to the politics of America's continuing nation building and reconstruction that Coles is most valuable to our striving for a deeper historical understanding of the more recent chapters of our nation's life.

With his medical training as both a calling card and a form of personal and social capital, Coles went wherever the action of reconstruction would send him—to New Orleans, to Mississippi, and even back to his hometown of Boston—asking questions to all sides in order both to report events and attitudes and also to clear a space for honest communication between members of conflicting constituencies. Even though Mr. Coles's appearances in Washington on behalf of Head Start or migrant families caused him to work especially closely with liberal Democrats such as Robert Kennedy and Walter Mondale, he nonetheless retained his independence and reminded liberals of how limited and narrowly self-interested their plans and visions could sometimes be.

FROM MOVING WORDS TO MOVING PICTURES "IN LIVING COLOR"

Despite developing a deep interest in the unique properties of still photography to draw out much that lies beyond the surface image, Robert

Coles was, first and foremost, a man of words and a humanist with an abiding interest in other humans. In this connection, it bears mention that, although Coles would become nationally known as the author of a now classic series of books of social observation, key parts of this writing first appeared in *The New Republic,* the leading journal of liberal opinion. In its pages these short essays were noteworthy for their ability to construct spare but powerful word pictures of individual scenes and episodes which told a larger story of injustice and social contradiction. These essays packed the punch of hard-won documentary truth in high resolution for the primary journal of liberal opinion of the 1950s and 1960s.

Nonetheless, Coles was a key figure who was influential even though he was not known to television audiences. In the 1950s, the most widely seen and best-remembered scenes of the Second Reconstruction are not to be found on television; they appear in the expansive and glossy pages of the picture magazines such as Henry Luce's flagship publications, *Time* and *Life,* which remained the first source for news from various fronts of human conflict. Television posed no threat to these publications in the 1950s because, as a public medium entrusted to private corporations, television was not yet then really in the news business; rather, its stewards expended their considerable efforts and talents exploring, organizing, and reflecting the cultural politics of everyday life.[85]

As Lynn Spigel has brilliantly demonstrated, the formative architects of American television organized their enterprise around a vision of family that, in the 1950s and 1960s, resonated with the public. At the center of television's early years was Pat Weaver's conception of "new electronic towns" that, as Lynn Spigel writes, "were purified of social unrest and human misunderstanding."[86] At the center of this utopian polity was the "young upwardly mobile middle class family."[87] Television producers and sponsors used their powers of rigorous editing to perform a function very similar to that performed by local zoning regulations and even the rules of the Federal Housing Administration to exclude or "redline" certain people out of the social picture—older people, gay and lesbian people, and people of color. Whether on television or in the structuring of everyday life in suburban communities, Spigel finds that, in general, these categories of person "were simply written out of community spaces" or relegated to marginal spaces within both the social scene and the television screen.[88]

The founders of American commercial television expanded on tried and true programming genres and advertising techniques to sell a more luxuriant version of the American dream of continuous upward mobility. Sociologist Todd Gitlin summarizes well the long-term cultural and political consequences of these trends in programming and promotion: "By the mid-twentieth century, 'middle-class' had become a catch-all label of choice beloved by pollsters and politicians and editorial writers, and a brilliantly flexible one it was, enabling office and technical workers to share status with doctors and corporate managers."[89] This new cultural homogenizing of a more complex and enduring social reality gave new power to an old American message: "those who failed to ascend had only themselves to blame for not being up to snuff."[90]

When trouble came—seemingly suddenly and unforeseen—in the form of protests over racial segregation, television was there because a crisis beckoned its network correspondents to the scenes of outright and angry conflict. Sociologist Herman Gray is absolutely right to remind us that, to the extent that television did indeed contribute to changes in public opinion and conduct, it was in spite of itself. It was only through the regular crisis coverage of the 1950s and 1960s that black Americans entered the television picture, either as "decent or aggrieved [individuals] who simply wanted to become a part of the American Dream, or as threats to the very notion of citizenship and nation."[91] As we move forward into "communities of the air" and the "electronic towns" and "neighborhoods" created by Bill Cosby and Joan Ganz Cooney, we need to keep the memory of this preexisting and continuing cultural condition—and conditioning—front and center in our own minds.

4

WILLIAM H. COSBY, VICTORIAN REFORMER, AND THE INTEGRATIVE PROPERTIES OF HUMOR

America's resistance to giving the black man a fair shake is unbelievably strong. . . . If white America chooses to withhold equality from the black man, the result is going to be disaster for this country. But if whites allow the black man the same civil rights as they themselves take for granted . . . this country will turn into the coolest and grooviest society the world has ever seen.

—BILL COSBY, *Playboy* interview (May 1969)

The trials of black people . . . are similar to those of all poor and alienated groups, regardless of race. We can all learn from each other and be allies in changing the behaviors and institutions that limit our people's chances for success.

—BILL COSBY and ALVIN F. POUSSAINT, *Come On, People: On the Path from Victims to Victors* (2007)

There is little doubt that, from the beginning of his quest for a public life, one of the things William H. Cosby Jr. most wanted to be was a teacher. As Cosby told an interviewer for *Senior Scholastic* in 1965, "Some part of me will always want to go back to school and teach—not because I was once a dropout and have a lesson to teach, but because the one kid who could have gone the other way is worth everything."[1] Three years later, in a foreshadowing of his work to come on *Fat Albert and the Cosby Kids,*

Cosby made the same point a little more sharply in *Life* magazine: "I mean it when I say [that] I'll be teaching junior high in a few years—in an underdeveloped neighborhood."[2]

Teaching and succeeding as a comedian on the largest stage of all required Cosby to be a cultural politician. As many defeated candidates can attest, winning the ultimate contest meant far more than assembling a program of popular policy positions (or one-liners in the temporary communities created by the "cathartic, integrative ritual of laughter");[3] the other hard and fast requirement of Cosby's cultural office was broadly the same as those faced by the most successful candidates for national political office: to understand the cultural contours of the surrounding polity and to fit one's personal narrative credibly within them—to seem to be one of "us."

Like Dick Gregory, his contemporary in the field of stand-up comedy, Cosby understood that, in its essence, "comedy is friendly relations."[4] Unlike Gregory, Cosby stayed away from debates about race and, for that matter, he avoided politics entirely. His mission, beyond the laughter, was to lead his audience to say, "Yeah, that's the way I see it too. . . . That must mean we're alike."[5]

Cosby's most recent widely reported public statements, made on the fiftieth anniversary of *Brown v. Board,* in which he took "the lower economic people" to task "for holding up their end of the deal" as members of American society, may make it seem too much to ask that Cosby be recognized as a notable participant in the Age of *Brown,* who contributed to the creation of a socially democratic kind of solidarity.[6] Of the children in these families, Cosby said, "They're standing on the corner and they can't speak English. . . . And I blamed the kid until I heard the mother talk. . . . You can't be a doctor with that kind of crap coming out of your mouth."[7] It was then that Cosby made a mistake that contravened his calling, both as a cultural politician and as a teacher when, as historian James T. Patterson aptly put it, Cosby engaged in "blaming more than explaining."[8]

Many years earlier, Cosby had ventured onto the same territory and received nary a criticism. Cosby chided the African American working class for an alleged narrowness of vision. At their best in times of struggle, "we Negroes are people working together in the fields, sharing together . . . like prisoners on a chain gang." And yet when one of them is called to "work in the big house where the white man lives," envy and resentment divide those in the fields from their former compatriots, "like Sidney [Poitier], Harry [Belafonte] and me." The field hands declare that "the guy no longer belongs. He's got the softer life."[9]

Still, according to Cosby, African Americans have not supported those, such as Dick Gregory and Cassius Clay (Muhammad Ali), who have come down from the big house and said, "I think it stinks here." And "what happened to Dick Gregory and Cassius Clay? They are broke and broken. And it's not all the white man. . . . what have the people in the fields done? Have they passed the hat around? No. Gregory and Clay risked their necks for them." At the bottom of it was not hardheartedness but a myopia born of hardship. "The men in the fields are not really used to giving," Cosby said. "A dollar is very hard to earn. A guy, come Friday nights, wants a few drinks, anything to escape. So if you go up to him and say you want five dollars so this other guy can live, he'll say, 'What? Five dollars to build a hospital? Do you know how long it took me to make two dollars?'"[10] In the same interview, Cosby cautions against handouts from the government to the poor. "I don't like the government saying they'll do something and the kids waiting for the bread with their hands out. It also gives some senators and congressman the chance to say, 'We'll take the money away because you were bad.'"[11]

Cosby is an ideologically complicated and contradictory figure. Along with the genial public persona is a genuinely progressive individual who understands the systemic nature of large social problems. In fact, one of the most significant yet overlooked points made by Professor Michael Eric Dyson, in his extensively researched and thoughtful response to Cosby's attack on the most economically disenfranchised blacks, discusses exactly this point: "Cosby's over emphasis on personal responsibility [as opposed] to 'structural features' [in the economy]" not only "wrongly locates the source of poor black suffering—and by implication its remedy—in the lives of the poor," it directly contradicts Cosby's own thinking. As Dyson notes, Cosby's doctoral dissertation presented a "more humane and balanced" sense of the forces at work, which included a heavy dose of "institutional racism."[12]

Cosby is also part of another long American tradition: he is a classically individualistic self-made man who has fought for and won a unique degree of personal success, and one who sees the same capacity existing in others left untapped, perhaps by poor judgment. Being possessed of these contradictory impulses is, in fact, one of the qualities that Cosby shares with many of the millions who have enjoyed his comedy over the years.

Cosby's public life also marks him as a thoroughgoing Victorian reformer, imbued with a faith in the individual whose integration into an emerging democratic capitalist order is made more certain by an allegiance to the values of thrift, hard work, and personal responsibility. To fully understand Cosby as a Victorian reformer, we must follow the lead of cultural historian Daniel Wickberg, whose innovative account of where the modern sense of humor originated introduced us to another side of the Victorian social vision and sensibility. Leading articulators of Victorianism recognized humor as a key social instrument of a democratizing society, a crucial factor that "bridges over the spaces which separate the lofty from the humble."[13] The idea of the self-made man was the product of a new sense of the self that emerged with modernity and a more democratic and less hierarchical ethos. In this context, as Wickberg explained, humor served "as a lubricant protecting against the constant friction of social life." In a new order in which one's rank and position were no longer as set and clear as before, humor served to "ensure that elaborate machinery of living continued to function in a regular way."[14]

The socially and politically integrative power of laughter resides not only in its ability to smooth and soothe, but also in the way it can facilitate debate and dissent. As cultural anthropologist Donna M. Goldstein has written, "humor is a vehicle for expressing sentiments that are difficult to communicate publicly or that point to areas of discontent in social life. The meanings behind laughter reveal both the cracks in the system and the masked or more subtle ways that power is challenged. Humor is one of the fugitive forms of insubordination."[15]

Cosby's public life as humorist and pitchman belongs in the American history of domestic nation building because he—along with other African American participant symbols—was at the very center of a potential cultural transformation that political sociologist Herbert H. Hyman identified in 1972. Just as nation building in countries around the world had grown from and encouraged a "revolution of rising expectations," especially among the youth, a similar process was underway in the United States in the aftermath of the civil rights revolution. In addition to well-known political accomplishments in the United States, Hyman witnessed a change in "ego ideal types."[16]

As in the new African nations, the United States was undergoing a cultural revolution of its own: "As the African past becomes prominent in [American] literature and [American] schoolbooks, as Negro history is being rewritten," Hyman wondered "which of the many diverse types that are represented become internalized as the ideal by white youth?"[17] It is a testament to Cosby's skills as a "cultural politician," a well-known contributor to a new national ethos, that he became the face of Coca-Cola, Jell-O, and other American brands over the 1970s and 1980s. To minimize this achievement is to forget that, in 1963, the year in which Cosby first received national attention, this specific arena (appearing in a television commercial) was, in the words of Norman Hill of the Congress of Racial Equality, the "'Ole Miss' of the broadcast industry."[18]

As civil rights protests dominated the airwaves in the spring and summer of 1963, Lever Brothers, a leading soap manufacturer, came forward in the name of "good business" and demanded that the advertisers for their products (and the producers of the shows they sponsored) make a more concerted effort to diversify their representation of American life. In tandem with this announcement, on August 14, 1963, during a break in the daytime broadcast of the game show *Password* on CBS, the first television network advertisement featuring an African American came on the air (and was pictured on the front page of *Advertising Age* on August 19). The ad for Wisk stain remover showed a young African American third baseman tagging out a white "sliding base runner." This scene is followed by the appearance of the white boy's mother on-screen, extolling the virtues of Wisk to clean the badly soiled seat of her son's uniform. The action taken by Lever Brothers had been a result of the company's outreach to the New York Branch of the Congress of Racial Equality, which was leading an effort to achieve "a better representation of American life" in advertising across all media.[19]

Two years later, as a costar (with Robert Culp) in the series *I Spy*, Cosby himself became a participant-symbol in prime-time television's gradually increasing receptivity to African Americans appearing on screen playing a new variety of character types. The fate of this television series, like so many public events of the time, was carefully watched for the evidence it might give about changing racial attitudes among white Americans, particularly in the South. Only a decade earlier, Nat King Cole, a figure whose broad popularity had seemingly been proven beyond doubt, had been unable to find sponsors for his variety hour on NBC. Network affiliates also refused to carry the program.[20]

By 1965, organized mass protest in favor of racial equality, coupled with the increasing importance of social progress in race relations to the image of the United States during the Cold War, meant that *I Spy* would have plenty of sponsors and plenty of viewers, even in the South. As the *New York Times* reported, 180 NBC affiliates had booked the weekly series, with only three refusals, from stations in Albany, New York; Savannah, Georgia; and Alexandria, Louisiana. Even in the civil rights battleground city of Birmingham, Alabama, *I Spy* would be shown, although on a newly founded UHF station rather than a local network affiliate.[21] On the issue of commercial sponsorship, producer Sheldon Leonard assured, "We have more sponsors than we need."[22]

When *I Spy* placed Cosby before a far larger audience than the substantial one he had already won with his comedy records, Cosby sought, in his own carefully calculated and calibrated way, to make the point that his life and his relationship to the world were far more complicated than the idealized relationship between the characters Kelly Robinson (Robert Culp) and Alexander Scott (Cosby). To the extent that *I Spy* had a political message, it was in its representation of a new American ideal. Culp expressed the sentiment well: "We're two guys who don't know the difference between a colored and a white man. . . . We're showing what it could be like if there had been no hate."[23] The symbolism went beyond the on-screen relationship. "It's the chemistry of those people playing together that builds a following," Culp said on another occasion, "And I guess it's pretty obvious on-screen as well as off that Bill and I have a great regard for each other."[24]

FAMILY MAN

Cosby came on stage with a special key light directed at his every word and move. Even the most recent analysts of Cosby's forty-year career begin by remarking upon his attempt to present "color-blind" comedy. According to journalist Gerald Nachman's analysis, Cosby's significance is best seen when placed in direct contrast to the comedy of his most famous and controversial contemporary, Dick Gregory: "Gregory got extra points by making his liberal white audience feel better about themselves for accepting a dark skinned Negro comedian. Cosby scored even more points with whites by not mentioning race at all. He made it all go away, if only for an hour or two, focusing on human race issues. It was a harmless but meaningful deception and it worked wonders. Cosby played to audiences of all hues, who gave themselves credit for ignoring blackness."[25]

Mel Watkins, the leading historian of African American humor, came to a more measured and accurate conclusion: "Whether intended or not, Cosby's outward congeniality was crucial to his quick ascendancy. At a time when racial confrontations were escalating in the streets, his relaxed, chatty style and surface image of a clean-cut sanguine black man was the antithesis of the menacing figures on the streets. And mainstream America, though it could abide the slashing wit and the more easily perceived anger of a Dick Gregory, seems to have been consoled by the playful brilliance of Cosby's approach."[26]

In addition, obvious only in retrospect, Cosby's seeming silence on race, coupled with his easy work with the most intimate material of human relations—family life—marked him as culturally revolutionary. As Watkins observed, "No previous comic had attempted or been allowed to step so boldly into this nonracial territory. . . . Cosby was quietly asserting that there was no difference between the races—a suggestion of equality that would have been instantly silenced."[27]

If this much is absent from Cosby's material, what is actually there? On his first record, *Bill Cosby Is a Very Funny Fellow Right!* the humor of family and childhood, which would emerge in the next album and become a mainstay in later years, is absent. In this first outing, Cosby demonstrated a fresh inventiveness with some of the stock comedy routines of the late 1950s and early 1960s—applying the rhythms and idioms of modern society to prehistoric man and to biblical characters, ridiculing the overblown claims of television advertising, and poking at the absurdities behind the alleged modernity and sophistication of urban life.[28]

Childhood and family life became a larger proportion of each succeeding album—*I Started Out as a Child* (1964); *Why Is There Air?* (1965); *Wonderfulness* (1966); and *Revenge* (1967)—until it composes three-quarters of the time on *To Russell, My Brother, Whom I Slept With* (1968).[29] The portrait of childhood drawn there is quite historically specific; it is the childhood he shares with his adult audience. In *Wonderfulness, Revenge,* and *To Russell, My Brother, Whom I Slept With* he begins addressing the problems of parenting in the affluent society, territory that is more contemporary to his own life and that of many in his audience.

The version of childhood Cosby drew is also a portrait of poverty, one of overwhelmed and economically hard-pressed parents and often-incompetent teachers. On *I Started Out as a Child,* listeners first meet Cosby's father (the giant) as a "boozed-up" character Cosby and his brother stole money from. That album opens with Cosby's recollections of playing street football in Philadelphia, where the problems of wearing cheap sneakers are at the core of the humor. On *Why Is There Air?* listeners are introduced to a preschool whose redeeming quality is that attending it "teaches you how to say good-bye to your parents without crying." Once inside, chaos reigns, supplemented by bad food ("lukewarm milk and old graham crackers"). The curriculum, to the extent that one exists at all, seems to be little more than a series of intellectually empty exercises (a child repeats the equation "one and one is two," pausing to ask, "What is two?"). In *Wonderfulness,* listeners meet an incompetent shop teacher (renamed Mr. Nasty) trying to bring order to chaos. ("We had gotten rid of five shop teachers in about three months.") According to Cosby, this is a classroom full of students "on the brink of becoming either killers or priests." This shop teacher was famous for coercing confessions from guilty students by degrading their parents. Mr. Nasty is so dumb that, when he appropriates a comic book from Cosby with the promise that it would be returned at semester's end, Cosby retorts, "Why? Does it take you that long to read it?"

In the world of Cosby's childhood, siblings sometimes slept two to a bed, and some kids were so poor that they "chewed water" and lived in dwellings with "walls so thin that you could hear a fly in the other room crawling on it." The world portrayed on the vinyl recordings is tougher and grittier than the television version provided by *Fat Albert and the Cosby Kids* and far less directly didactic. If Cosby steered resolutely clear of sending an explicitly social message, he sent very specific cues that he was talking about a society in which, sometimes, the wrong people hold authority and power. Evaluating the social and political content of Cosby's comedy requires including his advice, shouted at the family radio to Tonto every time he went into town at the Lone Ranger's request. For Tonto going into town would lead to being attacked by bad guys. Cosby remembered yelling to Tonto that he should tell the Lone Ranger to "go to hell."

Many of the young adults of the 1960s grew up in a world that was not only economically poor and more rigidly stratified by class but also far less aware of children with special developmental imperatives and needs. That Cosby, who "arrived in 1937, just ten days before the birth of Superman,"[30] was speaking to "Depression babies" is very clear from his references to the defining elements of kids' culture of the 1930s and 1940s, as evidenced by radio shows such as *Inner Sanctum* and *The Lone Ranger* and movie characters such as the Mummy, the Wolf Man, Frankenstein, and Dracula.

When describing what Cosby's audience thought of him during the 1960s, speculation is based primarily on what journalists covering Cosby intuited. This is unavoidable, and Watkins, writing on this point, is both properly restrained and wise. The absence of solid information about audience reactions, which were available to a degree in regard to *Fat Albert* and especially for the *Cosby Show,* should raise caution. Cosby's 1960s routines about his childhood disturb a settled image of Cosby as a comedian whose vision of family has no sharp edges, no sense that money matters in how families function and how children are raised—or raise themselves.

Cosby's 1976 doctoral dissertation on the impact of *Fat Albert and the Cosby Kids* among child viewers also adds to this image. In that manuscript, Cosby expressed the belief that providing black children with "positive images" that promote a constructive kind of "racial awareness" is entirely compatible with transcending "racial barriers." The *Fat Albert* series would not "exploit a black world." This world would provide a background against which "they explore the child's world." In so doing, Cosby was striving to "bring children together in the formation of common alliances and common pleasures"[31] just as he united adults on his comedy albums.

These stories can easily be read in a way that entirely dilutes any connection to poor children in the present. For many other "Depression babies" who, with a college degree and the GI Bill, could become economically comfortable and secure, these stories can be received in a triumphal frame of mind, one in which a conservative color blindness is seen as being authenticated, without any prod toward the idea that, in the "lifting up by the bootstraps," some got an extra boost, while others, equally situated and deserving, did not because institutional racism made it even more difficult to reach that ideal.

When he committed some of these routines to paper in 1991, Cosby added a layer of explicit meaning by fitting them into a very hallowed and comfortable narrative that seems to be reenacted with every generation: an affirmation of his generation being more affluent than its successor, proof that yesterday had been better than today. Adversity, now distant in fact if not in memory, provided the perfect salve to heal those wounds. Cosby and his cohorts developed positive strengths from the adversities of a childhood in those "happy days before children knew that center-fielders liked sex and Batman was . . . manic depressive," the generation before parents became "social directors" for their children.[32]

Cosby's reframing of his childhood experience in 1991 is especially interesting when compared to some of his coverage of the same territory—on the stand-up stage and in print—twenty-five years earlier. In addition to the softer backlight of nostalgia, there is also an important continuity. In his comedy albums of the 1960s and in his reflections on childhood and parenting in the 1980s and 1990s, Cosby is unsentimentally observant of the behaviors of the middle-class child, especially the sense of entitlement—to material things and to emotional attention—that were not a feature of his own childhood.

Cosby, like millions of Americans of his generation, grew up in one class and, by middle age, lived in another. There is nothing simple or easy about social mobility, especially in a society where many members insist, in the face of substantial evidence to the contrary, that it is "classless." In the 1960s and 1990s, Cosby did well, in part because he was, in journalist Alfred Lubrano's phrase, a "straddler," one who succeeded because of his ability to live in those two very different worlds, fully at home in neither.[33]

THE COSBY CLASSROOM

Nation Time

The political cataclysms of 1968 gave Cosby his first public opportunity to explicitly act as a teacher when he hosted an episode of *Of Black America,* a short-term CBS documentary series broadcast that summer. The episode, titled "Black History: Lost, Stolen or Strayed?" addressed an issue of urgent concern to Cosby. The first scene finds Cosby standing in an empty classroom announcing that "the fable agreed upon until now is that American history is white on white." The mention of token African American "exceptionals" only underlined the general African American exclusion. This omission is a modern-day reflection of a historical attitude: "There was a master race in this country and there was a slave race, and although there isn't any political slavery any more, these same old attitudes have hung around." As this introductory scene progresses, the camera moves back so that the viewer can see black and white children working together. Against this new backdrop, Cosby continues his indictment: "Nowadays we're getting these integrated schools, and most people think that if we get enough teaching and jobs everything's going to take care of itself, but there's a scar of history running through kids as young as these."

The remainder of the broadcast is devoted to an itemized examination of the various ways in which, from the beginning, American culture was organized against black people, whether in the slave codes of the mid-nineteenth century, the reels of *Birth of a Nation* in the early twentieth, or the advertising of modern consumer society, all of which sent the message that, in the words of the unseen narrator, if you were black and wanted to get "as rich as possible," you needed to get "as white as possible."

In its substance, "Black History: Lost, Stolen or Strayed?" repeats some themes that by the late 1960s had gained a wide currency. The *Brown* decision of 1954 had made a point of positing the psychological damage inflicted by a segregated society upon black children (although the court remained entirely silent on the damage done to whites by the same institutional setup). Only one year before this broadcast, in *Children of Crisis,* Robert Coles used black children's self-portraits to document how acculturation to racist patterns in American culture led to distorted self-perceptions among black children. Psychiatrist Emmanuel Hammer repeated this experiment in "Black History: Lost, Stolen or Strayed?" The argument that a desire to "become white" was the tainted seed from which some African Americans nourished dreams of upward mobility revived the theme sociologist E. Franklin Frazier explored nearly a decade earlier in his acidic and impressionistic final book, *The Black Bourgeoisie.*

The program's segments, which focused heavily on damage and victimization, were an overture to a final segment in which the issue of "black power" is addressed. Near the end of the program, another classroom is shown where black children are drilled in the essentials of an "Afro-centric" curriculum, in which black self-assertion and pride are taught in tandem with the rudiments of arithmetic.

At the end of this episode, Cosby challenges his audience to reconsider the impulse to regard such an approach as dangerous. "It's three hundred years—three hundred years—that we've been in this American melting pot, and we haven't been able to melt in yet, and that's a long wait." Cosby closes with the following, which turns the fist of black power into the extended hand of respectful mutuality and cooperation: "Listen, we've been trying all kinds of parts to make the American scene—we've been trying to play it straight and white—but it's been just bit parts . . . from now on, we're going to play it black and American because we're proud of both."[34]

The Cost of Dreams Deferred

When considering Cosby's ambivalent feelings about the African American working class, it is important to note one Cosby vehicle from 1971, a film titled *To All My Friends on Shore,* directed by Gilbert Cates. The film is a hard-edged portrait of an African American family's struggles during the economic "depression" afflicting African Americans in the early 1970s. In the film's first scene, a background portrait of John F. Kennedy, Robert F. Kennedy, and Martin Luther King Jr. telegraphs its political sensibility and sympathies—Bandy Blue and his family, like millions of other Americans, have been pursuing a dream more important than money and material things; in this pursuit of belonging to an enlarged community, they have also experienced great pain and loss.[35]

Cosby stars as Bandy Blue, a hardworking and hard-pressed jack of all trades (chauffeur, baggage handler, junk collector). Blue is tired of living in a world in which "living right is some kind of show [that] all we get to do is watch" and obsessed with achieving an economically secure place for his family. His wife, Serena (played by Gloria Foster), is his equal partner who works "cleaning white ladies' houses" while studying to become a practical nurse. Although she shares her husband's desires, she worries that the ferocity of his commitment to buying a "rotten, never-be-nothing shack" will consume him.

The drama is propelled by the tragic news that their son, Vandy, has sickle-cell anemia. His treatment absorbs all of the family's meager financial and emotional resources. In the course of this tremendous crisis, Gloria guides Blue to the understanding that, for all his strength, his rejection of the seductions of the "live for today" consumer culture, and his ability to "find value in things other people throw away," his focus on the family's future has put an intense strain upon life in the present. Blue's wife and son teach him that there can be great danger in a life defined too exclusively by "savin' and cravin'" and profound value in being a "today person" focused on the emotional and spiritual needs of his loved ones.

These lessons naturally lead to one of Cosby's most famous creative ventures, the long-running Saturday-morning cartoon series *Fat Albert and the Cosby Kids* (1972–84), another of Cosby's efforts to capture life as seen and lived by those in the African American working class. Fat Albert and other characters on the show made their first appearance in "Buck, Buck," a routine on Cosby's 1967 record, *Revenge*. The series was also the subject of Cosby's University of Massachusetts doctoral dissertation, "An Integration of the Visual Media via *Fat Albert and the Cosby Kids* into Elementary School Curriculum as a Teaching Aid and Vehicle to Achieve Increased Learning." Thus, there is an unusually strong record of what Cosby had in mind with the series.

Measured against the tenets of the very fragile moderate-to-liberal consensus that emerged between the mid-1960s and the late 1970s (in universities, corporate America, the corporate world, the federal courts, the federal government, and especially the armed forces), what is most remarkable about Cosby's dissertation is not his commitment to "combat the insidious nature of institutional racism which our schools perpetuate" but his insistence that such racism affected whites as well as blacks. Although blacks "bear the deepest scars" from such racism, Cosby believed that "whites suffer in a more subtle way. . . . They are raised with a countermyth of white supremacy. . . . Neither myth is healthy. Each breeds a negative ego position. On the one hand, there is a feeling of abject failure and inferiority, while on the other, there exists a super ego that is fed by continuous and demonstrated successes, leading to an aggrandized sense of superiority. In combination, they are the combustible ingredients of a divided society."[36]

In making this point, Cosby was doing something particularly important: he was expressing a finding in the work of Kenneth and Mamie Clark, whose research on the formation of racial attitudes in children had received much selective attention in the years following the recognition of the *Brown* decision as a milestone. Much has been said and written about the psychological damage done to black children by racism and racial segregation. At the same time, the Clarks emphasized the damage done to white children by delusions of mastery and power coupled, perhaps, with deep inner doubts about the morality of this unearned privilege. This side of the psychological color line has received very little attention.

Before 1969, when *Sesame Street* revolutionized the look and feel of educational television aimed at children, children's television, whether "educational" or purely "recreational," was, like the rest of television, an all-white world. The white experience was the default experience. By setting its action on a New York City street and by bringing together a racially diverse cast of characters, *Sesame Street* broke this mold. Nonetheless, it did so from a distinctly emergent and secondary platform in the American media world of the 1960s and 1970s: public television.

Cosby fashioned a way to break the color line and bring children's programming with an overtly "pro-social message" to eight million viewers of Saturday morning commercial television. By the late 1960s, this programming universe had become primarily a vehicle for merchandising toys directly to children. As a popular television pitchman for Coca-Cola and Jell-O products in the 1970s and 1980s, Cosby was an important actor in this trend. The commercials in which Cosby starred played quite naturalistically upon his winning ways in conversations with children. At the same time, he used his pull in commercial television to experiment with its capacity to be a constructive social messenger.

Cosby's accomplishment is no small matter. In addition to mixing learning and fun in a new way, something even more important was going on. Prior to this time and for a good many years to come, children's shows assumed that the norm was white. By using the experiences of black children as the norm, Cosby gently challenged this cultural default position. He attempted the same experiment in 1984 with the Huxtable family, asking Americans to accept a black family as a generic representative of family. In that case, the enduring cultural politics behind commercial prime-time television (in which "middle class" status possesses a social solidity and ubiquity that does not exist off-screen), as well as the cultural politics of representing an African American family as normative, added several layers of affluence to the Huxtable household.

In the immediate aftermath of the civil rights movement, *Fat Albert* could be a bit more experimental. Also, as an occasional rather than weekly series, perhaps the rules could be a bit looser. Although set in the "center city today," Fat Albert's neighborhood did not conform to the stereotype of the "slum." It did contain some dubious characters and some criminals, but these figures did not define or dominate the scene. More numerous and visible were good adults—caring parents, attentive teachers, and compassionate neighbors.[37]

How does one teach such a large and ideologically diverse audience about an issue so freighted with such significance as money? How, for instance, should a child learn about the social power of money? The program's advisory panel of experts did not deny that it would be important for a child to learn about money as something "used to gain power over others," but how should this important message be taught to young minds? Even Cosby's expert consultants "had to ask, 'do we really want this message to come across?'"[38] As scholar Heather Hendershot concluded, "*Fat Albert* was about poor black kids, which made it a radical innovation on Saturday morning TV, but the show had difficulty addressing the kids' poverty, except at the level of background design.[39]

Despite these hazards, the issue was not entirely avoided. The first season comprised two episodes, "Creativity" and "Take Two—They're Small." In "Creativity," Fat Albert and his friends decide to start a band but have no instruments. The Cosby Kids fan out, offering to do various chores around the neighborhood, only to be paid pennies or with nonmonetary rewards such as cookies or a stick of gum. As Cosby himself acknowledges, the gang has had "a lot of luck, most of it bad." Feeling defeated, the gang bounces back by creating instruments from things others have thrown away and form the "junkyard band," which becomes a staple of the series. Fat Albert, for instance, makes an accordion out of a heater, while another character learns how to make music by strumming on a mattress frame.

Cosby's moral is that sometimes you have to "make do with what you got." In Cosby's hands, this was not to be a form of resignation to one's circumstances but a way of moving forward when others expect you to remain still.

This moral can also be read in another way: being poor is tough—make the best of it. Cosby is encouraging people to *invest themselves* in solutions, making the most of their "social capital." Consider as well the lesson conveyed by the kids' failed fundraising efforts. The problem was not with the quality of the product offered but with the miserliness of the market's response. The lesson here is one that Marcus Foster applied daily as he made his way through the school system in Cosby's beloved hometown of Philadelphia: the rules and the system don't always work as advertised; intelligent creativity is the answer.

Cosby's social message can also be found in *The Wit and Wisdom of Fat Albert,* a small book of sayings authored by Cosby and published in 1973. What emerges from these pages is another example of gently subversive humor that looks askew at accepted rules for success: "A friend is somebody who doesn't mug you." "Stop crime in the streets—stay home." Several other sayings reflect a sharp awareness of life's unwritten rules, the social and economic facts of life:

> Ben Franklin might've invented electricity, but the dude who invented the meter made all the money.
>
> Give your landlord an inch—and he rents it.
>
> Money doesn't talk—it just goes without saying.
>
> There's one thing about being poor—it's expensive.
>
> The best things in life are free—like clothing? Food? And shelter?[40]

Cosby's greatest commercial success, the *Cosby Show,* again prompts consideration of his work as a "cultural reconstructor." What do these projects, which run counter to Cosby's persona of an affably apolitical personality, tell us about the man? Like Frederick Douglass, Cosby is a Victorian reformer whose sometimes-pointed forceful advocacy for change is interwoven with its opposite—a failure sometimes to appreciate that success is not simply a matter of one's values and attitudes. Upward mobility, especially in a modern industrial and postindustrial order, depends on structural factors that sometimes lie well outside of the individual's control.

That Cosby's advocacy for a reformed society, like that of others, should at times be mixed with anger, bitterness, and narrow-mindedness is a reminder that "upward mobility," whether the more common experience of those who migrate from the working class to the middle and upper-middle class or the more extraordinary migration like Cosby's, is a difficult journey—physically, emotionally, and psychologically. Its psychological dimension continues well after the material process of "moving up in the world."[41] Cosby's range of analysis about his working-class childhood also reflects the complexity and power of the network of values, images, symbols, and associations that are the foundation of American culture and of American politics. This is dense and complicated territory, with tensions, contradictions, and possibilities for innovation and retreat all bundled together. The Cosby story shares a cautionary theme: To reach the most exclusive heights of entertainment (or politics) as a harbinger of change requires not only a clearly drawn blueprint of future plans and directions but a deep and abiding sense of how they are related to and rooted in the established order. It is no easy task to simultaneously *take in* and *take on* one's home culture; the danger of missed connections and crossed wires is constant.

PRIME TIME

1964–1984

In addition to the pages of celebrity journalism generated by the *Cosby Show* that focused rather narrowly on the personality of Cosby and his co-stars, this series also produced some well-placed reviews that were efforts at social analysis, at understanding the *why* of the *Cosby Show*'s historically impressive popular success; it was the most popular prime-time television program in the United States between 1984 and 1989, attracting sixty-two million viewers a week at its peak.[42] What did this sustained popularity say about Americans and American society? Was it a true reflection of African American life? Did it need to perform this role? This dialogue, though ultimately grounded in the politics and political economy of the

1980s, had surrounded Cosby's public life for more than twenty years. Seen through this long historical lens, the journalistic and scholarly debate over the program is an early indicator of a crucial point: the *Cosby Show* was a culminating rather than an innovating event.

The *Cosby Show* was the last great hit of the three-network era. In fact, Cosby argued in 1985 that his sitcom succeeded because it was providing a kind of old-fashioned family style of entertainment that was bringing success to Nickelodeon and Ted Turner's entertainment networks. Within a few years, competition from cable would shrink the audience for the major networks to such a degree that such audiences would be impossible to achieve, even by the most successful series. Also, the *Cosby Show* culminated a twenty-year cycle of African American representation on American television. In 1984, as in 1964, "racelessness" was stressed, and its meaning was a cause of debate among observers. In 1984 the *Cosby Show* was seen in much the same way as previous Cosby efforts had been: either as refreshing indications of a more accepting and inclusive society or as cunning accommodations to the symbolism and iconography of a society stubbornly resistant to fundamental change. In 1984, as in 1964, American commentary on race relations had quite visibly but selectively internalized James Baldwin's insight that "the Negro is the key figure in his country, and the American future is precisely as bright or as dark as his.[43]

The *Cosby Show* arrived and thrived in the latter stages of a period in which mass media were still seen as a potential harbinger and reflector of positive social change. Civil rights advocates understood television news coverage as a powerful ally in shaping public opinion. They also reasoned that the same pressure that had brought some major victories in the legal and political realms might also be directed toward television to help reshape American culture itself. Television was the newest mass medium; television and the aspirations of African Americans (if not necessarily African Americans themselves) were both being integrated into American public life and ritual at the same time.

The 1950s had established television's dominance as a mass medium for escapist entertainment, just as radio had done twenty years earlier. By the years of the greatest civil rights conflict and advancement, television had supplanted radio as the primary source of news and entertainment to the public. Television coverage of civil rights crises and advances in the 1950s and 1960s did for television what war coverage had done for radio in the previous generation—it provided the context in which television proved its necessity and effectiveness in covering history as it happened.

By 1984, to a degree not evident in 1964, optimism about television's positive power competed with a more world-weary sense of the limits and illusions in television's ability do more than convey tried-and-true conventional wisdom in occasionally unconventional wrappings. Then, as now, television's dominant role has been to broadcast escapist entertainment, not news or public affairs programming. According to journalist Donald Bogle's careful research, in its first few years, when television production and broadcasting were local affairs, affiliate by affiliate, and when filling hours of airtime was a stiff challenge, "postwar television sometimes took a chance on the offbeat and opened its doors to African American performers."[44]

Nonetheless, when technological integration came to television, African Americans found themselves on the losing end of a one-sided transaction. With the firm linkage of local affiliates to national networks through coast-to-coast coaxial cable, the opportunities for African American performers did not increase. By the end of the 1950s, this regressive trend coexisted with another that was perceptively discerned by Daisy Fullilove Balsley, the author of the first sustained treatment of African Americans on television.[45]

Entertainment television was not entirely impervious to racial questions, but extreme caution was the order of the day. According to Balsley, some of the most popular Western dramas of the late 1950s—*Have Gun—Will Travel, Broken Arrow,* and *Cheyenne*—compassionately address prejudice against Native Americans but only as a problem in the distant past. In her pioneering study, Balsley related screenwriter Rod Serling's experience between 1956 and 1958 as he tried to get a drama produced on the murder of Emmett Till. Serling was one of the most successful and admired screenwriters of that era. The final product, a broadcast of *Playhouse 90* on June 19, 1958, bore little resemblance to Serling's original idea. The setting of the drama had been moved from Mississippi to New Mexico, its historical time changed from the present to 1870, and the victim of racial violence changed from an African American to a Native American.[46]

Lessons Learned

The *Cosby Show* played a large role in Cosby's own experience as a committed cultural and social reformer. Two quotations from Cosby, one from 1969 and one from 1985, convey lessons learned from the long years in this work. In Cosby's 1969 *Playboy* interview, he argued that an accurate television series about a black family would fail because in the course of being faithful to their experience of American life, "you're going to have to bring out the heavy, and who is the heavy but the white bigot?" Cosby said. "This would be very painful for whites to see, a show that talks about the white man and puts him down. . . . it would be called controversial and whites wouldn't want to tune in."[47] Sixteen years later, in an interview with writer Alex Haley, Cosby explained why he had created the *Cosby Show* and speculated on the reasons for its outstanding commercial success. At the heart of his comments was a feeling of disappointment. "I grew up loving television; to me it was a wonderful, magical invention. . . . Television is a *fantastic* medium and . . . could be something and *should* be something that a family can look at and get a good feeling from."

Looking back to the mid-1960s, when he and Culp were starring in *I Spy*, Cosby "felt that at least the television industry was making some inroads and I hoped it could lead the way in race relations. But as the years went by, I didn't notice any change for the better." Instead, the loosening of broadcast standards that in a very salutary way brought some new voices and new stories to the television schedule also, according to Cosby, opened the floodgates for programming that exploited sex, crime, and violence and created new opportunities to "say 'boobs' or 'butt.' . . . Prime-time shows were rife with stereotypes. Anytime you saw a black actor or actress you knew something negative was going to happen. Anytime you saw a beautiful woman, you knew she was the romantic link."[48] Cosby's strategy was, in his words, to "go back to basics," to highlight the best values in the American prime-time tradition while discarding the rigorous racial segregation that also accompanied its formative years.[49]

Cosby's testament of disillusionment is significant beyond explaining why he chose to design the *Cosby Show* as he did. Experience has taught that using television to change society is a far more complicated and intricate matter than first believed. If the objective is enduring mass appeal, the rules of the road of the American enterprise that is prime-time network television requires a vast softening and simplification, if not an outright avoidance, of the social complications present in everyday life. Messages, if delivered at all, need to be delivered in a soft, reassuring voice, preferably woven with delicacy and subtlety into the seams and the fabric of the thirty-minute situation. The scene and set thus arranged, the viewer is given a cumulative series of choices that, repeated over time, collectively compose the act of interpretation. As Cosby himself said in reference to his treatment of Clair Huxtable's career (and his decision to avoid addressing her struggle to achieve it), "If I threw a message out hard and heavy, I'd lose viewers. . . . if the message is subtle people who want to find it will find it, and if they want to make changes they will."[50]

Such caution was well founded. In the decade and a half before the *Cosby Show* entered the prime-time schedule, the pressures of social discord had led the television networks to experiment with programs that reflected on the polarization in American society. Pioneering producer Norman Lear, for instance, took up Cosby's challenge of showing white America the "heavy," the white bigot in *All in the Family,* with much commercial success but with some troubling implications. According to Bogle, unpublished audience research by CBS found a surprising degree of support for the "lovable bigot" at the center of the Bunker clan. Lear's clear intention was to create a character whom many viewers, whatever their politics and social views, might identify and empathize with without agreeing with—a nerve-wracking trick if ever there was one.[51]

In the situation comedy *Good Times,* Lear brought the life of a struggling African American family in Chicago to prime-time television—only to see audiences choose as the focus of their adulation a character remembered primarily for his outrageous locutions of slang and his accompanying body movements, with little evidence of residual understanding of or solidarity with the family and its challenges.

The *Cosby Show* has been evaluated as a sociological event by many commentators. Understanding the cultural framework of this "social program" takes us back to James Baldwin's famous words from *The Fire Next Time.* In that path-breaking essay, Baldwin argued that the survival of American democracy depended upon Americans recognizing a truth that was both venerable and overlooked: the early choice to distinctively enslave African Americans by law, followed by the collective decision to continue institutionalized exclusion, carried special consequences in the present for the entire American political community "he who has so long been rejected must now be embraced, and at no matter the psychic or social risk."[52] Over the next generation, as the "western" was replaced by the police drama, this symbolism, in its shallowest sense, became an underpinning metaphor in national life. It was most powerfully rendered in the motion picture *In the Heat of the Night* (and its cinema and television sequels). This new formula placed African Americans front and center in positions of civic honor and responsibility: as judges and as police officials—those who had been historically excluded now becoming the symbolic guarantors of fairness and helping their white colleagues gain insight and understanding.

At the same time, as the nation moved further and further away from the immediate and pressing crisis in race relations of the mid- and late 1960s, the commitment to doing more lessened as guarded efforts at continuing reform gradually lost out to economic stagnation at home, foreign policy failures, and the conservative counterrevolution these issues generated. The election of Ronald Reagan to the presidency in 1980 was both a culminating event many years in the making and a break with a more recent past. Reagan, like Richard Nixon, eschewed explicit appeals to racism among white voters while utilizing coded language to convey his solidarity with the desire of some Americans to end if not reverse the Second Reconstruction.

As president, Ronald Reagan was as important a cultural figure to the 1980s as FDR had been to the 1930s—representing not only a program but a general outlook for which there was a large constituency both within the electorate and beyond. While it is important to make the point that Reagan's economic policies "resulted in the largest redistribution of wealth to the top fifth of the social stratification order since the Gilded Age," it is but one important part of a more lasting campaign to reverse an admittedly fragile but nonetheless real dynamic in American cultural politics created during the struggles of the 1960s, a struggle for the legitimacy of black claims upon the nation for the institutional racism of the past and present that was first formally acknowledged by President Lyndon Johnson in his 1965 commencement address at Howard University, and brought to its fullest and most explicit public recognition in the aftermath of the assassination of Dr. Martin Luther King Jr. in 1968. As sociologist Herman Gray explains, the primary goal of "Reaganism" was to "take away from blacks the moral authority and claims on political entitlements won in the civil rights movement of the 1960s."[53]

Looking back over the initial public debate over the *Cosby Show,* the belief that the upper-middle-class Huxtable family appears as an affirmation that African Americans had reached the "promised land" of American life is not the only theme that stands out. More important is the way in which the symbolic logic stated by James Baldwin in *The Fire Next Time* remained an unacknowledged frame of discussion. In 1963, Baldwin had posed that "the American future is precisely as bright or as dark as" the Negro's."[54] It is a measure of the degree to which this insight had graduated into being an almost banal truism that, twenty years later, journalists who had begun their careers at the peak of civil rights protest subjected the *Cosby Show* to this part of the Baldwin test without perhaps ever actually realizing it.

What did its success tell us about race relations in the United States? Had the dynamics changed? Was one of the messages of the show's success that the situation in the country was indeed substantially improved? Was the program's avoidance of race as either a celebratory or cautionary subject a sign of bravery or cowardice? Although Reagan, who was in the final weeks of a landslide reelection campaign as the *Cosby Show* began its eight-year run, is seldom mentioned, it is difficult not to see his profile in the background of the scene these reviewers create.

The predominant critical reception to the show was that it was a perfect, placid, unproblematic affirmation of Reagan's "morning in America," the shorthand phrase used in television spots by the Reagan reelection campaign in 1984. It conveyed the Reagan campaign's central message: that a recent history of economic stagnation and unwarranted national introspection had been conquered by the strong leadership and economic policies of President Reagan. Of the journalistic essays that present the *Cosby Show* as a new cultural milestone to be observed and measured, Harry F. Waters's "Bill Cosby Comes Home" in *Newsweek* stands nearly alone, with Waters deeming the show a social as well as a comedic and commercial success. Not only is the series an "irresistibly charming, flawlessly executed sitcom," but it also derives its strength from the way it innovates on the past: "At a time when the sitcom genre is in eclipse and gory crime dramas are in ascendancy, it dares to restore our sense of humor about the daily absurdities of daily familyhood. It is the first all-black [show] to eschew jivey jargon and negative stereotypes. The Huxtables are a pair of affluent, highly educated professionals . . . whose libidinous urges lead to—not even randy Fred Sanford got away with this—moments of on camera, if under the covers, foreplay."[55]

For Waters, the Huxtables' emotional maturity provided a kind of interpersonal authenticity that, if by no means absent from prime time since the 1970s, had yet to be fully integrated into television's portrayal of the African American family. Mark Edmundson, who wrote about the show two years later in *Channels,* also saw signs of thoughtful creativity. Cosby's Cliff Huxtable succeeded because he represented a new synthesis of two opposed styles of parenting. In the aftermath of Vietnam and Watergate, the "imperial Papas" dispensing wise homilies unchallenged from the living-room easy chair or the den was no longer a credible image of authority. The success of *All in the Family,* in which Archie Bunker faces continual challenges not only to his rules but also to his very right to rule from sympathetic "proletarians" (his wife, daughter, and son-in-law especially), had seen to that. Prime-time television had let in just enough representations of a new and more complicated society that a credible authority symbol had to synthesize qualities from two opposed styles of leadership: "an image of American authority that is authentically humane, inventive and capable," made credible by the success of the civil rights, antiwar, and feminist movements, and the generalized "ethical appeal" of the "imperial Papas of the first generation of television fathers."[56] Cliff Huxtable represented a moderate and measured step away from the images of fatherhood previously conveyed on television. Cliff Huxtable, unlike the embattled Archie Bunker, "outwits rather than outweighs" his children; Cosby/Huxtable, again unlike Bunker, "always scores his point, but he allows his child to win a round too. . . . Cosby lets everyone preserve his or her dignity—indeed he often, if grudgingly, makes room for his wife . . . in the circle of his authority."[57]

John Leonard, in *New York Magazine,* was among the first to advance the claim that the *Cosby Show* was entirely "a throwback, atavistic in its yearnings: *Leave It to Beaver* in blackface."[58] While it is certainly the case that Cosby and the *Cosby Show* were looking back to the most tried-and-true format of commercial television (the classic family sitcom), the phrase "*Leave It to Beaver* in blackface" added a caustic spin, a suggestion that the series was not about an authentic African American family. It cannot be authentic because, although it "may be the best-acted new series of the merchandising season . . . it never gets out of the house" to deal with the real world of African American experience. The Cosby images that radiated from the sitcom, as well as from the many advertisements Cosby appeared in, operated as a kind of cultural "comfort food" whose primary function was to reassure white audiences that *his* success proves that *they* have overcome the racism of the past. "Cosby sells reassurance. . . . He's been selling it ever since the demise of the *I Spy* series . . . and he's selling it again very successfully." According to Leonard, Cosby succeeds because he ignores "the street" altogether: "Cosby bears no resentments; he won't hurt. He won't talk to us like Jesse Jackson [who first campaigned for president in 1984], he won't be killed like Martin Luther King Jr. He sells Jell-O."[59]

Terry Teachout, in the *National Review,* reached a very similar conclusion. According to Teachout, the series succeeded because, "for white middle class viewers, the *Cosby Show* is an exercise in face value . . . an electronic pipedream, a pristine vision of a successful nuclear family in the age of the working mother . . . a parable of ambition, a golden vision of upward mobility."[60] Like Leonard, Teachout was troubled by Cosby's refusal to "dramatize its vision in the context of the world outside the four walls of the Huxtable household. . . . Racist slurs are never heard, racist behavior never encountered by the Huxtable family." This decision means that larger questions about the Huxtables' upward journey are never asked. "One feels in the end that Bill Cosby and his writers are too gifted at aiming so low, too smart to be telling us so little about how we live now."[61] While Richard Zoglin did credit the *Cosby Show* with having a "refreshingly mature treatment of the matter of race" when it chose to make no "special point" about it, the overall verdict was negative: "If any new ground is being broken, it may just be that TV comedy is putting its head back into the sand."[62]

Some saw the *Cosby Show* as an implicit endorsement of "morning in America," even if, on a personal level, Cosby and Reagan shared only two important qualities: a gift for making us feel comfortable and a pride in being "self-made" men. Because the *Cosby Show* refused to go outside the house and engage with the world—and its racism and its stereotypes—it was seen as avoiding a social responsibility that was not expected of other prime-time entertainment programs. In its silence on the presence of race and racism at work and at school and how this outside world underscores the need for an all too elusive loving stability in the home, the *Cosby Show* was seen as implicitly endorsing a status quo in which achieving the Huxtable life was especially daunting if one were African American. For this reason, two leading scholars in the study of mass communication, Sut Jhally and Justin Lewis, charged, in a study funded by Bill and Camille Cosby, that "whatever Bill Cosby's intention . . . the result [of the show] is extremely damaging. The Huxtables' achievements ultimately lend credibility to the idea that 'anyone can make it,' the comforting assumption . . . that sustains a conservative political ideology blind to the inequalities hindering anyone born on the mean streets and privileging those born on easy street."[63]

It is striking how little attention was given to the possibility—indeed, the demographic fact—that the Huxtables did represent a distinct trend in American life. Between 1960 and 1980, the numbers of African Americans in the American middle class more than quadrupled. It fell to Professor Alvin F. Poussaint, MD, of Yale University, a consultant to the *Cosby Show* and to Cosby on his best-selling book *Fatherhood,* to make the case in *Ebony* magazine four years after the show's debut that the Huxtables did represent "one aspect of black reality." Poussaint also asserted that the continuing social distance that separated black and white Americans from each other had obscured the greater typicality of the Huxtable family among African Americans: "Like Whites, Blacks should be portrayed in the full spectrum of roles and cultural styles, and no one should challenge the existence of such an array of styles in a pluralistic society."[64] Nonetheless, could the *Cosby Show* have found some way to address the unique problems of these black Americans in the Reagan years (the abrupt retrenchment on efforts to racially integrate the corporate world where Clair Huxtable worked, for instance)? Was the nation's progress on social and political reconstruction still so fragile and tentative that the show would lose not all, or even most, of its popularity, but much of the "crossover appeal" that made it so dominant for five years? This is speculative territory, of course, exploring a road not taken, perhaps one that was made off-limits from the beginning by the requirements of the success that Cosby sought.

Cosby and his colleagues' decision not to portray these issues brings us back to the lessons Cosby learned in his years on center stage, ones about which he was quite plainspoken. In an interview with *Playboy* magazine in 1985, Cosby considered the consequences of a plot line in which the eminently deserving attorney Clair Huxtable, like many similarly situated African Americans, was denied a promotion at her firm: "If I put a situation that's behaviorally negative on the show, then I'll put some lawyers on the defensive. And what's the result? They'll say, 'Listen, I don't want to hear this. If somebody doesn't want to give you something, they're going to continue not to give it to you, regardless of what you say. And if they find in you something they don't like, they will, at some point, explain that they were about to give it to you, but now that you've done something they don't like, they won't give it to you.'"[65]

Cosby contrasts this with having Clair receive her promotion: "I feel that when the show is rerun and rerun, there will be lawyers out there who'll see it and who will give a black, white or Asian female the promotion that those women may deserve. We always try to put out a positive [message]. . . . The result is that we won't have lawyers saying, 'Don't tell me the rotten guy who turned down Clair is *me*.' They'll want to be smart, like the lawyer who gave Clair the promotion."[66]

These passages convey Cosby's deep sense of the reluctance and indeed the brittleness of white America's acceptance of black advances. It is important to remember that Cosby's career in front of the camera as pitchman and performer had a backstage dimension as well, one that acquainted him with the risk-averse mind-set of many in the corporate world; secondly, he understands how to build the kind of audience coalition implicit in the word "broadcasting": to cast a message broadly. To do so comes with some pretty tight limits, whether imposed by private enterprise or public officials, on who gets to cast the message across the undifferentiated "mainstream." The mass media are excellent at radiating themes for which there is wide agreement. When it comes to questions where there is deep division, the mass media cannot, by the strength of its sheer ubiquity, create by some magic a consensus that has otherwise eluded human beings. As an entertainer, Cosby has the power to create an image of what sometimes does happen in our present and what may happen, with much effort, in the future. To portray that social effort and its consequences would lose Cosby and his show valuable audience share. Being a certified "big man in show business" came with some power but at a great price. As Cosby himself put it, "Right now it may look like I'm the boss, but the ratings dictate who's the boss, and when the numbers drop you get a visit from the network SS men."[67]

Establishing how any piece of popular culture is actually received and how it actually fits as part of its times is difficult, even if we are working with an example such as the *Cosby Show* for which there is some compelling audience research. What are we to make of the fact that, in mid-1980s America, Bill Cosby and Ronald Reagan both enjoyed a high degree of personal popularity? They may share a trait (likeability) that can market a political program, a commercial product, or a performer's personality, but they are not ultimately in the same business. Reagan was a political figure whose fate rested ultimately on how voters answered certain policy questions (most memorably, "Are you better off than you were four years ago?"); Cosby is an entertainer whose "audience coalition" depends not only on his ability to be funny but also on avoiding the kinds of issues that a politician must confront.

How does their simultaneous popularity connect them to one another? In a cover story for *Time* in 1987, Richard Zoglin made the case that "Bill Cosby is more than a showbiz success story. He is a force in the national culture. Like Ronald Reagan, another entertainer with a warm, fatherly image who peaked relatively late in life, Cosby purveys a message of optimism and traditional family values. At a time when real-life families are weathering problems of drugs and divorce, the Huxtable clan . . . is the very model of a strong, close-knit, parent-dominated unit. The fact that the family is black . . . is an encouraging sign of maturity about race. For whites as well as blacks, the *Cosby Show* is a weekly source of comfort and wisdom. 'I hear white working-class families quoting the *Cosby Show* as though it was the last church sermon they heard,' says psychiatrist Robert Coles."[68]

There can be little doubt that Jhally and Lewis's research accurately portrayed the reactions of many white viewers that the Huxtable family performed a politically reactionary role because they were taken as proof that either (1) morning had come to America (and that the civil rights movement had done its work and could safely be treated as one troubled chapter in a glorious family history); or (2) *some* African Americans had what it took to succeed while others did not (and were exceptions to the rule).[69] Jhally and Lewis were right to situate the *Cosby Show* within a larger trend in 1980s entertainment television, away from representations of the working class and toward celebrations of wealth and affluence, with a concomitant decline in the representations of African Americans.[70]

At the same time, the details of dialogue and set design that place the Huxtables as members of an extended African American tradition may render the series "emotionally true" to black viewers regardless of income, operating as signals to a shared experience of struggle and to a shared understanding that the Huxtable brownstone is, like many African American homes, a refuge from a world that must be approached with care, strength, and dignity.[71] According to Jhally and Lewis's audience research, the cues to "blackness" in the series might explain why such a broad cross-section of African Americans "saw themselves, their fathers and mothers, their brothers and sisters, and situations from their own history in the show."[72]

When we try to understand how viewers established a personal connection between themselves and the Huxtables, we need to consider the possibility that viewers have a fairly sophisticated sense of what makes a television program relevant to them. Viewers who are not as affluent as the Huxtables may nonetheless form a bond with them because viewers see an authentic connection between how they create and sustain family relationships and how the Huxtables do so. Perhaps it was because viewers appreciated the nonmaterial essentials of family life that they were able to find common ground.[73]

A black working-class viewer need not be engaging in a kind of willful blindness when telling an investigator that the *Cosby Show* "provides an objective story-line [of] how a black family lives and sees things," or when recoiling at the suggestion that the Huxtables are not authentically black ("Just look at them and you can see they are black. You're not talking to white folks now. What kind of question is that for black folk?").[74] And, as sociologist Andrea L. Press wrote, working-class viewers were not fooling themselves when they saw the Huxtable family as being "typical." In comparison to the families in other hit shows of the era (such as *Dynasty* and *Dallas*), the Huxtables were closer to reality in a whole host of ways.

The question of where the Huxtables fit in relation to other American families, and especially whether they are an authentic representation of African Americans in the late twentieth century, can be addressed with advice from psychologist James P. Comer: "I have often heard middle-class people characterize [parental emphasis on education, achievement, and discipline] as cultural imperialism, the imposition of middle-class values on low-income people. Of late it has been dubbed 'white' behavior by both blacks and whites. I prefer to think of it as preparing low-income people to hold a job and function comfortably in the mainstream of our shared world. Hard work, fair play, individual rights and responsibilities, compassion, delay of gratification and respectable living—all these elements of the Judeo-Christian ethic are essential to . . . mainstream American culture and our church-based black culture."[75]

THE SOCIAL POLITICS OF CULTURE

Cosby's relationship to his public persona and his appeal to a large segment of the expanding white middle class in the postwar years run parallel to the historical significance of what was happening to the black middle class and why. Most obviously this is a requirement of a discourse in which, as Baldwin first argued, the fate of African Americans was now a direct barometer of the social and political condition of the United States. For Martin Luther King Jr., Baldwin, Vincent Harding, and others, this symbolism would have been properly acted upon if it had led to a reconsideration of American social values.

This debate did take place in American culture during the mid- and late 1960s, reaching its greatest legitimacy in the immediate aftermath of King's assassination and leading to a measured and timed acceptance of a policy known as affirmative action. This political consensus ended with the Reagan's election in 1980. It did not lead to the end of some further ameliorative action in the civil rights field, but such action was now intended to preserve past gains against a more explicit political attack than to expand on national reconstruction. Although President Reagan did not succeed in either shrinking the size of the federal government or slowing the rate of its growth, he was able to curb discretionary spending on programs that had a special significance to many black Americans, such as the federal School Lunch program, aid to primary and secondary education, and community-services block grants and federal aid to cities.[76]

In the same year that Jesse Jackson mounted the first of two politically impressive presidential campaigns within the Democratic primaries (the second and most successful effort was in 1988) in direct response to Reagan's domestic agenda, the *Cosby Show* debuted. In fact, it debuted the fall of that year as the nation entered the last phase of the 1984 presidential election, with Walter Mondale as the Democratic nominee. These electoral surroundings are essential to understanding the decisive and defining first series of responses to the *Cosby Show*.

The unprecedented success of the *Cosby Show* provoked a strong debate over whether it was an accurate representation of the conditions faced by African Americans. Was it a constructive reflection, validation, and vindication of the American Dream? Or was it the expression of something more cynical and culturally accommodating—the assumption of many Americans that they now lived in a post–civil rights or even post-racial era? This cultural question was repeated more than two decades later as Senator Barack Obama moved from being a compelling contender to being president of the United States.

Further social excavation will provide an additional prism through which to think about the sustained popularity of this program, especially among African Americans. It is no doubt true that many white viewers received the *Cosby Show* as confirming their fair-mindedness in creating a society in which race no longer mattered. Consider also the bond that may have existed between Cosby and black viewers. In the years after the Second Reconstruction, African Americans who were neither famous nor infamous remained on the front lines of a very tense situation. In the aftermath of the crises that had drawn national and international media attention, African Americans, though out of the collective public eye, remained symbols of a change in social priorities, which many white Americans remained uneasy about, if not outright opposed to it. As journalist Sam Fulwood wrote of his own experience as a member of the black middle class, "I was . . . fully aware that race was a factor in my life and I wanted to prevail in my role as a Negro ambassador. . . . I wanted to be equipped to "hold my own." I would do even better than that. I would succeed with grace and skill. I wanted to do my people proud. . . . I, too, would knock out all comers, like the Brown Bomber, with a nod, a smile and a gracious word. 'I glad I win,' Louis said after every victory. I could not wait to say it, too . . . only I would use proper English."[77]

Doors of opportunity had been opened, especially to African Americans who had or could secure a college education, but the opening was often a grudging one. Between 1960 and 1970, the share of black workers whose incomes placed them in the middle class doubled. During each year of the prosperous 1960s, according to sociologist Bart Landry, the black middle class grew robustly at a rate of between 7.9 percent and 12.4 percent per year.[78]

As the economy slowed and a fragile and tentative political consensus for social reform began to come apart, black economic advancement was hit especially hard. The experience of African Americans living in Yonkers, New York, offers a tangible sense of how these changes reached African Americans. According to sociologist Bruce D. Haynes, although African Americans had a long and significant history as residents of the city, they were not hired into the more lucrative rungs of the industrial economy until the early 1970s, just as this sector of the economy was beginning to shrink dramatically. Between 1968 and 1982, the number of jobs available from the city's largest private-sector employer, the Otis Elevator Company, fell from 1,300 to 375, leaving the city government and the school district as the major source of full-time work in Yonkers.[79]

African Americans were hit especially hard during the recession of the mid-1970s. Eight years later, in the deepest recession of the postwar years (1980–83), the black middle class experienced a net loss of 5,000 jobs, while the skilled and unskilled members of the black working class lost a net total of 179,000 jobs.[80] These figures underscore the fragile and contingent nature of African American gains. As the economy began not only to slow but also to redistribute gains and losses in economically and socially wrenching ways, the social and political atmosphere many African Americans lived and worked in remained a difficult one, even if it was not widely acknowledged except among those who bore its brunt.

As this day-to-day work of nation building and reconstruction continued through difficult times, so, too, did "blatant, subtle and covert discrimination"; some of those associated with keeping account of compliance with the employment titles of the Civil Rights Act of 1964 were dismissed in private conversations within some corporations as "coon counters."[81] For these Americans, and for many millions of others from all walks of life whose accomplishments were presumed to be entirely the product of some government-sponsored special benefit, the *Cosby Show* may well have provided an affirmation that the struggle was worth all the continuing resistance. For some viewers, the *Cosby Show* was a blend of present and future vision, showing a picture of family life that many African Americans recognized as resembling their own and looking forward to a time when the world outside might be prepared to acknowledge this reality. As Bogle recalled, the Huxtable family was not conjured out of some Reagan-era exercise in cultural hegemony but a definite mark of a long-running hegemonic project. According to Bogle, the salient fact was not that families resembling the Huxtables did not exist. He, in fact, saw significant elements of his own family's life represented on the *Cosby Show* and knew of many other examples. What was remarkable to him was that such a family experience—shared by millions—now had a place on prime-time television. He wrote, "I had never seen such a family on television." That more Americans did not see such a family was because they simply could not; residential segregation remained unofficially but very strongly in force.[82]

In his convincing analysis of the popularity of the *Cosby Show* in South Africa during the protracted State of Emergency, historical sociologist Ron Krabill has argued that this series was so positioned (in relation to other political events) as to finally expose the erosion of support among whites about the absolute, indeed biological, necessity of racial separation. As a result, Krabill argues, "Although Bill Cosby never stood for election in South Africa," his intimate presence on TV One—familiar and familial—helped clear the way for the eventual acceptance of Nelson Mandela, once an official enemy of the apartheid state, a man denied a public face in the culture and polity of his nation, as the legitimate founding father of a new South Africa.[83]

In the United States, a different historical trajectory gave a different meaning to the *Cosby Show*. Indeed, the *Cosby Show* gave some viewers in both societies a reason to confirm their own "color blindness," and to replace a biological racism with an equally pernicious classism.[84] For many other Americans, however, the *Cosby Show* was a sign of hope and affirmation in difficult times. The civil rights era had long ended by 1984, but it had left an important legacy: it had gone a long way toward ending the "structured absence" of African Americans and other groups from the American political system.[85] To understand the unusual popularity of the *Cosby Show,* we need to go beyond seeing it as what it may have represented to white viewers: an affirmation that the "recent unpleasantness" of the 1960s and early 1970s with regard to race was over and done with. Many African Americans—across lines of class and region—saw Reagan as a giant step (and potentially several significant steps) back from the commitments made in the 1960s. As political scientist Adolph Reed Jr. wrote at the time, "black people are acutely aware of suffering under the Reagan administration," and dramatic increases in voter registration and participation in the early and middle 1980s were not primarily a tribute to the considerable political skills and appeal of Jesse Jackson to black voters in the Democratic presidential primaries in 1984. This mobilization preceded that campaign and "represents the autonomous determination of black citizens to oppose that regime."[86] For these Americans, the *Cosby Show* may well have been an extension of the Jackson campaign—a sign of hope and encouragement in the midst of retrenchment.

THE CULTURAL POLITICS OF RECONSTRUCTION

Much has rightly been made of Cosby's importance to the racial integration of television advertising. Thinking about the social and cultural place of advertising in modern life, however, can also help in the understanding of Cosby's other work on television and in the (vinyl) public record. At their most effective, advertisements have a power beyond their narrow commercial function because, as historian Roland Marchand wrote, they operate as "social tableaux [of] an ideal modern life."[87]

Sociologist Michael Schudson went further and argued that the cumulative social impact of advertisements is that "they offer a public portraiture of ideals and values consistent with the promotion of a social order in which people are encouraged to think of themselves and their private worlds."[88] This analysis of the portraits and tableaux of advertisements can be extended to the television programs they punctuate, bracket, and subsidize, such as the *Cosby Show.*

That these pictures cannot well serve as documents of how life is lived even by those fortunate enough to occupy the broad middle ground in the class system is a given. But these images become such a part of public and private life and experience that they become "molds for thought and feeling," the very substances with which (and within which) people imagine their own lives and aspirations.[89] For a cultural politician aiming to influence the fabled mainstream, these images encapsulating "life as we know it or would like to know it" constitute the palette—the range and shades of images—he or she must work with.[90]

Working within the range of possibilities offered by these powerful representations is often limiting and confining. First of all, as Schudson points out, these images are celebrations of "satisfactions [that] are invariably private. . . . They do not invoke public or collective values."[91] Let us consider how this insight might help us to both appreciate Cosby's gifts as a cultural politician while also seeing clearly the limits inherent in working in that realm of cultural "portraiture." As a general matter, the personal and familial sacrifices, the exacting professional training and—perhaps most especially—the cultural and financial savvy that enabled the Huxtables to achieve their life—are not avoided so much as they are honored as facts not in need of proof or demonstration.

If adjusting to the psychology of an economy in which inflation is a fact of life is important to understanding American life in the 1970s, it is equally the case that, as chronic inflation eased in the early 1980s, high deficit spending—by government and by consumers—became another new fact of life. Derrick Bell provides an important insight into how a life dependent upon credit-card debt undermined the continuation of a broad-based social democratic politics aimed at making possible entry into a more solidly grounded middle-class life. Bell sees a great danger to social democratic politics in a "consumerism that nourishes the upward mobility belief system through credit card debt." This system enables "individuals to meet basic needs such as food and rent and to acquire material goods that are expected—yet ultimately fail—to satisfy deeper needs. Substituting the acquisition of material goods for real economic and political power literally consumes financial resources while simultaneously disempowering, through debt, any inclinations to protest."[92]

Think now of the hardworking middle-class person who aspires to the kind of social triumph of the Huxtable family but who, for all the knowledge and savvy he or she possesses, may not have the sophistication to see past a "teaser rate" on a mortgage. In today's America there are thousands of middle-class people, with high degrees of training and education, whose lives have been ruined by systematic predatory lending practices. For these and other people to realize the Huxtable dream requires a frank and messy public discussion of how the American financial world really works and the formulation of policies worthy of the "good society" (and, by the way, we have been engaged in this debate, and it has not been going terribly well).[93] The *Cosby Show* was and is constructive, useful, and important, but it can do only a small portion of the work that needs doing to realize its family portrait in a more collective sense.

We cannot leave this scene without noting the circumstances under which the *Cosby Show* left the air on April 30, 1992. On that day, a riot erupted in Los Angeles in protest against the "not guilty" verdicts rendered by a jury against policemen who had actually been caught on videotape as they beat a man named Rodney King. Here was palpable evidence that the inequities that had been exposed during the 1960s remained very much in force. And here, taking on a role familiar to those who remembered the response to the rioting after the assassination of Martin Luther King Jr. twenty four years earlier, Bill Cosby was called upon to go on the air and ask for calm. Herman Gray captures the meaning embedded in the stark contrast especially well: "The television landscape that evening dramatically illustrated that no matter how much television tries to manage and smooth them over, conflict, suspicion and rage based on race and class are central elements of contemporary America. Next to the rage that produced pictures of Los Angeles burning, the representations and expressions of African-American life on the *Cosby Show* . . . seemed little more than soothing symbolic props to affirm America's latest illusion of feel-good multiculturalism and racial cooperation."[94]

Cosby's public work places him squarely within a well-established tradition of Victorian "racial uplift." Like his historical predecessors in that tradition extending back almost a century and a half, Cosby understood the socially toxic role of antiblack stereotypes rooted in the minstrelsy tradition in preserving a racially segregated society. Like his distinguished predecessors in the uplift tradition, Cosby had an acute awareness and sensitivity of the pervasiveness and power of those destructive assumptions and images. Consequently, Cosby, again like his predecessors, fought against these images by associating fervently and uncritically with Victorian notions of family organization and personal virtue. These ideas were so acutely attuned to associate themselves with dominant representations of virtue and probity that they sometimes invoked the very stereotypes they labored against in order to separate themselves from those "bringing down the race."[95]

The *Cosby Show* fits less neatly within the pernicious tendencies of the uplift tradition than some of its critics have argued. Viewer testimony strongly suggests that some viewers understood better than some experts that the point was in the values, not in the products on the set. If the *Cosby Show* was silent on the hidden social costs of the process of urban gentrification that allowed the Huxtables to live in their nicely appointed brownstone, it nonetheless never descends to being a "celebration of class *against* class."[96] Instead, media scholar John D. H. Dowling argued, the series offers a compelling alternative to the "grinding everyday realities of racial tension and mistrust in the United States" by providing "some vision of what a financially secure family life might look like. The hopes and fantasies nurtured . . . in this communication are also the stuff of continuing resistance to a harsh reality, not simply its denial."[97]

THE CURTAIN FALLS

In the last months of 2014, Americans witnessed the dismantling of a cultural institution named Bill Cosby. His career as a pitchman for commercial products had long ago ended, but what had remained largely intact was something far more important, and far more difficult to create and sustain: Cosby's longevity as a participant symbol of positive social change. This is what finally came apart at the end of 2014: the *Cosby Show* was suddenly removed from the air, Cosby's philanthropic gifts reconsidered and returned, performance dates canceled.

Credible accusations made on the public record that Mr. Cosby, over a period of many years, had been a serial rapist struck at the heart of what had made him such a long-lasting and powerful participant symbol of the Second American Reconstruction. Bill Cosby resonated with a broad cross-section of twentieth-century Americans not because he was just an updated version of a traditional African American symbol. Though Cosby was absolutely carrying on the cultural work of Frederick Douglass by challenging Americans to reset their social and political house on the more secure ideological foundations offered by a more genuinely inclusive set of social democratic values, his specific relation to that ongoing cultural process was nonetheless quite different.

In the 1960s and 1970s, Cosby came on the scene as one of many new faces whose presence was meant to legitimate racial equality. On the public stage of the Cold War and civil rights years, Cosby was not the seemingly solitary messenger that Douglass had been one hundred years earlier: it was deeply pragmatic progress of a nonetheless significant kind that Cosby was not received, as Douglass had been, as the best and highest-ranking representative of his people to the rest of America. He was, instead, one member of a generation of pioneers whose public lives further elaborated what African Americans could do, be, and represent in the American world. Cosby became singularly important because he represented an elaboration of that earlier form of reception into new social territory: he was a figure that white Americans could think of in more ideologically intimate terms. The continued strength in recent years of Cosby's standing in the midst of earlier public disclosures of predatory behavior confirm the strength not only of his celebrity armor but also of the depth of the media's faith (as a representative of the public) that Bill Cosby, though sharing profound character flaws with other powerful men, was nonetheless still a trusted member of American culture's official family.

From 2014 forward, that public role is simply no longer possible for Cosby to fulfill. The pulling down of the Cosby cultural presence has occurred for reasons fundamentally opposite to the reasons that other African American icons of the Cold War era came down. The generation of black public figures for whom W. E. B. Du Bois and Paul Robeson were orienting participant symbols witnessed the public marginalization of these figures as the result of the coordinated action of an angry and powerful ideological elite, who could demand and receive compliance from the public. The action that we began to observe in 2004, and which returned with deliberate speed in late 2014, came from within the public itself. The dismantling of authority originated in the organized public's nearly universal demand that Cosby provide specific answers to specific charges from specific people who have gone on record in court and elsewhere.

At the time that this book went to press in the first days of 2015, the ritual of disclosure and Cosby silence continued. Enough of lasting consequence has happened that we must grapple with a central question: How should we now think about the Cosby past, and its relationship to our own? I do not believe that the emotions of love, respect, and understanding that Cosby generated among so many different kinds of people were passing and ephemeral; they were real and historically meaningful. What about the man himself—who was that "masked man"? Do we now consider Cosby to have been unmasked, and thus no longer worthy of any consideration as an honest and honorable historical actor? The backstage life of another modern national fable is being exposed as deeply corrupt and corrupting. I cannot—and we cannot—look back at the Cosby of 1963 to 1992 in the same way that we once did; but the present must not be taken as another license to simplify and distort again: we do not provide an honest historical accounting of ourselves and of Cosby if we now distort his image in an opposite direction and remember that career as nothing more than a cynical and self-serving ruse that was perpetrated upon us.

Whatever the final fate that awaits Mr. Cosby , his career is a cautionary tale to us all. Even if these repeated abuses of private power had never happened, there is a steeply challenging moral here which applies directly to all of us: participant symbols ultimately make their best contribution by the decisions we make when they are done, or we are done with them. These early inspirational figures should remain with us, but we must make them far less important as we learn and act, not through imitating their imagined lives, but in the actions that we actually decide for ourselves to take.[98]

5

JOAN GANZ COONEY'S *SESAME STREET* AND THE REBROADCASTING OF SOCIAL CHANGE

All children have very uncomplicated instincts and reactions to their world . . . and the reaction of a black child to never or rarely seeing another black child, a black man, or a black woman on television is that something must be wrong with . . . being black. This is the kind of emotional burden . . . that we must strive to remove.

—JOAN GANZ COONEY, founder of the Children's Television Workshop, testifying before the U.S. Senate Select Committee on Equal Educational Opportunity, July 30, 1970

Sesame Street, the most enduring offering of public broadcasting in the United States, began its life on the airwaves only a few years before *Fat Albert and the Cosby Kids* and has become a fixed part of American children's culture. Like *Fat Albert, Sesame Street* made the city its home as a clear signal that, while any child would feel at home in its neighborhood, the disadvantaged child would finally also belong and have a secure home in the American television neighborhood.[1] The company that produced *Sesame Street,* the Children's Television Workshop (CTW), was established by Joan Ganz Cooney, along with influential leaders in education and philanthropy, to produce children's programming for the nation's fledgling educational network. The goal was to create shows that would capitalize on children's strong attraction to fast-paced and colorful shows, but to convert this moment into an opportunity to actually prepare preschool children to meet the academic and social challenges ahead. *Sesame Street* was the first of its many successful series. Cooney's view of children's "instincts and reactions to their world" is an essential starting point because it provides a link between this part of the Second Reconstruction and *Brown v. Board,* which, among its accomplishments, officially made the point that the problem of racism was historically integral to the nation's culture—its values, priorities, and meanings.

PUBLIC TELEVISION AND AMERICAN TRADITIONS

The great early success of *Sesame Street, Mr. Rogers' Neighborhood, The Electric Company* (which, it must be noted, featured Bill Cosby), and countless shows since has made the association of American public broadcasting with the education of the young appear to be something natural and present from the beginning. In fact, the early supporters of public television, going back to the early 1950s, saw it as a way of continuing lifelong learning among adults. What was then colloquially referred to as simply "educational television" (or ETV) was most effectively popularized as a children's network because of circumstances in which it emerged as a truly national force. The vast Baby Boom popularized the debate over the child's capacity to learn and tested the physical capacity of a K–12 educational system that was itself still in the early stages of becoming a universal institution.

In the first years of television's introduction into American life, it was welcomed as something that kept families together. As television's role as a purveyor of entertainment continued to increase, its programming aroused congressional attention, and television joined comic books in the minds of some critics as a cause of an increasing tide of juvenile delinquency. Often lost in the public debate was the point made by some of TV's most careful observers: "The violence on the television may stimulate aggression in an already frustrated and aggressive child. . . . No child is likely to be much harmed by television if he has warm, secure social relationships, and he has no serious psychological troubles."[2] By the early 1960s, there was a consensus among opinion leaders that commercial television was a "vast wasteland" that posed a special danger to children because of the violence of some of its most popular entertainment programming and because of unregulated targeting of children as consumers.[3]

The declaration of what became a child-centered War on Poverty in response to the demands of the civil rights movement also added a more urgent reformist thrust to ETV's efforts to reach out to a national audience. It is no historical accident that public broadcasting took its first decisive steps toward becoming a truly national network between 1963 and 1967—decisive years in the Second Reconstruction and in the chapter in American reform covered by the New Frontier presidency of John F. Kennedy and the Great Society presidency of Lyndon B. Johnson. In these years, federal support, culminating in the Public Broadcasting Act of 1967, was provided so that a dispersed collection of ETV stations sharing programming through the U.S. Postal Service might become an actual "fourth network," with affiliates connected through satellite technology rather than the mail.[4]

Sesame Street's formative years reveal how public broadcasting met the social and political challenges of the Second Reconstruction. Could a fourth network not supported exclusively by advertising provide a broad-based alternative to the Big Three? Or must it forever meet the expectation of many that it must compete with (and lose to) the commercial broadcaster who would "sell his mother for an ad," while ETV takes the road less traveled because it "bores his audience to death for their own good?"[5] Can this now-ubiquitous social institution transcend the limitations on the social and educational systems to provide high-quality education to those deprived of one? Can television be a medium for finding common ground in a nation once again divided? The framers of *Sesame Street* held out that hope when they noted in an early issue of the *Sesame Street Newsletter* that both Chicago-based community activist Jesse Jackson (and the members of his Operation Breadbasket) and First Lady Pat Nixon were enthusiastic supporters of the program. The First Lady went so far as to say, "I love it. I wish I had more time to watch it every day instead of working."[6]

The American version of publically supported television differs fundamentally from its most famous counterpart, the British Broadcasting Corporation (BBC), in the implications of the word "public." Both political establishments believe that the airwaves of radio and television belong to the public, and both are subject to consequential parliamentary oversight.

The British system is funded by a tax tied to owning a television set, which ensures a stable flow of monies to the BBC. On the other hand, the Public Broadcasting Service (PBS) in the United States is especially vulnerable to political pressure because of its need for regular congressional appropriations and because it must rely on annual support from local viewers. Ultimately, although both the British and American political systems recognize the airwaves as a public good subject to oversight, the responsibility for what goes over them in the United States is entrusted to private entities; in Britain, these airwaves have a stronger public guardian.[7]

Founding ETV was the work, not of government policy makers (although federal and local regulations were an important factor from the beginning), but local elites with sometimes overlapping interests. The Ford Foundation supported ETV as a vehicle for adult education. Some of the earliest advocates for ETV were local business leaders who sought to bring "cultural enrichment" to their communities. Add to these supporters states, school districts, and leaders in higher education who pushed for a new venue for basic education in school systems already filled beyond capacity.[8]

The tight local control of primary and secondary education is another value of the American political tradition that extended to the design and development of ETV. As with the operation of schools themselves, a strong local option on what could be broadcast enabled ETV to develop even in the South, a region hostile to nondefense government spending. In 1963 Alabama's statewide network, the first in the nation, had a regular viewership of two hundred thousand (out of a potential audience of two million).[9]

Established by the state legislature, this network projected a "state service personality." It featured locally produced educational programming and "made little use of NET [National Educational Television] programming." Despite extensive coverage of the emerging civil rights crisis by NET, the Alabama network reflected the priorities of a local political community in which racial segregation was an explicit fact of life and social policy from the governor's office on down.[10] As journalist James Ledbetter pointedly observed, at the height of civil rights conflict in Alabama and other parts of the South, the Alabama Educational Television Commission engaged in a consistent pattern of censorship surrounding civil rights issues—or what Ledbetter calls "political program discrimination": "The longest running and most notorious political program discrimination was practiced by the Alabama Educational Television Commission. . . . It is no exaggeration to say that in Alabama, the issues of segregation and civil rights could incite some people to violence. The response, therefore, of the AETC was to avoid these issues in nearly any form. The resulting irony was that on those occasions when educational . . . television viewers across the nation were watching programs about civil rights battles in Alabama, the . . . viewer in Montgomery or the . . . viewer in Birmingham would generally not see them."[11]

As federal funding came online during the Kennedy administration, some saw a greater role for ETV in meeting certain national priorities. Anticipating by four years Cooney's rationale for *Sesame Street,* Professor Lester Asheim of the University of Chicago argued, "The real potential of preschool educational content [on television] lies in providing a background about people, places and things which would equalize the experience for all children. Thanks to television, there need not be so many underprivileged children whose limited experience and environment handicap them in their early years of formal schooling."[12]

Others, such as James R. Killian, chairman of the board of the MIT Corporation and chair of the Carnegie Corporation Commission on Education Television, and Roger Revelle, dean of research at the University of California, certainly accepted the formal educational mission of ETV but held to a broader sense of what public broadcasting might contribute to the life of a modern democracy. According to the Killian commission's 1967 report, public broadcasting went well beyond the transmission of academic curricula to include being a forum for "debate and controversy" and provided a "voice for groups in the community that may otherwise be unheard."[13] Testifying a few years earlier before the U.S. Office of Education's Television Advisory Panel, Revelle expressed the hope that ETV could provide ideological diversity to counteract the "very low level of conformity" encouraged by commercial television.[14] Lawrence Dennis of the American Council on Education hoped that ETV could play a leading role in the developing national "civil rights crisis" and the coming "crisis in jobs and poverty," in which African Americans would be especially vulnerable to long-term unemployment.[15]

As historian Steven D. Classen has noted, the opponents of desegregation in Mississippi had strong allies among local broadcasters. These supporters of segregation not only refused to air national news segments on civil rights protests in their own states, but they were among the three hundred broadcasters in forty-one states who carried the *Citizens Council Forum* as part of their programming.[16]

The close relationship between American cultural and political arrangements and the content of mass media (whether public or private) is reflected in how social relations are reproduced in the media. Even at the high point of conflict over civil rights issues, the image of African Americans improved only slightly, and perhaps even lost something of value in the process.[17] As sociologist Herman Gray has written, the portrait of black Americans on "fictional television" was of "invisibility" made necessary by a political calculus rooted in an assumption of "color blindness . . . driven by the discourse of assimilation."[18]

This conservatism was not new. In its earliest years, television was celebrated for allegedly fostering family togetherness.[19] Television historian Lynn Spigel has argued persuasively that, while the leaders of the commercial television industry certainly did not hold or transmit a bias in favor of racial integration, the recreational content of their networks played an important role in idealizing another kind of social movement involving another kind of integration—the integration of upwardly mobile white Americans into suburban communities often rigidly segregated by race.[20]

THE LOCAL COMMUNITIES OF ETV

The success of programs such as *Sesame Street* in the 1960s and *Antiques Road Show* a generation later has enabled PBS to become a genuinely national network. For this reason it takes considerable imaginative effort to think back to what National Education Television (NET), as the service was known in the 1950s and 1960s, might have been like. At that time, NET was a collection of independent stations, some linked to local school districts, colleges, and universities and some to local community foundations, with a potential viewership, in 1961, of twenty-six million and actual national viewership estimated at just over one million.[21] According to three expert observers, the typical NET station "comes on the air at 9:30 a.m. with a class in mathematics . . . taught by a master teacher," followed by some science education, going dark occasionally at designated periods in the afternoon, when no programs were available. The evening brought some educational offerings for smaller children, followed by "cultural programming"—folk music, classical music, or perhaps more offerings in science or public affairs featuring Eleanor Roosevelt, Newton Minow—the chairman of the Federal Communications Commission—or some other esteemed public figure, with the broadcast day ending a little more than twelve hours after it had begun.[22]

Anthropologist G. Alexander Moore's observation of educational television at work in the classroom of an urban elementary school provides a nice snapshot from those tentative early days:

> The reception is not very good this morning and it is sometimes difficult to understand the woman who is presenting the program, which is called *Science House*. . . . The children . . . sit on large adult-sized chairs in the back two rows. . . . At one point the person on the TV program demonstrates a xylophone and asks, "Which of the keys is lower, the short one or the long one?" When she asks this question, three or four of the children raise their hands, as if in a classroom situation, while others begin to call out the answer. Later in the program, one of the music boxes plays the tune of "Three Blind Mice" and several of the children begin to sing the song spontaneously. . . . Mrs. Schwarz did not prepare the children for the program, and after they returned to the classroom she refers to it only very briefly. There is no actual discussion of the material.[23]

This scene, then, is part of a report on a failed experiment. "The TV program has not been an appreciable addition to the school day. . . . On the contrary, the reception was poor and it might be asked what was in the program which could not have been taught by the teacher herself. On the other hand, she had neither prepared [her students] for the program nor made use of it afterward. In short, she had allowed her autonomy, her independence of action, to be limited by this 'aid.'"[24]

When the children in that room raised their hands and spoke to the on-screen teacher, they demonstrated the unusual power of television, even when the technical reception was weak. Marshall McLuhan, an early expert in television, wrote that "even teachers on TV seem to be endowed by . . . student audiences with a charismatic or mythic character that much exceeds the feelings developed in the classroom or the lecture hall."[25] In 1963 educational television was a mere ten years old; the "pedagogical richness of its mosaic image" was a seemingly distant potential rather than an inexorably approaching reality. Six years later, Cooney and the "brains trust" behind *Sesame Street* made that potential a reality. They brought academic enrichment to a large and loyal audience and were able to demonstrate a significant growth in knowledge among this audience. The experts at the CTW fulfilled McLuhan's aspiration for this medium because they followed his advice. As McLuhan had recommended in *Understanding Media,* Cooney and her colleagues at CTW drew children to the colorful and fast-paced commercials and cartoons on commercial television and created an educational vehicle creatively utilizing these qualities. Like Cosby, they were engaged in building audience coalitions that might endure beyond the moment of performance. Also like Cosby, they had to contend with the "soft solidarity" among the public when it came to addressing fundamental questions of race and poverty.

The CTW took techniques that had worked well in prime-time commercial TV and applied them to early learning, including the introduction of key academic knowledge to children as young as three and four. *Sesame Street* held the attention of its young viewers better than its direct competitors, such as *Romper Room* and *Captain Kangaroo,* because it took the spirit of what "hit best" on television: the "hip, fast and funny" look and feel of two great hits of late 1960s prime-time commercial TV: *Rowan & Martin's Laugh In* and *Batman.*[26] During the summer of 1966, Cooney not only immersed herself in the latest research on early learning, but she also took to the road and observed children as they learned in a variety of settings. As she wrote in her first report to the Carnegie Corporation, which explored the unique possibilities for television to provide early childhood education, "It is difficult not to find a young television viewer from Harlem to Greeley, Colorado, who does not cite *Batman* as his favorite television program. Beginning at an early age . . . children are conditioned to expect pow! wham! fast-action thrillers from television and certainly highly visual, slickly and expensively produced material. It is [also] clear that . . . children graduate rather quickly to the same shows that their parents view and enjoy."[27]

Television for children needed to appeal to this sensibility and curiosity. Those seeking to reach children realized that they must also reckon with their fascination with commercials: "Anyone who has small television viewers at home can testify to the fascination that commercials hold for children. Parents report that their children learn to recite all kinds of advertizing slogans, read product names on the screen . . . and sing commercial jingles. . . . If we accept the premise that commercials are effective teachers, it is important to be aware of their characteristics, the most obvious being frequent repetition, clever visual presentation and clarity. . . . Unfortunately for our children, many teachers may have forgotten what Madison Avenue . . . has cribbed from them."[28]

These techniques were put in the service of a particular political and social sensibility: a desire to reach the most disadvantaged children and their families, millions of whom still did not have easy access to the Head Start program despite their clear need and desire for it. Even before she decided to try to use public broadcasting to fulfill the promise of that initiative, Cooney had established herself as a pioneer in public broadcasting. In the early and middle 1960s, Cooney was one of the people working in local educational television to bring news about civil rights protests and social activism to viewers of educational television in New York City. Among the programs that Cooney produced were *Poverty, Anti-Poverty and the Poor* (1965–66), "a three hour 'teach-in' on the poverty program with officials from Federal, State and City government in a dialogue with the studio audience, composed of clients of the anti-poverty program," which won a local Emmy award; *Speak-Out in East Harlem,* a "three-hour 'live' remote from a church in East Harlem on the problems of that area"; *Harlem: The Winter After,* which combined "still pictures and interviews. An hour-long examination of the mood of Harlem in the winter after the riots [in the summer of 1964]"; and finally, *A Chance at the Beginning,* "taped at PS 68 in Harlem, a documentary about a cultural enrichment program for four-year-olds in Harlem. I25 [*sic*] prints of the program were later bought by the Office of Economic Opportunity to be used as training films in Project Head Start."[29]

Cooney was blunt in one of her earliest public statements about *Sesame Street.* Although she was "producing a *national* show . . . that will be relevant to all children," she considered her "mandate" to be reaching "the inner-city poor"—exactly the kind of children G. Alexander Moore visited in the early 1960s.[30] Like Moore, Cooney wanted to connect with "the least fortunate [public] in the city" and be able to convey a full picture of urban life—not just "the squalid and dirty streets" of fact and stereotype but also the "lively street life" also in evidence to anyone who does more than speed by on the expressway.[31]

Sesame Street was effective because it blended the fast action of 1960s entertainment television with a commitment to representing city life and the possibility that people from different nations and cultures might be able to live as neighbors. When the scholarly team led by Wilbur Schramm, a pioneer in the academic study of television, first formally addressed the capacity of the medium to expand and enhance educational opportunities, the "disadvantaged child" discovered in 1965 as part of the War on Poverty's Project Head Start was nowhere in sight. Instead, in keeping with the priorities of Cold War political culture between the late 1950s and the early 1960s, the researchers asked, "Can television not offer more challenge to bright children. . . . It seems to us a disappointment, and a waste of potential, that television should . . . have its influence with children so overwhelmingly as a fantasy medium rather than as a source of reality experiences. No one can doubt that it can be a great reality medium. It seems to us that it might be a matter of pride with television people to do more toward making it a reality medium. . . . Do we really think that this is the best way to make leaders and thinkers?"[32]

From ETV's beginnings in the early 1950s, the prospect of a government-sponsored network had few allies. New York governor Thomas E. Dewey, the embodiment of moderate Republicanism before the election of Dwight D. Eisenhower, feared that a noncommercial network, because it was not accountable to the market, might be used to broadcast "un-American ideas."[33] The steady growth of ETV during the 1960s from the very loose confederation of the 1950s into a more tightly interconnected national network exposed a major difference of interpretation among its advocates about what ETV should do. In 1961 Raymond Hurlbert, general manager of the Alabama commission, testified about the great importance of ETV to his state. For Hurlbert, such broadcasting would enable his state, "with one of the lowest per capita incomes in the nation, to afford an equal opportunity to every student in the state." Making much the same point, Representative Robert W. Hemphill of South Carolina noted that his constituents "have a limited source of revenue for all school purposes." In South Carolina, school overcrowding was caused not by a shortage of actual classrooms, as was the case in other parts of the country, but "because we are unable to pay teachers."[34] In Miami, Florida, where fifty thousand students received some televised instruction in courses ranging from language arts and the sciences to history and driver's training, this medium was primarily used to compensate for an acute teacher shortage. In addition, television was used in shifts with groups numbering between three hundred and six hundred, relieving classroom overcrowding in core courses for at least part of the school day.[35]

A different interpretation of ETV's public mandate was followed elsewhere. In San Francisco, Boston, and New York City, the definition of public television, while it did not exclude the transmission of narrowly instructional programs, included the extensive coverage of local controversies over civil rights, education, and urban renewal. This variety closely matched the definition offered in an influential report to the Carnegie Corporation: "Public Television programming can deepen the sense of community in local life. It can show our community as it really is. It should be a forum for debate and controversy. It should bring into the home meetings, now generally untelevised, where major public decisions are hammered out, and occasions where people of the community express their hopes, their protests, their enthusiasms and their will. It should provide a voice for groups in the community that may otherwise be unheard."[36]

One of the obstacles to the establishment of a public broadcasting network in the United States was the fear of some that this powerful resource could, to quote Mississippi congressman G. V. (Sonny) Montgomery "get into the wrong hands . . . and put out the wrong kind of information" because it recognized the importance of local control.[37] Montgomery imagined a network committed to ending segregation, which could broadcast over the heads of local school boards and PTAs. He needn't have worried. In the same way that the national priority of providing elementary and secondary education was reserved to localities by a century of political tradition, the legislation establishing a national public broadcasting network reserved a large degree of local control when it came to determining what was broadcast in individual communities.

Sesame Street as Urban Renewal

Sesame Street sought to provide a new vision of American social politics in opposition to a prevailing stereotype of the city best described by sociologist (and future U.S. senator from New York) Daniel Patrick Moynihan as "ugly, incoherent, sprawling cultural wastelands."[38] In this sense, we can appreciate *Sesame Street* in a new way: as a key reconstructive institution in the national process of creating a new polity no longer organized around racial hierarchy. By portraying harmonious social relations on "an imaginary block between 104th Street and Second Avenue," *Sesame Street* was both representing and enacting a potentiality that might someday become reality.[39]

By representing a defining aspiration of its time, *Sesame Street* brought something quite new—indeed, revolutionary—to a medium made cautious and conservative as a condition of its universal reach. Cooney and the CTW made their plans at a time of unprecedented national crisis described by Bayard Rustin, best remembered as the organizational genius behind the March on Washington in 1963. As Rustin put it, "Having escaped the bombs of two world wars, we are not familiar with the horror of burned-out buildings, smoking rubble in our streets, the blasts of Molotov cocktails, the ring of sniper bullets from rooftops. Today we look at sections of Detroit and think of war-torn Berlin. We see rampaging, looting mobs and think of the unstable politics of underdeveloped countries. A nation's identity has been overturned."[40]

Against a backdrop of struggle and violence, with middle-class whites fleeing cities at the rate of 345,000 a year, Cooney, like Cosby, wished to inject hope and optimism while overthrowing the default assumption underlying much of American culture that the United States was a white man's country, with all other figures consigned to supporting roles at best.[41] She and her colleagues at the CTW, also like Cosby and his collaborators, offered a vision of what was now possible, if efforts continued and created a new scene and setting in which a group of people lived together as part of a policy that had moved forward from mere tolerance and desegregation to a more robust sense of community in which people are both independent and connected, freely living and working together in a state of dynamic peace. Like the alternate universe of *Star Trek*, another cultural staple of this era, the world on *Sesame Street* was rooted in a potential embedded in a contentious present whose ultimate direction seemed to be very much up for grabs. The *Sesame Street* world brought the real world of some of the most disposed Americans into focus, not as an amendment but as the front-and-center point of reference where all were welcome.

The setting and general atmospherics of *Sesame Street* were yet another expression of the hope that part of building a truly Great Society was rescuing the American city and revitalizing it. Consider *Sesame Street*'s urban family portrait beside these words by political activist and theorist Jane Jacobs, an early voice in the effort to rethink a definition of "urban renewal" that envisioned little more than "wiping away slums and their populations, and replacing them with projects intended to produce higher tax yields or lure back . . . populations with less expensive public requirements."[42] Four years before the first of the "long, hot summers" erupted in American cities, and eight years before *Sesame Street* aired, Jacobs was imagining American cities reinvested with "all kinds of diversity, intricately mingled in mutual support. We need this so city life can work decently and constructively, and so the people of cities can sustain (and further develop) their society and civilization."[43] It is not too far of a leap to see *Sesame Street* suggesting what it would be like to live in a city neighborhood envisioned by Senator Robert F. Kennedy when he argued for the establishment of community development corporations (CDCs) such as the one he championed for the New York neighborhood of Bedford-Stuyvesant. CDCs could enable city people who were previously without power and voice to "act together on matters of mutual concern with power and the resources to affect the conditions of their own lives."[44]

Social Reconstruction through Television

The *Sesame Street* experiment was part and parcel of a larger struggle to reconstruct American society, as evident in Cooney's testimony before Senator Walter Mondale's Senate Select Committee on Equal Educational Opportunity in the summer of 1970. Cooney made the case for the special power of socially conscious television broadcasting to contribute to achieving these ends. As "the most democratic of media" that more than 95 percent of all American preschool children had access to, the right kind of show might reach those who were otherwise excluded, with knowledge they were otherwise locked out from, by a system of education tied to the wealth of its neighborhoods.[45]

When Cooney testified, she repeated a point first pressed by students, parents, and teachers allied with the civil rights movement: "Poor mothers and fathers want this education for their children just as much as their middle-class counterparts want an adequate education for their children. And minority-group children and their parents need to see people like themselves in constructive, warm, entertaining and educational circumstances on TV."[46] Echoing themes found in the work of Kenneth Clark and others, Cooney asserted that the city-block community portrayed on the Astoria, Queens, CTW soundstage was doing important reconstructive work: "All children have very uncomplicated instincts and reactions to their world, to the people they encounter, to what they see on television; and the reaction of a black child to never seeing another black child, a black man, or a black woman on television is that something is wrong with being black. This is the kind of emotional burden . . . we must strive to remove."[47]

In her testimony, Cooney presented evidence of dramatic changes in children's perceptions: "A Head Start teacher in New York told us: "The black children in our group feel very good about having so many black children on the show." A New York day care center aide quoted a white boy, who said: "Look at the black boy: he knows all the right answers." The aide added that some children were surprised that black children knew as much as the white children on the show."[48]

Images of black and white children working together seemed to have a powerful impact on young minds: "A five-year-old white boy in Pennsylvania told his parents [that] he didn't like Matt Robinson, who plays Gordon on the show because he was 'different looking.' After a few weeks of watching Gordon and the others, he told his father, 'Gordon's my friend. I like him.'"[49]

Even in the nine states of the Deep South, where *Sesame Street* was shown on fifty stations, Cooney noted that "there has been no protest registered." Even in Mississippi, where the "public TV authorities originally hesitated to carry the show," *Sesame Street* had made friends across an enduring divide.[50]

The creation of a safe and friendly city block symbolized a larger change in how the American world was depicted in textbooks. According to anthropologist Otto Klineberg, whose research had done so much to begin to discredit scientific racism in the 1920s and 1930s, the children's readers published a generation later suggested that some of this revolution in thought had yet to move beyond the already persuaded members of the academy. He wrote that, judging by the content of these elementary school readers, "Life in the United States . . . is . . . easy and comfortable, frustrations are rare and are usually overcome quite easily, people (all white and mostly blond and 'North European' in origin) are almost invariably kind and generous. There are other kinds of people in the world, but they live in far-off countries or in days gone by; but they evidently have no place on the American scene."[51]

Consider, for example, the popular basic readers developed by educator Helen N. Robinson and her colleagues at the University of Chicago. Until 1965 these texts featured only white children living in an idyllic suburban setting of neat lawns and sprawling homes. When the series incorporated black characters, the family was also upper middle class, with dad dressed in a blue suit and carrying a briefcase, confirming Klineberg's earlier verdict that, in American school texts, "poverty exists, but usually only in fairy tales or those set in foreign lands." While Klineberg conceded the debatable assumption that "Americans are generally well-to-do," he pressed ahead and asked about the child from a family for whom struggle and scarcity are mandatory facts of life. The child, he noted, is left alone to contemplate difficult questions such as, "Are there no other families as poor as ours? Does everybody else live in a pretty white house?"[52]

This contrast was particularly harmful when teaching minority children in the nation's cities. As anthropologist Eleanor Burke Leacock noted in 1969, "comparison of the content in [traditional basal readers] with the life circumstances of . . . children from a . . . school in an all-Negro lower income neighborhood illustrates the distance between the white textbook family and the reality of their world. . . . Instead of a house studded with trees and bushes, the children [live] in apartment houses or city projects. In the housing projects there was chained-off greenery; around the apartment houses there was no greenery but an occasional tree. In place of the neat and inevitable three-child family, three-quarters of the children had three or more siblings and one-third had uncles, aunts, grandparents, or boarders included in the household."[53]

The creators of *Sesame Street*, by taking city life as their starting point, sought to meet the problem identified by Klineberg and Leacock. If educators wished to reach children, shouldn't their materials also better reflect their diverse worlds? In making this choice, Cooney and company were bringing something new to television programming for children. In a larger context, however, they were also acting as rebroadcasters of change. Whether they realized it or not, these founders were bringing to television an approach already ventured in the medium of textbooks. It has been well established in historian Robert Morrow's authoritative account of *Sesame Street*'s founding and development that the organization favored a more ambitious academic curriculum for early learners than what was favored at New York's famous Bank Street School.[54] But the two parties shared something important in common. Like the television pioneers at the CTW, the framers of the Bank Street Readers aimed to reach out to city kids by accepting the axiom that "to represent in textbook story and picture is to accept, and to accept is to dignify."[55]

In explaining the need for the Bank Street Readers, John Niemeyer, president of the Bank Street College of Education, asserted that "for many years reader textbooks have presented a stereotype of a typical American family: father, mother, dog, two or three exemplary children. The books have excluded many things deeply known by millions of boys and girls, both urban and rural. Increasingly, educators fear that this exclusion alienates many of our children and stifles their aspirations." The world of *Sesame Street* and the world of the Bank Street Readers were both infused by a sense of mission to create the foundation for understanding between people who were different in many ways. In the Bank Street Readers, as on *Sesame Street*, cities are presented as places where there is a "positive cross section of life." As concerned as Niemyer and his colleagues were with making sure that, through these readers, "the urban child will meet [themselves], affirming their daily experiences of city kids," they also hoped to reach out, as *Sesame Street* would, to "the rural and suburban child" who would receive his or her first exposure to "a world and ways of living that [they] may not have encountered." In the process, this child "will meet people who, whatever their skin color, social status or economic position, think, dream and feel—just as [they do]."[56] When it arrived, *Sesame Street* offered a city block that could act as an effective middle ground where children, whether they were from the city or the suburbs, and no matter what the wealth or ethnicity of their family, could virtually gather. As two observers wrote in the *New York Times,* "The genius of *Sesame Street* is that it has created a world that is neither 'Dick and Jane' antiseptic nor a slum. It has its garbage cans, and its inhabitants are not villains, heroes, or supermen."[57]

This change in both setting and sensibility was limited. The Bank Street Readers and *Sesame Street* shared something in common with widely used textbooks of the era. What was true of the textbooks Klineberg reviewed in 1963 and the Bank Street Readers that meant to supersede them was that "Not only is there no poverty, but work seems to be readily available to everybody and is on the whole not only easy but 'fun.' In fact, life in general is 'fun,' filled almost exclusively with friendly, smiling people, including gentle and understand parents, generous and cooperative neighbors and even warmhearted strangers."[58]

To go more deeply and explicitly in this direction, however, would be to enter a hot zone rigorously patrolled by politically active parents and other interests groups with sharp and strong counterclaims. To reach a new, more inclusive "all" meant trusting in symbols to do their full and necessarily subtle work of suggesting deeper meanings below a safe and agreed-upon surface image. Even these gentle efforts faced strong critics. Consider the words of one educator in the 1961 edition of *Controversial Issues in Reading*: "The value systems and social customs portrayed in primary basal readers have been criticized as 'middle class' and therefore not in harmony with the background many children bring to school. To these critics we may ask, what is wrong with middle-class values? Is working diligently, helping with a family project, caring for a family pet, treating friends and neighbors with kindness and respect a poor set of values to develop? We may also ask these critics, 'What values system would you substitute?'"[59]

The leaders of the "cultural arm" of the Second Reconstruction gave a solid and thoughtful answer. Whether it was Robert Coles traveling the social battlefields of the Second Reconstruction; Marcus Foster working in Philadelphia and Oakland; Bill Cosby broadcasting varying versions of his Philadelphia childhood; or Joan Ganz Cooney and Gerald Lesser, a leading academic consultant on *Sesame Street,* providing public testimony as witnesses and partners in cultural reconstruction, such values are not the property of any one class or race. The power and effectiveness of those human endowments varies depending on one's place in society. Striving for equal opportunity is inherently and unavoidably an unequal process that demands more from some than it does from others. The job of the parent—the first and most influential teacher—is to prepare future citizens to succeed within this reality of modern society.

WHOSE KNOWLEDGE?

A television program that emphasized good neighborliness—even set on a New York City block—would have fit well with the conventions of children's television in the 1960s. The goal of preschool was to orient the child to his or her immediate social environment and introduce the basic rules of entry into a warm and supportive world. This was indeed a strong element of the program. Consider a sequence on parts of the body filmed on the streets and playgrounds of sun-splashed New York City that ends with the children running in their Keds sneakers toward the storied Brooklyn Bridge. These vignettes convey some fundamental life facts within the framework of a world without threats or divisions. In addition, however, the CTW decided to emphasize academic preparedness. This approach had been gathering the support of affluent young parents, especially those living in or near college and university towns. Having seen their own fortunes rise through the educational intervention of the GI Bill, these Americans were especially eager to see their children get ahead, not only in the race to "beat the Russians" but in the contest closer at hand to rise to the top of an emerging meritocracy founded on standardized tests and postgraduate education.[60] As columnist Joan Beck, whose words on child development reached a national audience through syndication by the *Chicago Tribune,* reported, recognizing the formative importance of the home and school environment were essential if the "genetic potential of each child will be realized."[61]

The principal features of this trend can be seen in the literature devoted to the Montessori movement from the late 1950s through the 1960s. Montessori placed a high priority on creating a classroom devoted to structured exploration where the child became his or her own teacher. This movement was also built in opposition to some trends that some affluent suburban parents found disturbing. Montessori parents were skeptical of a preschool curriculum too focused on "pro-social education," represented by activities such as "bead stringing and block play," which, they feared, produced nothing more than a "well-adjusted illiterate," at home in a vulgar mass culture in which "emotion and feeling have replaced thought."[62]

As the War on Poverty took center stage in 1964–65, the American Montessori movement's leader, Nancy McCormick Rambush, transferred her energies from the Whitby School in Greenwich, Connecticut, to working with Puerto Rican children in New York City, with the belief that the Montessori system could provide "the first step in educating children from culturally barren backgrounds."[63]

This background information provides us with an additional insight into the anger of the disadvantaged parents in Stockton, California, whom anthropologist John Ogbu interviewed in the late 1960s. They welcomed the possibility that Project Head Start might give their children the help they needed to get ahead (learning the alphabet, how to count and how to write their own names), but they had become suspicious of a curriculum they believed was overly devoted to "going there and eating some food and laying about on the floor . . . playing with balls and all that crap."[64] The solution was for the school to invite parents to become partners in the design and execution of "compensatory programs," not thrown-together crash courses promising results that would be both instant and unrealistic.[65]

The ubiquity of television, coupled with what social critic Michael Harrington called "the first militant movement of the poor since [the Great Depression]" had brought the gospel of early learning from faraway Greenwich and the much closer community of Berkeley into the lives of these Stockton parents.[66] Because they were not "culturally barren," they expected Head Start to teach the fundamentals of modern literacy. One of the chief accomplishments of the civil rights movement's Freedom School movement and of the Great Society's Head Start program in the North and South was that they brought parents who were not socially connected into the national discussion of what early schooling could and should accomplish. As Commissioner of Education Francis Keppel acknowledged in 1964, "for years, we have talked of the disinterest and apathy of slum parents. We have argued that we can't reach their children because they are not interested in education and because their parents have not taught them to be interested. . . . But now, out of the civil rights movement we are learning that many of these parents *are* interested and have finally found a way to express their interest."[67]

Sesame Street's neighborhood was more than just a set; it invited the target children into a world they recognized and lived in for at least some part of their day. It was also something more essential. Just as New York City teacher Herbert Kohl discovered when he started the 1962–63 school year, the materials with and the framework within which he was expected to teach were not only "flat and uninteresting" but alienating to these children, inspiring "anxiety and hostility . . . alternate indifference, suspicion and curiosity. . . . The people in the stories were all middle class and their simplicity, goodness and confidence were unreal." *Sesame Street* sought to answer this world, not by rejecting or parodying it but by showing that the city, too, was home to goodness and to well-motivated confidence.

Reaching these children was the motivating force that pushed Cooney and her colleagues forward. As they developed their vision, they came to believe that they must find a way to give to the poor child a head start in life. The best way to do this, they concluded, was not a new form of an old educational concept of "tracking" or "ability grouping" but by building a virtual world that resembled theirs, while leaving the door open wide enough to let other children and their parents in. *Sesame Street* used the medium of television to create a virtual educational community projected into the single-family homes and apartments, public housing facilities, day-care centers, and Head Start classrooms. The early years of *Sesame Street* were also the years in which school desegregation accelerated in the South and finally reached communities in every other region of the United States. Looking back on the thinking of his colleagues in the late 1960s from the vantage point of 1990, Lloyd Morrisett, who, as vice-president of the Carnegie Corporation, was in the cockpit in *Sesame Street*'s early days, conveyed the way in which *Sesame Street* was to operate as a quiet support, supplement, and reinforcement to the surrounding atmosphere of constructive social change: "We believed television could be an element in creating a universally available, educationally supportive environment in which schools could do their jobs and in which children would have the opportunity to the limits of their capacity."[68]

BUILDING THE *SESAME STREET* COALITION

Devising a message that would reach the nation's children posed a special challenge that previous generations of broadcasters had not needed to confront: how to use the programs of this ubiquitous social medium to transmit knowledge to "have-not" families without alienating the "haves." The record of the early planning meetings for *Sesame Street* clearly reflect a concerted effort to come to grips with this challenge. What survived of these proceedings is not verbatim transcripts but summaries of key comments and agreements and the names of those in attendance. These lists feature some of the leading figures in American psychology and sociology, including Lawrence Kohlberg, Jerome Bruner, Jerome Kagan, and Hylan Lewis.

"If the program is to reach the urban disadvantaged," read one passage, "the programmers will have to understand him. First of all, the ghetto is not all of one piece, including as it does family units as well as black militants and the alienated." In a fairly direct reference to the debate over the condition of the black family sparked by the Moynihan report, one comment read, "Nor is the Negro family devoid of strengths."[69] At all costs, the producers must avoid "track TV"—that is, programming aimed exclusively at one particular group of children. Such a program would, in all likelihood, fail both economically and politically with the people it was most determined to help.[70]

Here, of course, the brain trust of *Sesame Street* seemed to possess an advantage, one that the brain trusts of the New Deal and the Great Society never did. The program designers at the CTW were sending information out to the world, not engaging in the most controversial work of social provision—moving income from one group to another. The road to achieving a rough equality in early learning among young children would be easier: "Despite differences in their backgrounds and environments, four-year-old children have more in common . . . than divides them. . . . Often the ghetto child's problems are simply exaggerated forms of all children's problems."[71] Television also permitted these children to experience a type of "integration" that would cost society very little. Both sets of children could, for one hour, share a common television world without having to engage in the geographically and sometimes politically complicated task of busing.

Class division was deeply implicated in racial inequality. One participant in the planning sessions asserted, "What I want the show to do is prepare my three-year-old daughter to react properly the first time somebody calls her a nigger."[72] How could this mission be fulfilled without alienating children who might—and, more importantly, whose parents might—classify some people as "niggers"? Showing the world as it truly existed was a special challenge because what McLuhan called the "television child" lived in a world saturated with all kinds of information, much of it not intended for children. As the CTW summary document, written only a few weeks after the assassination of Robert F. Kennedy and a few months after the killing of Martin Luther King Jr., acknowledged, "From the adult television fare he sees, he may have the idea that adults can do anything, including murder."[73]

Trying to come to terms with the tension between public acceptance and the equal need to "tell it like it is" by addressing the larger concerns of children was very difficult. It was probably especially wrenching for this assemblage, since they were meeting in the middle of a season of unprecedented social turmoil. The desire for realism, the group concluded, would also need to be carefully balanced against the "real danger in dealing with what could be wounding issues for the child. . . . If the program helps as many as two million but hurts a few thousand, it would not be worth it."[74] As with the question of violence, the challenge of prejudice was also difficult. The producers of *Sesame Street* "placed their trust in the power of constructive images and symbols to overcome negative ones." As Lesser remembered, "We decided to try it both ways, to show the world as it is and some aspects of the world as it could be. . . . As we went along, our drift toward the sweet side of life emerged. . . . In order to depict reality, *Sesame Street* should not add more to the stridency and bitterness . . . already present in the child's life. . . . We wanted to show the child what the world is like when people treat each other with decency and consideration. . . . The harsh realities of a child's world surely exist. But, at the risk of sugarcoating these realities, perhaps we can suggest the vision of better things."[75]

Several surveys completed for the CTW demonstrated that *Sesame Street* largely succeeded in reaching its target audience at a time when public television did not enjoy the degree of universal access enjoyed by the Big Three commercial networks. This success became a subject of intense debate. Although the long-term benefits of early learning can be difficult to sustain, in reaching its goal, *Sesame Street* did not entirely avoid the perception that, like other social programs, it was involved in a zero-sum game in which some would be better served than others. In 1971, in response to strong protests from Chicano activists, the producers began presenting some instructional segments in Spanish. For one observer this "recognition of a basic cultural difference" as legitimate exposed a serious inequality of treatment between black and Hispanic children. "Black Language . . . is not recognized on *Sesame Street* . . . [as] a legitimate linguistic system." Those behind *Sesame Street* evidently believed that "Black children are verbally destitute" and in need of "large doses of middle-class verbiage. American Standard English, therefore, is the primary language of instruction on the program."[76]

SESAME STREET AS A SOCIAL PROGRAM

Sesame Street spoke to millions of parents and children during the last years of the Second Reconstruction not only in its concern with extending education and perhaps rebuilding American social relations through the educational process but also in its commitment to demonstrating its worth and effectiveness through a science. Going back as far as the litigation that culminated in *Brown v. Board,* the quantification of consequences had been key, demonstrating the resource gap that was the real essence of this misnamed doctrine and the psychological implications of unequal treatment by all quarters of American society. *Sesame Street* was entrenched in this ethic not only as a necessity of successful public advocacy in an age that placed an increasing value on professionalization, specialization, and expertise but also, above and beyond that, as the best way of seeking and then knowing what was true. The testing arm of the CTW was led by distinguished academicians Lesser, Edward Palmer, and Valerie Lovelace. In the earliest work at framing the project, experts in education and sociology had been present. Setting significant goals and measuring their attainment were the CTW's highest priorities.

From the beginning, according to Lesser, the goal of the CTW was to reach three- to five-year-olds who were classified as "disadvantaged." Lesser and the other builders of the *Sesame Street* coalition were in agreement that it was not an absence of "middle-class values" that created poverty, nor would the broader "distribution of middle-class paraphernalia" bring prosperity.[77] The goal was to cast a net wide enough that, with additional work, disadvantaged children would be reached and helped across "the basic literacy line which is the key to education and later entering the mainstream of American life." Lesser reiterated the point Cooney had made to the affiliates as the show was being planned: if the CTW failed to "reach inner city children in particular, we would have failed."[78]

A strategy of targeting only the disadvantaged was not favored. The stigmatization that would likely be the natural consequence of such an approach had no constituency within the CTW or, from what the CTW could ascertain, among the parents in question. In the same way that it was not appropriate to turn *Sesame Street* into a vindication of certain behaviors too often identified as "middle class," the program's planners also refused to "romanticize the presumably great benefits" of doing without. Lesser and his team believed (as Marcus Foster and John Ogbu had suggested) that those who headed disadvantaged families were not interested in theories about the roots of their alleged inadequacy; rather, "inner city parents [took] a utilitarian view and seek for their children the basic intellectual skills that have broad currency in our society."[79] Weighing the goal of the CTW against the very limited popular support for more sweeping strides toward social reform, it is hard to conceive of a children's program with a more explicitly social or political edge having any chance of, first, getting on the airwaves and then, if that barrier could be surmounted, winning the audience needed to stay there.

The CTW utilized television as a delivery system of skills and information to those without them. *Sesame Street,* unlike Social Security or Medicare, was in no sense redistributive—it did not take resources away from those in abundance in order to give a greater measure of security to those without it; and yet those who were already plugged into the

American social system by their social and economic position received the greatest benefit. In fact, in the most serious criticism the CTW would ever receive, social scientist Thomas D. Cooke and his team (which worked side by side with the CTW academic experts) found that *Sesame Street* actually increased the knowledge gap between the affluent child and the poor one.

Sesame Street succeeded in giving its target audience a "head start" if that meant the transmission of some essential knowledge (especially of the alphabet) the audience had not previously possessed before entering school. If a more ambitious standard suggested by Cooke and his colleagues is applied instead—that *Sesame Street* provided the powerful launch pad toward closing a gap in knowledge and opportunity that not only endures but grows over the school years—then the benefit is negligible.[80] For these "secondary evaluators," *Sesame Street* provides yet another example of "how the economically advantaged take greater advantage of universally available social resources than . . . the less advantaged."[81] In these analysts' opinion, the gains that *Sesame Street* did convey to those most in need, while neither absent nor necessarily negligible, were nonetheless small in comparison to its success at amplifying the preexisting advantage held by children who were already well off. In addition, viewing *Sesame Street* unaccompanied by the surrounding support of an older parent, teacher, or other caregiver brought little benefit.[82]

In view of the high aspirations and expectations embedded in the rhetoric of the Great Society years—whether expressed by Lyndon Johnson in his argument for the War on Poverty or by Marshall McLuhan, both explaining and envisioning the transformative powers of universal television—it would be natural to accept the assertion that *Sesame Street* failed in its most important charge: to do something significant to begin to close the educational gap between advantaged and disadvantaged children. Indeed, in her final proposal for what became *Sesame Street,* "Television for Preschool Children: A Proposal," dated February 19, 1968, Cooney led her brief with a discussion of this gap: "The educational problems of the disadvantaged child have turned a spotlight on the preschool period. Research has shown that the academic gap between the disadvantaged and middle-class children shows up very early in the school years and increases dramatically in the higher grades. This widening gap, which is of increasing concern to educators, has made the disadvantaged a crucial target in any educational effort. The earlier that the gap . . . can be narrowed, the easier the task will be and the better his educational chances. To many, the neglected years before school have seemed the best place to begin."[83]

What role was proposed for television in the "sandbox to classroom revolution" already underway in the upper-income schools and neighborhoods?[84] "What can be done to reach and stimulate our preschool population?"[85] The CTW made no claim for television's ability to advance dramatically against the learning gap. But in a time now recalled for more generous public spending on social needs, as more than half of the nation's school districts provided kindergarten classes (although many were understaffed by part-time people with inadequate training), the organization noted, "We believe that television, used in an imaginative, educational way, may provide an immediate practical answer" to a very basic shortage in properly trained teachers and even school space to provide any kind of early childhood education. Bluntly stated, "There may be a shortage of schoolrooms, but there is no shortage of television sets."[86] Perhaps well aware that the big early claims and promises made for Head Start were not being met and of the complexities in the achievement and measurement of learning, the CTW promised only to meet "a broad goal of fostering intellectual and cultural development."[87]

It is also essential to see the debate over *Sesame Street*'s long-term effectiveness in its full context. If the Great Society began in euphoric confidence about what new monies and new programs could accomplish—and how objective research could settle longstanding arguments over the nation's social problems—it did not take long for these easy verities to seem antiquated. New money could not simply be directly injected into that part of the body politic most in need; even very health systems insisted on further nourishment. Concentrated efforts to compensate for social and economic disadvantage through Project Head Start could show results while they were being applied, but not much beyond that point. If the early theorists of what became "community action" demonstrated a keen and sophisticated understanding of how social deficits interacted with and compounded each other within one "depressed community," the process of implementation through broad-based human participation also proved difficult to manage and sustain. What if the leaders of a political establishment were threatened by the "maximum feasible participation" of the poor? How are the mechanisms of participation made both legitimate and effective? What role was there for theory and expertise?[88]

As the first rigorous yet sympathetic critics of Project Head Start made clear in an ambitious report released in the summer of 1969, preparing disadvantaged children for school first required more than a summer program of enrichment.[89] Secondly, more attention was needed to how the potentially powerful impact of Head Start might be "contravened by the generally impoverished environment" of the larger community.[90] How might Head Start be reconceived or redesigned to provide an intervention of longer duration, perhaps extending downward toward infancy and upward into the primary grades?[91]

The modern public educational system and the research on childhood learning and human-development learning that surrounded it were in their infancy. This was even more the case for educational television. The available knowledge about television as an explicitly educational tool was impressionistic and fragmentary. Cooney and her collaborators, like the parents, teachers, and scholars working in Head Start, were striking out over unexplored territory. For Cooney and company, this was doubly true: they were pioneers in the field of early learning and in the use of television to do something more than sell and entertain. *Sesame Street* did succeed, but the sharp profile outlining the contours of its reach and effect require examination beyond this one program to the world around it. Surrounding both Head Start and *Sesame Street* was a fundamental assumption about the relationship between cognition and the achievement of greater opportunity for economically disenfranchised people. As Heather Hendershot has perceptively argued, some educators and policy makers embraced early learning and enrichment programs out of the belief that the human brain could serve as "the great equalizer" in the effort to transcend the barriers erected by an unjust social order.[92] Training and honing the intellectual capacities of individual children might, over time, achieve what the collective intelligence of the adult world had not.

Even with the passage of a half-century, there remain basic questions to answer and basic reconstructive work to do, such as bringing every school up to a minimum standard of safety and suitability. What can be done to improve and expand day care in the United States? What can be done to strengthen the economic standing and stability of families so that support at school can more smoothly merge with parental support in the home? What can be done to ensure that parents can and will take the time to be in their children's lives to the degree that a fully developed definition of childhood, citizenship, and parenting requires?

Many years ago, child development expert Urie Bronfenbrenner asked these kinds of questions. In the early 1980s, Bronfenbrenner proposed one way to alleviate pressures on the American family: trim the workweek by 25 percent without cutting wages. When Bronfenbrenner tested this proposal among a sampling of working Americans, it received a cold shoulder. One delivery man told him that such an idea is "inconsistent with what this country's based on." A white-collar worker disclosed that he would utilize the extra time to "increase my marketability." A cafeteria worker planned to spend this imagined benefit to spend more time cleaning her home.[93] In light of such "entrepreneurial values," how can we create a social order in which every child has an adult with an "irrational commitment" to their welfare and well being?[94] These questions must be answered more concretely in national social policy for the work of the CTW, or even Head Start, to have a stronger reach and a more lasting effect.

THE LIMITS OF VIRTUAL RECONSTRUCTION

What do the earliest years of *Sesame Street* convey about the ability of television to influence change? Was it realistic to expect even the most thoughtfully conceived and soundly researched television program to override or transcend entrenched divisions and inequalities within a society? It was unrealistic for the architects of the *Sesame Street* curriculum to expect that gaps in learning skills and knowledge could be narrowed by broadcasting in the same way that the tax code translates portions of a person's personal income into public revenues to be redistributed to those with fewer resources. Such social engineering is, in either case, more easily imagined than implemented. Sesame Street does provide useful knowledge and at least a temporary membership in a supportive community of learning. However, no mass medium can override its surrounding social environment and context. Without more attention to these surroundings, is there any prospect that the virtual community might become an actual one? Is it really so surprising that the benefits of early interventions fade without steady reinforcement over time?

Our sense of television's social role in the 1960s emphasizes the way it heightened contrast, clarified conflict, and helped galvanize the public in support of significant reform. The role that television plays is powerfully determined by the role it is given to perform, as evidenced by Mississippi governor Paul Johnson's strong opposition to the Head Start program offered by the Child Development Group of Mississippi, with his nearly simultaneous support for a federally supported public broadcasting network. Johnson embraced the Public Broadcasting Act because it would provide valuable resources for a new eight-station network in Mississippi. In the new political rhetoric that forced him to acknowledge the needs of new voters, ETV in the state of Mississippi became a "potential instrument for the maximum development of all of its citizens." ETV symbolized the hallmark of this particular Johnson administration: "education for progress."[95] This was a qualified victory for yet another "New South," elusive yet also real, in which past and present, agitator and established leader, were required to coexist, the power differential between them somewhat reduced, in a situation that resembled nothing so much as an uneasy truce.[96]

William R. Smith, who directed the educational television authority in Mississippi, gave voice to a reassuring and familiar vision of change-a-coming when he testified at a House hearing in the summer of 1967: "The social change and adjustment of attitudes between the two races making up the society of this state is a matter of crucial concern in Mississippi today and we must find new ways of communication and understanding—tolerance and respect—and welding what have traditionally been two separate societies dwelling within a single state. . . . We believe that all but a very small portion of our citizens are eager to broaden their horizons . . . to know more than they know now, to be more tolerant and understanding, better informed, better skilled people than they are today."[97]

Beginning in the late 1960s, a new politics and a new language emerged in the American South. The politics created by the Second Reconstruction ended much of the explicit and public race bating that had not so many years before been integral to southern politics. In its place was a rhetoric "seeking to unify . . . various factions in a common purpose," which was economic development through education. As astute observers of southern rhetoric noted, these leaders now acknowledged the presence of African Americans in the polity by speaking "frequently . . . in terms of 'all' citizens, asking for cooperation in pursuit of equal rights."[98]

Progress was often grudging, gradual, and manifestly incomplete; such progress came only as a result of a very determined application of public pressure from African American activists in the South and their allies within the region and beyond it. In 1968, as the planning for *Sesame Street* was just getting under way, Bob Roland, associate director of the newly established Mississippi Authority for Public Television, wrote to Cooney to share the news that ETV was "just getting started in Mississippi" and that new agency wished to work with the CTW to bring early childhood education to Mississippi: "The need for increased and improved pre-school education is a particularly critical one in our state, Mrs. Cooney. Mississippi has no public kindergarten or nursery school program associated with its public education. We also have one of the largest Head Start programs in the country. Yet, despite the private programs and the Head Start work, there are many indications that thousands of Mississippi children are entering school who are very poorly prepared for this new stage of their life. We hope that educational television can assist in preparing these children and are delighted about the availability of programs from the Children's Television Workshop to help us accomplish our goals."[99] In her reply, Cooney wished the new Mississippi network "all the luck in the world." Cooney regretted that the organization of the initial planning seminars for the as-yet-unnamed program would keep her staff, "which consists of two or three people besides myself," from meeting with Roland later that summer.[100]

Almost exactly two years later, on May 2, 1970, the Board of Directors of the Mississippi Commission for Educational Television, by a vote of three to two, declined to allow the broadcast of *Sesame Street* over Mississippi ETV. An unnamed member of the commission explained the decision to the *New York Times*: "Some of the members of the board of directors were very much opposed to showing the series because it uses a highly integrated cast of children."[101] That decision lasted only twenty-three days before the board reversed its decision. William Smith, the executive director of the Mississippi network, greeted the reversal with the opinion that "*Sesame Street* is an excellent instructional program for small children."[102] In addition responding to the public outcry, the board may have been moved to act by the very real prospect of litigation and that a commercial station, with a much wider reception area, was offering to broadcast *Sesame Street*.[103] As a result of protracted litigation by civil rights activists, the station in question, WLBT in Jackson, was coming under new management with a commitment to redressing past discrimination in the coverage and treatment of African Americans.[104]

The contrast between a continuing opposition to integration—especially when children were at the center—and an emerging rhetoric of conciliation and rebirth demonstrates the limits of "virtual integration." Although American society, if measured by where its families live and go to school, may in fact be more racially segregated today than it was forty years ago when *Sesame Street* entered the picture, the amount of actual interracial contact in daily life and in representations of it in the mass media have increased, which provides a sometimes too great a sense of progress that, if it is as full and deep as some too easily assume or as others would like, is nonetheless not an illusion.

In addition to providing help with numbers and letters, *Sesame Street* did "what many teachers are prevented by circumstances from doing . . . show blacks and whites living together in harmony."[105] At a time when court-ordered busing was proceeding unevenly, experienced not as a true national imperative but as a challenge and burden borne by some people in *other* places, this achievement should not be dismissed. And yet *Sesame Street* cannot actually transport anyone anywhere. To the extent it succeeds, it is because there are actual people—parents, child-care workers, and siblings—with an "irrational commitment" to particular children at the viewing site adding locally generated specific content that others not only do not want delivered but, indeed, oppose: "A is for African American, B is for 'Black is Beautiful,' C is for colored people and D is for dignity."[106]

This examination of *Sesame Street* returns us to an issue raised by the career of Bill Cosby: Is "audience solidarity" created by the simultaneous viewing of an experience through its broadcast over public airwaves? If this audience is brought together only in the virtual sense, how long does this unity last and how deeply rooted is it? Lasting political or social change is accomplished in part because people agree, perhaps reluctantly, to change long-established practices (and thus be newly inconvenienced) in the name of improving their community. Does the virtual solidarity created through television really constitute solidarity?

Similarly, Robert Coles is a kind of "good will ambassador" engaging in a one-man cultural exchange effort between affluent Americans and those whom Michael Harrington called the "other Americans." For the last forty years, *Sesame Street* has also sought to play such a role as it is exported to other nations. While the brain trust of the New York City–based Children's Television Workshop highlights the collaborative nature of the workshop's work in host countries, Heather Hendershot has raised significant questions about whether the producers of *Sesame Street* have fully thought through a commitment to real collaboration, especially with countries with colonial pasts and without the economic resources of the United States.

In Hendershot's extensively researched and carefully reasoned analysis, the question of who is in charge—who is the giver and who is the recipient—is raised immediately by CTW's insistence that its partners in Mexico, Jamaica, Morocco, and other countries set up "the same testing-production circuit as is used in the United States," and that the producers of the host-country program come to New York for extensive training.[107] In and of itself, this very high cost requirement puts meaningful collaboration beyond the reach of many local producers. Does this disparity need to feature so centrally in the coproduction process? I am not suggesting that this problem can or should be solved by simply paying to raise the production and testing processes to American norms. What if this meeting of minds and exchange of cultures began truly at the start—with the question of how CTW can assist the particular host country in using television to educate small children. It may well be that an open-ended dialogue does not begin with the offer of participating in the CTW production framework or the *Sesame Street* brand. What secondary support might CTW be able to offer an existing local effort (or one just getting underway)? Is there an opportunity here to reverse the colonial relationship of center to periphery—or is the bottom line here the export, with the best of intentions, of yet another American cultural technology as indispensably universal?

As in the case of *Fat Albert and the Cosby Kids* and the *Cosby Show*, the meaning of *Sesame Street* for audiences, like beauty, remains where even diligent researchers cannot easily find it—privately held in the mind's eye of the beholder. Knowledge that is merely beamed into some other place cannot by itself change the nature of a political and social community. Beaming a curriculum to individual viewers does not transcend barriers; it can contribute to the maintenance of an illusion, especially among those viewers who have the least desire for or investment in social change. The virtual solidarity provided by the television signal enables these viewers to stay in their privileged place while they participate in social change in only a superficial way. Television cannot bring societies together unless enough people are actually already moving toward one another.

6

LESSONS FROM A HISTORICAL REENACTMENT

> It seemed self-evident that segregation was the malfunction in the system that relegated blacks to inferior educational status and that integration was the only tool that was going to accomplish the necessary adjustment. From our vantage point racial segregation—enforced separation, with its degrading humiliations—seemed to be the great evil that had to be destroyed. . . . [I]t was not until *Brown I* was decided that blacks were able to understand that the fundamental vice was not legally enforced *racial* segregation itself; that was a mere symptom of the greater and more pernicious disease—white supremacy.
>
> —ROBERT L. CARTER, former general counsel, NAACP (1980)

I have attempted to show a culture at work on both the most enduring and urgent problem before it: taking up the work fitfully begun a century earlier, with the most nationally visible and symbolically resonant leadership of Frederick Douglass and Abraham Lincoln. In that earlier experiment, Douglass was the best-known outside leavening force, beckoning the polity which he and others had been able to join only at the cost of a convulsive civil war, to a place that only he and a few others had richly imagined and now intended to make real; Lincoln operated as the far more powerful senior partner in this team; he was the intellectually nimble and capacious (and more powerful) representative of a white majority which saw in its status and desires a natural order, which required restoration with some reluctant modification.

THE STUFF THAT DREAMS ARE MADE OF

It is one of the most crippling blows to the constructive and thoroughgoing development of this American society that an assassin's bullet denied that time and ours the continuation of this team effort, unequal in power though its two members were. Would the practical challenges of Reconstruction have moved Lincoln to a new understanding of what the past required of the present if more than a surface equality was to be achieved between whites and blacks in these United States? Would the argument over reparations have resulted in the creation of an administrative capacity capable of redistributing resources, power, and opportunity beyond that which has become the inheritance of the twenty-first-century polity? Would reconciliation by retreat—in the face of terrorist violence—still have become the stronger political emotion? Would the abolitionist vision have remained a marginalized one, held by people like W. E. B. Du Bois—roughly sidelined as someone made dangerous by a (potentially contagious) radical fever? I would like to think so, but I cannot do so with much hope and even less confidence.

Such questions cast stark light on how the First and Second Reconstructions are linked, and they suggest why the final dimensions and impact of the second were, as historian James McPherson long ago argued with great prescience and perception, so much narrower and inadequate to doing the work that they were announced to accomplish.[1] I do not mean, by posing these questions, to suggest that John Wilkes Booth's bullet denied Americans the more transformative experience that could have been theirs and ours. Such logic is best dismissed as a variety "of magical thinking." However, what I do find worth considering is whether a continuing Lincoln-Douglass debate might have widened the banks of the American political and culture mainstream just a bit more at the margins and left this polity with a more robust sense of how class operates in American society, as it does in others. Would this more persistent grappling with fundamentals have increased a sense of shared destiny and responsibility than actually exists in American political culture today, the frequent rhetorical tributes to indivisibility and a shared destiny notwithstanding?

As a child of the Age of *Brown* myself, "magical thinking" has played an important part in my own political and cultural socialization. Born in

1960, I first learned to read at a time when books on President Kennedy shared prominent space in school libraries with books about Lincoln (I was not aware of Martin Luther King Jr. beginning to receive such an honor until I entered junior high school in the early 1970s). First lady Jacqueline Kennedy's campaign to have her husband seen as Lincoln's direct heir, begun with her supervision of the funeral arrangements, succeeded.

My own first consciousness that I was part of a culture-wide exercise in historical reenactment took place in 1968, when Senator Robert F. Kennedy was assassinated as he sought the presidency. Like millions of other Americans, I have let my imagination roll away from its spool as I speculated over how much better things would have been if only Sirhan Sirhan had missed; or if Hubert H. Humphrey (probably the first politician I came to admire while he was alive) had done a little better in Illinois or in my home state, California, on November 5, 1968. On that day, former Vice-President Richard Nixon received 301 electoral votes to Vice-President Humphrey's 191, with former Alabama Governor George C. Wallace, still deep in the "Segregation Forever" phase of his career, receiving 46 votes.[2]

The education that I have received over the last twenty years, while living in my times and working on this book, has led me to imagine the following scene: yes, Vice-President Hubert Humphrey, perhaps the greatest champion of human rights produced from within the American electoral system during the Cold War, had closed the final gap in a few key states to win an Electoral College majority of 280 electoral votes (by carrying five states that he lost to Richard Nixon by less than 3 percentage points).[3]

If "victory" is measured by whether fundamental power relationships are significantly altered, whether racial privileges granted to some by long-running historical patterns of inequality are more candidly faced, discussed, and addressed, that is something that neither the system in the Age of *Brown* nor in our own time was built to prove—it is not "in the cards." In a final thought experiment about the election of 1968, let's think through the likely impact of a Humphrey presidency on the signal reconstructive project of his time—school desegregation. In view of the virulence of opposition to virtually any mandatory change in the link between residence and schooling, progress would have been slow, grudging, and would ultimately not have had any impact on the divide between black and white as it is registered most starkly in patterns of residence and school attendance. The evidence on this question, as Sheryll Cashin has demonstrated, is in: legislatures throughout this country have consistently thwarted efforts to share the wealth of affluent districts with poorer ones.[4]

Lest you doubt this, look North instead of South—to Chicago rather than Little Rock or New Orleans. In 1966, the commissioner of education, Francis Keppel (no relation to me, by the way), announced his intention to proceed on school desegregation in the city of Chicago—complete with the threat of a cutoff of thirty million dollars in federal funds if the effort was met with defiance. Nothing happened—except that Francis Keppel took the fall and found himself back at Harvard, presumably "returned to his first love—teaching," and now able to spend more time with his family.[5]

Keppel's superior, Health Education and Welfare secretary John Gardner, had to promise the overwhelmingly Democratic Congress that had passed the Voting Rights Act, the Elementary and Secondary Education Act, and Medicare not to pursue school desegregation aggressively as the price of retaining his authority over the issue. We must also add in Humphrey's own statements of strenuous reassurance to opponents of the Civil Rights Act of 1964 that the act would not be used to force desegregation through busing. The congressional record provides redundant evidence as to the depth of this fear all around the nation and among Democrats as well as Republicans.[6]

Members of Congress from outside the South well understood that, as historian Tomiko Brown-Nagin has written, "Residential segregation had intensified in the North at a time when [civil rights] activists hoped that the political environment had become more favorable to improvements in race relations."[7] Here again history was being reenacted: as Charles Lawrence emphatically reminds us, "segregation is Northern, not Southern in origin. The exclusion or segregation of blacks in public facilities was settled policy in the North before moving South in full force."[8]

Let us take this scenario a step further to something that came far closer to becoming a reality: what if neither Nixon nor Humphrey had reached 270? With no candidate at the magic number to certify election, and with Alabama's former governor, George C. Wallace, holding the balance, what kind of horse trading would have taken place? How would it have resembled the end of the First Reconstruction under a similarly politically pressured situation? As it was, from 1955 onward, the Supreme

Court proceeded with a heightened sensitivity to the powerful opposition that would inevitably develop.[9]

PARTICIPANT SYMBOLISM

A culture is a complex human creation of many parts with many authors, a few of whom have vastly more power than the much larger group of unorganized others. Cultural communities are rarely settled and tranquil places; they can generally be counted upon to be alive and thriving with tension and conflict. My interpretation of the dynamics of cultural change in the United States of the middle to late twentieth century involves an assemblage of people ranging from the highly visible and those with a high degree of access to the institutions of culture, politics, and sociality to those who, by the very nature of the system, have been dealt a weak hand in this process (individuals such as Septima Clark and Marcus Foster) and who must fight and labor to change at least some of the rules of a game whose ultimate outcome they know is rigged.

Robert Coles, Bill Cosby, and Joan Ganz Cooney were three cultural politicians who had influence and visibility at the center of a polity and a culture (and thus, some degree of power that most other people don't) and who used the opportunities that they created for themselves. My strategy of investigating these figures is my way of trying to capture the substance of a larger process: how certain ideas (and their symbolic representations) are formulated and advanced. After all, although cultures are collective processes and products, the fundamental unit of human experience resides in the lives of individual humans and their encounter with the world.

Americans have a much-declared regard not only for the rights of the individual but for the autonomy of the individual as the agent and author of her or of his own fate, despite considerable evidence that the reality that surrounds each of us is much more complicated than such individualism can grasp. Thus, if we are to understand the workings of such a culture—and the degree to which the strengths and liberating potentials of these ideas are densely mixed with the shared mythologies expressed most obviously in national advertising campaigns for brand-name products—we need to examine the forceful and creative work of key individuals.

But how do individuals create themselves into a "participant symbol," as Robert Coles and Bill Cosby did, or as Joan Ganz Cooney succeeded in doing, fulfilling the better recognized role of cultural entrepreneur and political power broker between constituencies that were advancing from the margins of culture to the mainstream and venerable institutions of official knowledge (such as the Carnegie Corporation and the Ford Foundation)?

I categorize Robert Coles and William H. Cosby Jr. as key "participant symbols" in the Age of *Brown* in different ways (and also to two different, if sometimes, overlapping, constituencies) within the American public. The quality that Coles and Cosby share, and that which defines them as participant symbols, is that they devote substantial parts of their public lives to representing in the present the attitudes and attributes of an America that was still very much off in the future (exactly how near or far in the future tense being determined in part by the actions of others who have also decided to take on this public work in their less well-known and less broadly visible lives).

Robert Coles was situated by both his material inheritance (generated from wise investments made by his parents) and ideological inheritance (through his marriage to Jane Hallowell) to be one of Howard Zinn's "new abolitionists." Unlike the students who also earned this title, or Professor Zinn, Coles had access to political influentials as an advocate who, unlike these others, was seen to possess special credentials as an analyst and observer of how humans respond to various kinds of stress, hardship, and suffering. Through his nearly twenty years of work in this vineyard, Coles created a record that is second to none in the Age of *Brown*.

Through his books and essays we see firsthand the push and pull of change among an exceptional range of people; we learn, for instance, that, although children are, in relation to many of the people around them, new to this world, this fact does not necessarily make them that much more receptive to change, although they can, in certain circumstances, demonstrate courage and the power to stand alone in dissent. Whether specific children or youths decide to act as pioneers and "participant symbols" of a potential transformation is determined by the formative adults in their lives. Advocates for change from outside this circle of intimacy cannot rely on any special power of perception among the young (tied to their innocence) to lead the rest of us.

Such insights were significant within a political culture in which children were especially numerous and were seen as possessing a unique and potentially powerful dynamism. Nonetheless, Coles's *Children of Crisis* series is even more valuable for its carefully rendered documentary portraits of those who, in respect to the most pressing challenge of their times, decide to draw a line of resistance around themselves—and a barrier between them and the change pursued by the "new abolitionists." These persons, Coles constantly reminds us, are easily caricatured; the power and strength of their resistance easily contributes to their ready-made construction as "the problem" and makes them easy for a scholar such as myself to see as captives to a cultural hegemony they do not see or, if they do occasionally acknowledge its presence in modern consumer culture, do not generally experience as imprisoning. Coles's record provides no formulas, theories, or answers—beyond underlining the importance to individuals, whether or not they are "new abolitionists"—of agency and of having a genuine feeling of power over one's own life without having to be above someone else.

Bill Cosby is, in the most classic sense, a participant symbol whose easy manner, fatherly bearing, and good humor once invited us to move forward in a way that did not (and perhaps cannot) address the real underlying social mechanics that actually make everyday life far more difficult for most people than our most beloved commercially sponsored representations of it often allow. And yet, I cannot, as a child of the Age of *Brown,* say that it all resolves into a small pile of pixie dust. *Fat Albert* and *The Cosby Show* opened the doors of social perception. If these warm depictions of community and family provided many of us with an oversimplified glimpse of something better that might be around the corner, they nonetheless did not ignore the fact that collective gains could not be made without collective struggle.

What Robert L. Carter said about why the litigation which underpinned the Age of *Brown* did not work as he had hoped applies with equal force with regard to the work of the participant symbol. Whatever they do or can contribute to a new and more expansive vision of that most contested of all ideas—what constitutes the "good society"—the following fact, Robert L. Carter proposed from his vantage point as a civil rights activist who became a member of the federal judiciary, remains the stronger force:

"our society is composed of a series of insulated institutions and interests antithetical" to becoming a more fully developed social democracy. "Effective regulation and control of those institutions must come not from the Supreme Court but from the bodies politic."[10]

The case of Joan Ganz Cooney is far more familiar territory to historians of American reform: the work of the well-connected agent of change, whose commitment to the "good society" is further strengthened not only by an unusually strong set of skills and abilities, but also by her ability to make connections with powerful people who share her interest in the channeling of potentially threatening social developments in more constructive directions. To the liberal foundation establishment with whom she worked, Cooney offered the possibility that a television program presented on a television network operating at least somewhat outside the standard commercial broadcast framework could accomplish what, in the Age of *Brown,* citizens and public institutions were finding to be extraordinarily difficult: closing the enduring inequalities created by the compound effects of racial and economic inequality. In fact, *Sesame Street* has contributed to the social and academic readiness of many individual American children. And yet it must be admitted that, over the same years, American society has grown more economically and socially segregated than it was in the late 1960s. As parents, producers, and others in the world attuned to *Sesame Street* did their work, the world which surrounded this urban pastoral portrait of urban life continued along its own path, honoring the iconography and symbolism of "integration" as it moved in more disintegrating directions.

GETTING SCHOOLED

For more than one hundred years now, there has been a debate going on in the United States about how to make schools "work" better, perhaps through their comprehensive reinvention. The key word here, of course, is "work": doing what, to what end, and for whom? A century of debate has clarified some issues, raised new ones, and settled very few others with finality.

John Dewey opened this discussion in a way which spoke eloquently to a vision of an American "imagined community" that was coming into being among the members of an emerging, university-trained middle class whose numbers grew significantly, especially in the quarter-century after the end of the Second World War. Dewey's definition of "Progressive education" was to enlarge, enhance, and humanize the whole mission and process of the public school by rejecting the traditional notion that it was "a place apart in which to learn lessons." Dewey boldly proposed that the school should strive to affiliate itself with life by having it become a publically supported "habitat" in which a child would learn a variety of skills through "directed living," including but not limited to building the individual's capacity to be part of a "social enterprise in which all individuals have an opportunity to contribute and to which all feel a responsibility."[11]

When we recognize the strong influence of Cold War ideology on the Supreme Court's decision in *Brown*, we must not allow ourselves to forget the extent to which that decision's description of the cultural and political function of the public school (and its implicit potential to inaugurate change) also reflects the pragmatic optimism of Dewey. In the same vein, the texts of *Brown I* and *Brown II* share something else with Dewey: a reluctance to acknowledge that at the heart of a society's most urgent challenges are conflicts so fundamental that they cannot simply be thought through or reasoned into resolution.

The social organization of education in the United States is an especially vivid case in point. Dewey wisely counsels us that the "range and outlook" of what citizens expect from the public school needs considerable enlargement; specifically, the blueprint for education must be a community's commitment to the principle that "what the best and wisest parent wants for his own child" must equally govern what the entire community does about all aspects of public schooling. "Any other ideal for our schools," Dewey warns, is not only "narrow and unlovely; acted upon, it destroys our democracy."[12] This vision of "imagined community" assumes decision making in town meetings in which all are free to speak and participate and in which each participant has an equal voice and vote.

Everyone who has ever attended school understands intuitively that "going to school" and "getting schooled" are two very different things. "Going to school," of course, refers to the formal act and process through which children enter the civic habitat outside their immediate family created expressly for them by some larger community. "Getting schooled" or being "taken to school" refers to the rougher and decidedly unofficial process through which we learn the actually operational "social physics" of our neighborhood and nation.[13] When we think about who "got schooled" through the Age of *Brown,* I contend that the advocates for "integration" were the ones who were taken to school and roughly taught a lesson in American ways.

If the public schooling of Americans over the twentieth century has taught us anything, it is that schools replicate the social and political structure of the supporting community. This is no accident; in fact, the system that Americans have devised demands it. The experiences of Septima Clark and Marcus Foster provide powerful evidence of how hard it can be for educators seeking to affiliate their institutions with life and to teach children through "directed living"—even when the public and their leaders seem to be on board. Localism, as administered in the United States, especially magnifies the great inequality in resources between communities within the same country, state, county, and city. When the Supreme Court, in *Brown II,* rather circumspectly and equivocally, laid out how parents, courts, and educators were to follow in order to desegregate schools, many white Americans resisted in a variety of ways because many parents believed that what the court now required violated the greater and stronger compact into which they had entered—that the location and investment in one's home was directly linked to the resources of the neighborhood as they resided publically in the quality of the school system. Residential housing and school attendance zones were linked to provide some with social protection from undesirable "others."[14] In words published in 1965, long before "white flight" became associated with school desegregation, educational sociologist Ronald Corwin spoke an important truth:

> Suburbia is not a return to nature. . . . it is not even purely a quest for the small town. . . . Most people have not turned to the suburbs to be near the birds and bees or to be active in a grassroots movement, but rather to escape the lower class conditions of central cities. "Child-Centered" parents are in search of middle-class playmates and segregated schools and play areas for their children. Suburbia is a class phenomenon. Those persons not fortunate enough to cross the barriers of restricted covenants, real estate monopolies, tax rates and fixed building costs into the most exclusive areas, move into

> the next subdivision and erect their own homogeneous ghettos. The cities have been left to the lower classes, the very young adults, and the very old.[15]

If many federal judges were ill-equipped by their social and political backgrounds to see much beyond well-established modes of thought, the same was true of the people who sat on school boards. Strengthening the ability of certain classes to assert a narrowly self-interested (and thus "private") ideological and social possessiveness over public schools (in the "public interest" of course) was the orientation of many of those who sought and often won election to local school boards; these were often, Corwin reminds us, "the same businessmen who prevent Negroes from eating in their restaurants and who think that lower-class students are lazy."[16]

Opposition to school desegregation efforts merely continued an existing trend. Sociologist Clarence Y. H. Lo gets right at the nub of the issue when he argues that many of those opposed to busing did so because "they sought to maintain advantages for their racial and ethnic group in the consumption of government services."[17] And when busing plans were issued by courts, the desire for social peace meant that certain socially and economically influential groups were "protected" while those without clout (whatever their race) were not. In addition, in a debate in which the fears of harm as expressed by white parents were featured prominently, the same fears, when expressed by black parents, went unheeded.[18] As the more rigorous phase of court-supervised desegregation ended its first decade in 1980, one pattern—which had first caught the attention of Marian Wright Edelman as she moved in the early 1970s to found the Children's Defense Fund—remained stubbornly alive: black students were at greater risk of being targeted by white students and were also far more likely to be more severely punished for any effort to retaliate.[19]

This historical record does not provide any alternative paths that could have been taken to a more satisfactory result. There is no one step that, if only *it* had been taken, would have left Americans less divided by race. The question becomes one of how best to reckon honestly with one's past, especially as it remains not just "in the present," but as the substance of the continuity between the past and the present. The architects of national litigation strategy for the NAACP deserve much praise for their formidable and indispensible contributions to modern nation building on the American home front. The NAACP spent years in local communities and courtrooms seeking to make separate truly equal. And yet, as they changed course once they had gone as far as they could on the "separate" issue, they ignored the lessons of the past, along with some of the teachers who had taught them, on the "equal" part. As Tomiko Brown-Nagin notes quite poignantly, some dissenting voices from allies in the earlier fight for equalization were ignored and sometimes even attacked by the national leadership as being captives to their own self-interest. The experience and wisdom of local teachers and administrators were by and large discarded when the dual systems created by the legal (and legalized) fiction of "separate but equal" were formally disestablished.[20]

Were he able to return to the early phases of the *Brown*-era litigation, Robert Carter would have brought professional educators together—presumably from both sides of the educational color line—to advise his team and ultimately the Supreme Court with a "concrete definition of the meaning of equality in education." Thus fortified, Carter would then "seek to persuade the Court that equal education, in its constitutional dimensions, must at the very least conform to the contours of equal education as defined by educators."[21]

Weighed against the persistence of institutionally supported racial separation in the United States, we cannot continue to believe that this approach would have brought forward a completely new day—such events do not really exist here or anywhere else. However, it might well have brought greater public and private resources and greater legitimacy in the American culture at large to historically black institutions as truly national partners in the work of the nation, as they continued in their efforts to enlarge the size and general capacity of the body politic to work toward a more substantive equality of opportunity.[22]

And finally, does this long and difficult chapter in American domestic policy deserve to be ranked with the most tragic failure of American foreign policy, American intervention in Vietnam? Was busing a "domestic Vietnam"?[23] In my view, the evidence, at even the most basic level, tells us that the answer to this question is no. This does not deny the problems that were inevitable with even the limited change that was attempted. In the main, however, the impact was to open up and improve the existing school systems. Jennifer Hochschild and Nathan Scovronick remind us of some important realities: "[D]esegregation . . . challenged racial prejudice and racial hierarchies as old as the country. It required change in the way that education has always been organized, particularly in the South. It threatened the preferences of whites to attend schools with people like themselves, and sometimes the preferences of people of both races to attend particular schools. It also helped millions of students to pursue their dreams, and enhanced citizens' ability to participate in shared democratic governance. Most centrally, it was a moral fight made for the sake of social justice; on that level it was necessary, long overdue, and a real victory."[24]

Hochschild and Scovronick also have an acute sense of how various calculations by groups and individuals have brought us to where we are today: "Desegregation created a high level of discord in society because it brought the values of the American dream into conflict. If Americans had not sincerely believed in the collective goals of the American dream, if they were not willing to make sacrifices for them, there would have been no victories. If the majority of Americans did not eventually come to believe that the risks to their individual goals were too high, the fight would not be over."[25]

NATION BUILDING RECONSIDERED

For most Americans, "nation building" is something done by others—distant from us in miles, history, and resources. Although a long history of social struggle has forced changes in national practices and institutions within these United States, these are most often treated as amendments or "new chapters" to a narrative in which the polity's most egregious problems have been solved. For the United States, as for other nations, the fundamental work of nation building remains undone—postponed by necessary compromises and the unavoidable realities of our particular social physics. It is my hope that the history presented here convinces you that we share some urgent problems with many others peoples in this world as we strive to develop a stronger and more participatory union of peoples and states.

Where might we start? There is ample evidence across the country that home-front nation building continues even when the national media aren't necessarily looking. As these local projects continue, and as some are elevated to national attention over others, we need to be wary of the purposes to which some would apply words such as "reinvention," "reform," accountability," and "progressive." The rhetoric of innovation and the mantle of progress are today being forcefully claimed on a bipartisan basis as both a corporate need and a necessity of national security. Under "No Child Left Behind," an appropriately ironic title for the era in which we now live, schools are treated as failing corporations that must be taken over (and closed if they do not succeed); also in the mix has been the creation of new "charter schools" (sometimes in the same buildings as the less well supported public schools that they are meant to compete with) in the belief that sometimes it is best to simply start over.[26]

This, Michael Apple argues, is the ultimate "de-integrative strategy" because it sends a very destructive message to the student citizen: "buying and selling . . . is the dominant ethic of society."[27] The key to applying the mass-production model to education has been the systematic "de-skilling of teachers" through the centralization of curriculum and the standardization of materials into prepackaged, "teacher proof" lesson plans.[28] The anticipated result, as well as the desired outcome, of such strategies, according to Apple, is to "create enhanced jobs for a relative minority" and "deskilled and boring work for the majority."[29]

There is an element of historical reenactment here, too, of course. This latest movement has some deep nineteenth-century roots in trying to provide a school experience geared not so subtly to aggressively acclimate the immigrants to American cities to the "experience of being a worker" on an industrial production line.[30]

To see nation building—in need and in action—in the United States requires only that we pay attention to what is and isn't happening in our schools—especially those where basic and genuine "domestic tranquility" (which makes robust debate and participation possible) and basic human care seem to have left the premises.[31] If we Americans can accept that, like other peoples, we have much fundamental conceptual nation-building work yet to do (and that we always will), we will be better citizens of our nation and of the world. This could be an important first step toward arriving at a sense of collective identity more realistic and fully dimensional than the idea that we are always being "remade" or "reborn" (and continually "losing our innocence" when crises come). This history of the collective schooling of the American people—my people—during the Age of *Brown* leads me to argue for a new sense of national identity in which experience has been leavened with the wisdom that comes from difficult lessons honestly learned. Such wisdom is not the enemy of positive, practical, and idealistic work, at home and in the world; rather, it is its proper and most reliable incubator.

NOTES

CHAPTER ONE

Note to epigraph: *The Life and Times of Frederick Douglass, Written by Himself: His Early Life as a Slave, His Escape from Bondage and His Complete History,* introd. Rayford W. Logan (1892; rpt. Mineola, N.Y.: Dover Publications, Inc., 2003), 264.

1. *Life and Times of Frederick Douglass,* 265.

2. I discuss this concept further in *The Work of Democracy: Ralph Bunche, Kenneth B. Clark, Lorraine Hansberry, and the Cultural Politics of Race* (Cambridge, Mass.: Harvard University Press, 1995); and "Kenneth B. Clark in the Patterns of American Culture," *American Psychologist* 57, no. 1 (January 2002): 29–37.

3. Danielle S. Allen, *Talking to Strangers: Anxieties of Citizenship since "Brown v. Board of Education"* (Chicago: University of Chicago Press, 2004), 19.

4. On this relationship, see especially John Stauffer, *Giants: The Parallel Lives of Frederick Douglass* (New York: Twelve, 2008).

5. Rebecca de Schweinitz, *If We Could Change the World: Young People and America's Long Struggle for Racial Equality* (Chapel Hill: University of North Carolina, 2009), 4; for a full discussion of this question, see Steven Mintz, *Huck's Raft: A History of American Childhood* (Cambridge, Mass.: Harvard University Press, 2006); Robert L. Griswold, *Fatherhood in America: A History* (New York: Basic Books, 1993); Elaine Tyler May, *Homeward Bound: American Families in the Cold War Era* (New York: Basic Books, 1988).

6. Derrick Bell Jr. "Serving Two Masters: Integration Ideals and Client Interest in School Desegregation Litigation," *Yale Law Journal* 85, no. 4 (March 1976): 473.

7. Quoted in Len Holt, *The Summer That Didn't End* (New York: William Morrow and Co., 1965), 128. These words originally appeared near the end of Zinn's essay "Education in Context: The Mississippi Idea," published in *The Nation,* November 23, 1964. I have quoted here from the version titled "Freedom Schools," reprinted in Howard Zinn, *The Zinn Reader: Writings on Disobedience and Democracy,* 2nd ed. (New York: Seven Stories Press, 2009), 562–73 (see 572–73).

8. There is a vast literature on this subject. The titles cited here represent some of the best work of the last fifty years. Excellent early accounts of desegregation in all regions of the United States are collected in Raymond W. Mack, ed., *Our Children's Burden: Studies of Desegregation in Nine American Communities* (New York: Vintage Books, 1968); Richard Kluger, *Simple Justice: The History of Brown v. Board and Black America's Struggle for Equality* (New York: Alfred A. Knopf, 1975), is an exceptional combination of social, political, and legal history; in the same category is J. Anthony Lukas, *Common Ground: A Turbulent Decade in the Life of Three American Families* (New York: Alfred A. Knopf, 1985); a compelling critique of the educational reforms that were brought forward during the Age of *Brown* is offered by Raymond Wolters, *The Burden of Brown: Thirty Years of School Desegregation* (Knoxville: University of Tennessee Press, 1984); Melba Pattillo Beals provides an unforgettable first-person account of what it was like to be one of the "Little Rock Nine" in *Warriors Don't Cry: A Searing Memoir of the Battle to Integrate Little Rock's Central High* (New York: Pocket Books, 1994); James T. Patterson, *Brown v. Board of Education: A Civil Right Milestone and Its Troubled Legacy* (New York: Oxford University Press, 2001), provides a perceptive historical account of the public debate that *Brown* has provoked on a number of fronts; on the persistence of racial distance in the southern Black Belt and beyond, Charles T. Clotfelter's *After Brown: The Rise and Retreat of School Desegregation after Brown* (Princeton, N.J.: Princeton University Press, 2004) is starkly revealing .

9. John H. Fischer, "Race and Reconciliation: The Role of Schools," in Talcott Parsons and Kenneth B. Clark, eds., *The Negro American* (Boston: Beacon Press, 1967), 491.

10. Deborah Meier, *The Power of Their Ideas: Lessons for America from a Small School in Harlem* (Boston: Beacon Press, 1995), 71.

11. "'The Mission of the War,' An Address Delivered in New York on 13 January 1864," in Frederick Douglass et al., *The Frederick Douglass Papers, Series One: Speeches, Debates and Interviews* (New Haven, Conn.: Yale University Press, 1991), vol. 4 (1864–80): 4.

12. Michael W. Apple, *Cultural Politics and Education* (New York: Teachers College, Columbia University, 1996), 98.

13. Michael W. Apple, *Educating the "Right" Way: Markets, Standards, God and Inequality* (New York: Routledge, 2006), 30.

14. Nat Hentoff, "Never Sell More of Yourself than You Can Buy Back," interview with Ossie Davis, *New York Times*, May 5, 1968, section D: 15.

15. Allen, *Talking to Strangers*, 18.

16. Ibid., 19.

17. U.S. Senate Select Committee on Equal Educational Opportunity, *Desegregation Under Law: Hearings Before the Select Committee on Equal Educational Opportunity, Part 3B*, 91st Cong., 2nd sess. (1970), 1, 396.

18. Dorothy C. Clement, Margaret Eisenhart, and Joe. R. Harding (with J. Michael Livesey), *Moving Closer: An Ethnography of a Southern Desegregated School* (Washington, D.C.: Department of Health, Education and Welfare, National Institute of Education, 1978) [ED 161 UD 013814], 68.

19. Ibid., 152.

20. Ibid., 204.

21. These lyrics are quoted from sheet music published by Shawnee Press in 1972. This edition contains the version recorded by Three Dog Night and the more historically explicit original version.

22. I obtained this episode of *CBS Reports,* "Pilot Plan for a Peace Corps: Operation Crossroads Africa," as a DVD from the archives of BBC America in Los Angeles.

23. "Billboard Hot 100," *Billboard,* August 12, 1972, 60; August 19, 1972, 52; September 16, 1972, 50.

24. The background summarized in the text is found in Earl Robinson with Eric Gordon, *Ballad of an American: The Autobiography of Earl Robinson* (Lanham, Md.: Scarecrow Press, 1998), 242–43. On the popularity of "Black and White" as a single, which sold more than one million copies, see Jimmy Greenspoon with Mark Bego, *One Is the Loneliest Number: On the Road and Behind the Scenes with the Legendary Rock Band, Three Dog Night* (New York: Pharos Books, 1991), 321. On Three Dog Night's status as the top rock group of 1972, see Ben Fong-Torres, "Three Dog Night: See How They Run," *Rolling Stone,* September 14, 1972, 30–34, 36.

25. On the matriculation of the song through American culture, see Robinson with Gordon, *Ballad of an American,* 342–43.

26. Benedict Anderson, *Imagined Communities: Reflections on the Origin and Spread of Nationalism,* rev. ed. (New York: Verso, 1991), 203.

27. On the opposition to busing in 1970, see George H. Gallup, *The Gallup Poll: Public Opinion, 1935–1971* (New York: 1972), vol. 3: 2248; on its role in the 1972 election, see George H. Gallup, *The Gallup Poll, 1972–1977* (Wilmington, Del.: Scholarly Resources, 1978), 51–52; on the widespread support in the late 1950s (outside the South) for school "integration" (as the holding in *Brown* was described to respondents), see George H. Gallup, *The Gallup Poll, 1935–1971* (New York: Random House, 1972), vol. 2: 1401–2, 1507, 1517.

28. George Gallup, "The Gallup Poll—Opposition Drops on Racially Mixed Schools," rpt. in U.S. Senate, *Hearings Before the Senate Select Committee on Equal Educational Opportunity, Part 1A: Equality of Educational Opportunity: An Introduction* (Washington, D.C.: U.S. Government Printing Office, 1970), 242.

29. Reuben Askew, "Gov. Askew's Noted Speech on Busing," *South Today,* May 1972, 2.

30. Ibid., 3.

31. U.S. Senate Select Committee on Equality of Educational Opportunity, *Hearings, Part 6: Racial Imbalance in Urban Schools* (Washington, D.C.: Government Printing Office, 1970), 3,106–7.

32. Alan David Freeman, "School Desegregation: Law, Promise, Contradiction, Rationalization," in Derrick A. Bell, ed., *Shades of Brown: New Perspectives on School Desegregation* (New York: Teachers College Press, Columbia University, 1980), 85.

33. On the firing of black teachers and administrators as unitary school systems were created, see Adam Fairclough, *A Class of Their Own: Black Teachers in the Segregated South* (Cambridge, Mass.: Harvard University Press, 2007), 393–420; on the "one-sided" nature of desegregation, see Barbara J. Shircliffe, *The Best of That World: Historically Black Schools and*

the Crisis of Desegregation in a Southern Metropolis (Cresskill, N.J.: Hampton Press, 2005), and David S. Celeski, *Along Freedom Road: Hyde County, North Carolina, and the Fate of Black Schools in the South* (Chapel Hill: University of North Carolina Press, 1994). On what was lost in the unequal treatment of historically black schools, see Hilton Kelly, *Race, Remembering, and Jim Crow's Teachers* (New York: Routledge, 2010), and Vanessa Siddle Walker, *Their Highest Potential: An African-American School Community in the Segregated South* (Chapel Hill: University of North Carolina Press, 1996).

34. Bell, "Serving Two Masters," 479.

35. For a cogent discussion of how profound differences in their experiences of day-to-day life continue to create a deep divide between how blacks whites see this society and its institutions, see Eduardo Bonilla-Silva, *Racism without Racists: Color-Blind Racism and the Persistence of Racial Inequality in America,* 4th ed. (Lanham, Md.: Rowman and Littlefield, 2014), 199–224.

36. "Address on Colonization to a Committee of Colored Men, Washington, D.C.," August 14, 1862, *Abraham Lincoln: Speeches and Writings, 1859–1865 (*New York: Library of America, 1989), 354.

37. "Speech at Cincinnati, Ohio," September 17, 1859, *Abraham Lincoln: Speeches and Writings,* 84.

38. "To the People of Sangamo County, New Salem," March 9, 1832, *Abraham Lincoln: Speeches and Writings,* 4.

39. "To Jesse W. Fell, Enclosing Autobiography," December 20, 1859, *Abraham Lincoln: Speeches and Writings,* 107.

40. "Proceedings of the State Convention of the Free Colored Freemen of Pennsylvania, Held in Pittsburgh, August 23–24, 1841," *Proceedings of the Black Convention Movement, 1840–1865,* ed. Philip S. Foner and George E. Walker (Philadelphia: Temple University Press, 1979), vol. 1: 113–14.

41. John Ernest, *A Nation Within a Nation: Organizing African-American Communities before the Civil War* (Chicago: Ivan R. Dee, 2011), 48, 137, 79.

42. "Report of the Committee on Education, Proceedings of the State Convention of the Colored People Held at Albany, New York, July 22–24, 1851, *Proceedings of the Black Convention Movement, 1840–1865,* ed. Foner and Walker, vol. 1: 73.

43. Ibid., 73–74.

44. Proceedings of the Second Annual Convention of the Colored Citizens of California Held in the City of Sacramento, December 9–12, 1856, *Proceedings of the Black Convention Movement, 1840–1865,* ed. Foner and Walker, vol. 2: 149.

45. "A Letter to the American Slaves from Those Who Have Fled American Slavery," *Frederick Douglass: Selected Speeches and Writings,* ed. Philip S. Foner, abridged and adapted by Youval Taylor (Chicago: Chicago Review Press, 2001), 161.

46. "Black Freedom Is the Prerequisite of Victory," speech delivered January 13, 1865, New York, *Frederick Douglass Papers, Series One,* vol. 4 (1864–80): 58

47. George Lipsitz, "The Racialization of Space and the Spatialization of Race: Theorizing the Hidden Architecture of Landscape," *Landscape Journal* 26, no. 1 (January 2007): 12. From

a systematic examination of Lorraine Hansberry's Chicago to a historically sophisticated analysis of the recent subprime mortgage crisis, Lipsitz builds upon this foundation in *How Racism Takes Place* (Philadelphia: Temple University Press, 2011). Also essential is Lipsitz's *The Possessive Investment in Whiteness: How White People Profit from Identity Politics* (Philadelphia: Temple University Press, 1998).

48. See my comments in Ralph Belaveau et al., "After Trayvon: Voices from the Academy Respond to a Tragedy," *Cultural Studies/Critical Methodologies* (Thousand Oaks, Calif.: Sage Publications, 2015), vol. 15, no. 2 (forthcoming).

49. Deirdre Cobb-Roberts, Sherman Dorn, and Barbara J. Shircliffe, eds., *Schools as Imagined Communities: The Creation of Identity, Meaning, and Conflict in U.S. History* (New York: Palgrave Macmillan, 2006), 1.

50. Ibid., 5.

51. Ibid., 1.

52. Gary Orfield, *The Reconstruction of Southern Education: The Schools and the 1964 Civil Rights Act* (New York: Wiley-Interscience, 1969), 7.

53. Ibid., 16.

54. Tony A. Freyer, *Little Rock on Trial: Cooper v. Aaron and School Desegregation* (Lawrence: University Press of Kansas, 2007), 13–14.

55. Ibid., 14.

56. Abraham Lincoln, Second Inaugural Address; endorsed by Lincoln, April 10, 1865, delivered March 4, 1865; Series 3, General Correspondence, 1837–1897; Abraham Lincoln Papers at the Library of Congress, Manuscript Division (Washington, D.C.: American Memory Project [2000–2002]), www.ourdocuments.gov/doc.php?flash=true&doc=38.

57. *Brown v. Board of Education*, 349 U.S. 294 (1955).

58. Sara Lawrence Lightfoot, "Families as Educators: The Forgotten People of *Brown*," in Bell, ed., *Shades of Brown*, 3–4.

59. Ibid., 4.

60. John Lewis (with Michael D'Orso), *Walking with the Wind: A Memoir of the Movement* (New York: Simon and Schuster, 1998), 54–55.

61. Ibid., 55.

62. Ibid.

63. Stephen J. Whitfield, *A Death in the Delta: The Story of Emmett Till* (New York: Free Press, 1988), ix, 11, 45, 91.

64. Tomiko Brown-Nagin, *Courage to Dissent: Atlanta and the Long History of the Civil Rights Movement* (New York: Oxford University Press, 2011), 139.

65. Herman Gray, "Remembering Civil Rights: Television, Memory and the 1960s," in Lynn Spigel and Michael Curtin, eds., *The Revolution Wasn't Televised: Sixties Television and Social Conflict* (New York: Routledge, 1997), 348–59; see also William Peters, "Visible and Invisible Images," in Ralph Lynn Lowenstein and Paul L. Fisher, eds., *Race and the News Media* (New York: Frederick A. Praeger, 1967), 81–82.

66. Harper Lee, *To Kill a Mockingbird* (1960, rpt. Harper Perennial Modern Classics, 2006), 173–75.

67. John Steinbeck, *The Grapes of Wrath* (New York: Modern Library, 1939); Richard Wright, *Native Son* (New York: Harper Brothers, 1940); James Agee and Walker Evans, *Let Us Now Praise Famous Men* (Boston: Houghton Mifflin, 1960); Jonathan Kozol, *Death at an Early Age: The Destruction of the Hearts and Minds of Negro Children in Boston Public Schools* (New York: Bantam Books, 1967); Sally Belfrage, *Freedom Summer* (Charlottesville: University of Virginia Press, 1965); Bel Kaufman, *Up the Down Staircase* (Englewood Cliffs, N.J.: Prentice Hall, 1964); Anne Moody, *Coming of Age in Mississippi* (New York: Dial Press, 1968); Pat Conroy, *The Water Is Wide* (Boston: Houghton Mifflin, 1972); Herbert Kohl, *36 Children* (New York: New American Library, 1967); John Holt, *How Children Fail* (New York: Pitman Publishing, 1964).

68. "Richard M. Nixon: Address on the State of the Union Delivered Before a Joint Session of the Congress," American Presidency Project, www.presidency.ucsb.edu/ws/?pid=3396.

69. WFM-ON Report, transcript of discussion with unidentified staff, Mondale Papers, Minnesota Historical Society, 154. K. 3. 4 (F), 23. On the political risks to Mondale of being seen as an advocate for busing, see Steven M. Gillon, *The Democrats' Dilemma: Walter Mondale and the Liberal Legacy* (New York: Columbia University Press, 1992), 135, 139–40. Mondale's major legislative contribution in the field of school desegregation as chair of the Select Committee on Equal Educational Opportunity was the provision of federal funds in the Emergency School Aid Act of 1972 to assist in the implementation of desegregation plans, a practice which occurred annually until 1978; see Jennifer L. Hochschild, *The New American Dilemma: Liberal Democracy and School Desegregation* (New Haven, Conn.: Yale University Press, 1984), 28 and 187. For a close-up view of how these funds were used in Portland, Oregon, during the 1973–74 academic year to ease interracial contact during and after the school day, see Ray C. Rist, *The Invisible Children: Scholl Integration in American Society* (Cambridge, Mass.: Harvard University Press, 1978), esp. 37–55. Mondale's autobiography (written with David Hage), *The Good Fight: A Life in Liberal Politics* (New York: Scribner, 2010), does not contain any discussion of his two years of work as head of the Select Committee on Equal Educational Opportunity.

70. Arturo Escobar, *Encountering Development; The Making and Unmaking of the Third World* (Princeton, N.J.: Princeton University Press, 1995), 52; see also Clifford Geertz, *After the Fact: Two Countries, Four Decades, One Anthropologist* (Cambridge, Mass.: Harvard University Press, 1995), esp. 17, 44.

71. I have been greatly assisted in developing my understanding of nation building, in theory and in practice, and as something relevant to understanding contemporary American political life, by many able scholars, not all of whom are thought of as having this expertise. Among these are the scholars interviewed by Gerardo L. Munck and Richard Snyder in *Passion, Craft, and Method in Comparative Politics* (Baltimore: Johns Hopkins University Press, 2007); Jeremi Suri, *Liberty's Surest Guardian: American Nation-Building from the Founders to Obama* (New York: Free Press, 2011); Hochschild, *New American Dilemma*; Jennifer Hochschild and Nathan B. Scovronick, *The American Dream and the Public Schools* (New York: Oxford University Press, 2003); Sheryll Cashin, *The Failures of Integration: How Race and Class Are Undermining the American Dream* (New York: Public Affairs Press, 2004).

72. Stokely Carmichael and Charles V. Hamilton, *Black Power: The Politics of Liberation in America* (New York: Vintage Books, 1967), 43.

73. Doug McAdam, *Freedom Summer* (New York: Oxford University Press, 1988), 14–15.

74. Howard Zinn, *SNCC: The New Abolitionists* (1964; rpt. Boston: South End Press, 2002), 9.

75. Theodore V. Purcell, "Hopes of Negro Workers for Their Children," in Arthur B. Shostack and William Gomberg, eds., *Blue-Collar World: Studies of the American Worker,* (Englewood Cliffs, N.J.: Prentice Hall, 1964), 147.

76. Hans Kohn, *American Nationalism: An Interpretive Essay* (New York: Macmillan Co., 1957), 15.

77. Gabriel Almond and Sidney Verba, *The Civic Culture: Political Attitudes and Democracy in Five Nations* (Princeton, N.J.: Princeton University Press, 1963), 9.

78. Gabriel A. Almond and G. Bingham Powell Jr., *Comparative Politics: A Developmental Approach* (Boston: Little, Brown, 1966), 71.

79. Zinn, *SNCC,* 217.

80. Ibid.

81. Warren I. Susman, in *History as Culture: The Transformation of American Society in the Twentieth Century* (New York: Pantheon Books, 1984), explores, with assistance from T. V. Smith and Roger Caillois, how the popularity of all kinds of games—from the Irish Sweepstakes to Monopoly—contributed to maintaining traditional values in a time of exceptional crisis: "these are not just foolish ways out of the rat race, but rather alternative . . . patterns duplicating in structure what institutionalized society demanded and normally assumed it could provide." Thus, Susman argues, rule-based recreations, giving special significance to luck and chance, provided "significant social reinforcement" (161–62). I am suggesting that we can think of American political culture as a deck of cards, but, like any other cultural creation, the deck is stacked in certain ways—making certain outcomes far more likely than others. The way the deck is not only dealt but how it is stacked in the first place—with what symbols, institutional capacities, and cultural possibilities—determine how "new," "fair," or "square" the "deals" offered by reformers actually are.

CHAPTER TWO

Note to first epigraph: Clifford Geertz, "The Integrative Revolution: Primordial Sentiments and Civil Politics in the New States," in Clifford Geertz, ed., *Old Societies and New States: The Quest for Modernity in Asia and Africa* (New York: Free Press 1963), 125–26.

Note to second epigraph: Allen, *Talking to Strangers,* xviii.

1. On Geertz's career as a contributor to American knowledge about what was once known as either the "Third World" or the "developing world," see especially his intellectual autobiography, *After the Fact.* Helpful appraisals of his work are offered in Jeffrey C. Alexander, Philip Smith, and Mathew Norton, eds., *Interpreting Clifford Geertz: Cultural Investigation in the Social Sciences* (New York: Palgrave Macmillan, 2011), and Susan Slyannovics, ed., *Clifford*

Geertz in Morocco (New York: Routledge, 2010); for a dissenting view on Geertz's legacy, see Daniel Martin Varisco, *Islam Obscured: The Rhetoric of Anthropological Representation* (New York: Palgrave Macmillan, 2005), 21–51.

2. Allen, *Talking to Strangers*, xvii–xviii.

3. Geertz, "Integrative Revolution," 109, 111.

4. Ibid., 109

5. Donald R. Matthews and James W. Prothro, *Negroes and the New Southern Politics* (New York: Harcourt Brace and World, 1966), 10. For a thorough understanding of the debates over the causes and meaning of the South's unique patterns of development within the United States in the twentieth century, see Natalie J. Ring, *The Problem South: Region, Empire, and the New Liberal State: 1880–1930* (Athens: University of Georgia Press, 2012), and Bruce J. Schulman, *From Cotton Belt to Sunbelt: Federal Policy, Economic Development, and the Transformation of the South, 1938–1980* (New York: Oxford University Press, 1991).

6. "Mississippi Freedom School Curriculum, Part II: Citizenship Curriculum, Unit 1: Comparison of Students' Reality with Others," rpt. in *Radical Teacher* 40 (Fall 1991): 9.

7. Philip E. Converse, "The Changing American Electorate," in Angus Campbell and Philip E. Converse, eds., *The Human Meaning of Social Change* (New York: Russell Sage Foundation, 1972), 306.

8. Almond and Verba, *Civic Culture*, 441.

9. Alan I. Abramowitz, "The United States: A Political Culture Under Stress," in Gabriel A. Almond and Sidney Verba, editors, *The Civic Culture Revisited* (Newbury Park, Calif.: Sage Publications, 1989), 183. On how the sample size limited Almond and Verba's ability to interpret apolitical responses, see 181–82.

10. Almond and Verba, *Civic Culture*, 452.

11. Ibid., 454–55.

12. Ibid., 452, 453.

13. Brown-Nagin, *Courage to Dissent*, 81–87; Fairclough, *A Class of Their Own*, 14–16.

14. The most insightful and persistent documentarian of this condition to the general reading public has been Jonathan Kozol; see especially his *Savage Inequalities: Children in America's Schools* (1991; rpt. Harper Perennial, 1992), and *Shame of the Nation: The Restoration of Apartheid Schooling in America* (New York: Crown Publishers, 2005).

15. U.S. Senate Select Committee on Equal Educational Opportunity, *Equal Educational Opportunity, Part 1A: An Introduction* (Washington, D.C.: U.S. Government Printing Office, 1970), 310.

16. Ibid., 325.

17. Ibid.

18. James W. Guthrie et al., *Schools and Inequality* (Cambridge, Mass.: MIT Press, 1971), 118–21. For an understanding of the intense financial pressures on local property tax in this period, see especially Paul E. Peterson's *City Limits* (Chicago: University of Chicago Press, 1981). An essential primary source is the final report of the President's Commission on School Finance, and Neil H. McElroy, *Schools, People & Money: The Need for Educational Reform: Final*

Report (Washington, D.C.: Government Printing Office, 1972). On the inherent problems faced by local governments in modern American federalism, see Clarence N. Stone, *Regime Politics: Governing Atlanta, 1946–1988* (Lawrence: University Press of Kansas, 1989).

19. U.S. Senate Select Committee on Equal Educational Opportunity, *Equal Educational Opportunity, Part 1A: An Introduction*, 312–13.

20. Ibid., 325.

21. Ibid., 332.

22. John H. Fischer, "Race and Reconciliation: The Role of the School," in Parsons and Clark, eds., *Negro American*, 491; Charles G. Spiegler, "Materials for Retarded Readers," in Helen M. Robinson, ed., *Materials for Reading* (Chicago: University of Chicago Press, 1957), 24.

23. James S. Coleman, *The Adolescent Society: The Social Life of the Teenager and Its Impact on Education* (1961; New York: Free Press, 1971), 3–6, 37–50, 68–142, 164–72.

24. Spiegler, "Materials for Retarded Readers," 24.

25. Ronald G. Corwin, *A Sociology of Education: Emerging Patterns of Class, Status, and Power in the Public Schools* (New York: Appleton-Century-Crofts, 1965), 43.

26. On the property tax revolt that began in California in the late 1970s, see Clarence Y. H. Lo, *Small Property versus Big Government: Social Origins of the Property Tax Revolt* (Berkeley: University of California Press, 1990), and David O. Sears and Jack Citrin, *Tax Revolt: Something for Nothing in California* (Cambridge, Mass.: Harvard University Press, 1982). Commentary on the grassroots tax revolt is sprinkled throughout the public record. For school-focused protests over ideology, curriculum, and funding in Long Island in the 1950s, see Joseph F. Maloney, *"The Lonesome Train" in Levittown* (University: University of Alabama Press, 1958); on the protracted struggle in Minneapolis in the late 1940s to avoid cuts in teacher pay and in the length of the school year, see H. Otto Dahlke, *Values in Culture and Classroom: A Study in the Sociology of the School* (New York: Harper Brothers, 1958), 503–4; for an analysis of taxpayer anger over schools in New England during the 1950s, see Neal Crasilneck Gross, *Who Runs Our Schools?* (New York: Wiley, 1958), 6, 70–73; on popular opposition to increased school funding in Oregon in the 1960s, see Harry F. Wolcott, *The Man in the Principal's Office: An Ethnography* (New York: Holt, Rinehart and Winston, 1973), 80–81.

27. Max Lewis Rafferty, *Max Rafferty on Education* (New York: Devin-Adair Co., 1968), 132.

28. Lo, *Small Property versus Big Government*, 8–9.

29. Ibid., 31–35.

30. Ibid., 31.

31. See Herbert T. Olander, "Children's Knowledge of the Flag Salute," *Journal of Educational Research* 35, no. 4 (December 1941): 300–305.

32. Jules Henry, "Docility, or Giving Teacher What She Wants," *Journal of Social Issues* 11, no. 2 (Spring 1955); Ray C. Rist, *The Urban School: A Factory for Failure: A Study of Education in American Society* (Cambridge, Mass.: MIT Press, 1973), 34–41; Rist, *Invisible Children*; John Ogbu, *The Next Generation: An Ethnography of Education in an Urban Neighborhood* (New York: Academic Press, 1974).

33. Kaufman, *Up the Down Staircase*; Kozol, *Death at an Early Age*; Kohl, *36 Children*.

34. Holt, *How Children Fail,* 43. The most naturalistic representation of this kind of classroom that I have found in the films of this period was in the internationally acclaimed *The 400 Blows* (Francois Truffaut, 1959; DVD, New York: Criterion Collection, 2006).

35. James S. Coleman, *Equality of Educational Opportunity* (Washington, D.C.: Department of Health, Education and Welfare, Office of Education, 1966) 12, 21–22.

36. Ibid., 66.

37. Eric A. Hanushek and John F. Kain, "On the Value of 'Equal Educational Opportunity' as a Guide to Public Policy," in Frederick Mosteller and Daniel P. Moynihan, eds., *On Equality of Educational Opportunity* (New York: Random House, 1972), 121.

38. See especially Patricia Hill Collins, *Another Kind of Public Education: Race, Schools, the Media, and Democratic Possibilities* (Boston: Beacon Press, 2009), 4–6; Daniel Pearlstein, "Teaching Freedom: SNCC and the Creation of the Mississippi Freedom Schools," *History of Education Quarterly* 30, no. 3 (Autumn 1990): 297–324; Daniel Pearlstein, "Minds Stayed on Freedom: Politics and Pedagogy in the African-American Freedom Struggle," *American Educational Research Journal* 39, no. 2 (Summer 2002): 249–77.

39. Interview by Holly Hill, *Stanford University Civil Rights Series, New York Times* Oral History Collection (Glen Rock, N.J.: Microfilm Corporation of America), A3.

40. Judith C. Hudson, "Freedom Teachers: Northern White Women Teaching in Southern Black Communities, 1860s and 1960s," EdD thesis, University of Massachusetts at Amherst, 2001, 91–92; Daniel Peter Hinman-Smith, "Does the Word 'Freedom' have a Meaning? The Mississippi Freedom Schools and the Search for Freedom through Education," PhD diss., University of North Carolina, Chapel Hill, 1993, 47–48

41. Zinn, *SNCC,* 3

42. Ibid., 9.

43. McAdam, *Freedom Summer,* 87.

44. Hudson, "Freedom Teachers," 198–99, 202, 211–15.

45. McAdam, *Freedom Summer,* 14–15.

46. Qtd. in Belfrage, *Freedom Summer,* 7.

47. Qtd. in McAdam, *Freedom Summer,* 40.

48. Hudson, "Freedom Teachers," 25.

49. Clayborne Carson, *In Struggle: SNCC and the Black Awakening of the 1960s* (Cambridge, Mass.: Harvard University Press, 1981), 113; 113–17; Mary Aikin Rothschild, *A Case of Black and White: Northern Volunteers and the Southern Freedom Summers, 1964–1965* (Westport, Conn.: Greenwood Press, 1982), 104; Holt, *Summer That Didn't End,* 49–50.

50. Rothschild, *Case of Black and White,* 104.

51. The Highlander Folk School, under the leadership of Myles Horton, played a crucial role in training generations of local leaders to organize labor unions and to register black voters in the South. Clark joined this work in the 1950s as Highlander came under especially intensive harassment and scrutiny from local, state, and federal authorities for this work.

52. Septima Poinsette Clark and Cynthia Stokes Brown, *Ready from Within: Septima Clark and the Civil Rights Movement* (Navarro, Calif.: Wild Tree Press,1986), 104.

53. Ibid. See also Septima Poinsette Clark and LeGette Blythe, *Echo in My Soul* (New York: E. P. Dutton, 1962), 38.

54. See the following interviews from the *Brown v. Board* Oral History Collection, Kansas State Historical Society: Eliza Briggs (May 19, 1995), 2; Annie V. Gibson (May 17, 1995), 3; and Ferdinand Pearson (May 17, 1995), 1. These former students describe using their laps as their desks and how they even shared paper and pencils.

55. Katherine Mellen Charron, *Freedom's Teacher: The Life of Septima Clark* (Chapel Hill: University of North Carolina Press, 2009), 70–71. Also instructive on the distinctive problems faced by the teacher working in the rural South is Valinda Littlefield, "An Open-Ended Education: Problems in Reconstructing the History of an African-American Classroom," in Ian Grosvenor, Martin Lawn, and Kate Rousmaniere, *Silences and Images: The Social History of the Classroom* (New York: Peter Lang, 1999), esp. 148–49, 154–55, 158.

56. Clark and Brown, *Ready from Within,* 106.

57. Margaret Washington Creel's *"A Peculiar People": Slave Religion and Community-Culture among the Gullahs* (New York: New York University Press, 1988) remains an essential study.

58. Clark and Brown, *Ready from Within,* 106–7 . For a clear sense of how common these improvisational instructional strategies were among Jim Crow teachers, see Kelly, *Race, Remembering, and Jim Crow's Teachers,* 72–89.

59. Clark and Blythe, *Echo in My Soul,* 49; Conroy, *Water Is Wide,* esp. 41–42, 58–59; Sandra Brenneman Oldendorf, "Highlander Folk School and the South Sea Island Citizenship Schools: Implications for Social Studies," EdD thesis, University of Kentucky, 1987, 34 note 1 (Dissertation Abstracts International, 48-04). On Conroy's limitations as a documenter of Sea Island people, see Juanita Jackson, Sabra Slaughter, and J. Herman Blake, "The Sea Islands as a Research Area," in Mary Arnold Twining and Keith E. Baird, eds., *Sea Island Roots: African Presence in the Carolinas and Georgia* (Trenton, N.J.: New World Press, 1991), 163 note 3.

60. Willie Lee Rose, *Rehearsal for Reconstruction: The Port Royal Experiment* (1964; rpt. Galaxy Books, 1976), 160.

61. Gerald Schwartz, ed., *A Woman Doctor's Civil War Diary: Esther Hill Hawks' Diary* (Columbia: University of South Carolina Press, 1984), 41.

62. Ibid.

63. John M. Glen, *Highlander: No Ordinary School,* 2nd ed. (Knoxville: University of Tennessee Press, 1996), 188–200.

64. Oldendorf, "Highlander Folk School and the South Sea Island Citizenship Schools," 31–33.

65. Septima Poinsette Clark, "An Experiment in Individualizing Instruction in Reading in a Sixth Grade Class," master's thesis, Hampton Institute, 1946, 37–43, 45. On how the ideological themes of the Second World War and the popularity of progressive education among educators in the urban South created limited opportunities for black teachers to teach against racism, see Fairclough, *A Class of Their Own,* 340–41.

66. Clark, "An Experiment in Individualizing Instruction in a Sixth Grade Classroom," 56, 83.

67. On the skepticism about poverty and the absence of English as a primary language in the home as reasons for difficulty in reading, see Helen M. Robinson, *Why Pupils Fail in Reading: A Study of Causes and Remedial Treatment* (Chicago: University of Chicago Press, 1946), 93–96. On the potential of children "born into homes and cultural ebb tide," see Spiegler, "Materials for Retarded Readers," 24–29.

68. Robert P. Moses and Charles E. Cobb Jr., *Radical Equations: Civil Rights from Mississippi to the Algebra Project* (Boston: Beacon Press, 2001), 13.

69. Ibid., 119.

70. James E. Clyburn, *Blessed Experiences: Genuinely Southern, Proudly Black* (Columbia: University of South Carolina Press, 2014), 124.

71. Clark and Brown, *Ready from Within,* 121; Charron, *Freedom's Teacher,* 545–55.

72. Davison M. Douglas, *Jim Crow Moves North: The Battle Over Northern School Segregation, 1865–1954* (New York: Cambridge University Press, 2005).

73. "Parents Claim Gangs Rule Gratz High School," *Philadelphia Tribune* (March 8, 1966), 1, 3.

74. William C. Green, "Simon Gratz Hi [*sic*] Changes are Being Seen, Felt, Heard," *Philadelphia Tribune,* February 24, 1968, 5.

75. "Gratz High Student Injured in Demonstration," *Philadelphia Tribune,* October 28, 1967, 1.

76. Ibid., 3.

77. Len Lear and John Brantley Wilder, "Negro History Courses Demanded by Students," *Philadelphia Tribune,* November 4, 1967, 1.

78. Ibid.

79. Marcus A. Foster, *Making Schools Work: Strategies for Changing Education* (Philadelphia: Westminster Books, 1971), 119–20.

80. Green, "Simon Gratz Hi," 5; Foster, *Making Schools Work,* 121–22. In his doctoral dissertation, Foster makes clear that he had developed the strategy for Gratz some years earlier as principal of the Octavius V. Catto Remedial Disciplinary School. See Marcus A. Foster, "Utilizing the Sellin-Wolfgang Index of Delinquency to Determine the Efficacy of a Treatment Program for Delinquent and Pre-delinquent Boys," EdD thesis, University of Pennsylvania, School of Education, 1971), esp. 64–96.

81. Foster, *Making Schools Work,* 135–36.

82. John Brantley Wilder, "School Board Defies Mayor; Votes to 'Take' White Homes," *Philadelphia Tribune,* February 27, 1968, 1–2.

83. Lawrence Geller, "Gratz Bus Brigade Blasts City," *Philadelphia Tribune,* February 27, 1968, 1–2.

84. Ibid., 23.

85. John Brantley Wilder, "Marcus Foster, Gratz High Head Recuperating," *Philadelphia Tribune,* October 21, 1967, 2; Wilder, "Gratz Students Lodge Complaint against Unsanitary Eating Place," *Philadelphia Tribune,* October 28, 1967, 4.

86. John Brantley Wilder, "Strain from Overwork Cited by Physician for Marcus Foster," *Philadelphia Tribune,* April 22, 1969, 1.

87. "School Chief Talks Reform," *Oakland Tribune,* April 4, 1970, 1.

88. For a full discussion of Oakland in these years, see Robert O. Self, *American Babylon: Race and the Struggle for Postwar Oakland* (Princeton, N.J.: Princeton University Press, 2003).

89. "School Chief Talks Reform," *Oakland Tribune*, April 4, 1970, 1.

90. Ibid. That comment is attributed to Paul Cobb of the Oakland Black Caucus. See also "Caucus Raps School Board Chief Pick," *Oakland Tribune*, April 8, 1970, 8.

91. John Palmer Spencer, *In the Crossfire: Marcus Foster and the Troubled History of American School Reform* (Philadelphia: University of Pennsylvania Press, 2012), 212–14; "Lawmakers Pledge School Funding Push," *Oakland Tribune*, November 2, 1972, 4; "2,200 "Oaklanders Plead for More State School Aid," *Oakland Tribune*, November 20, 1972, 1; Bev Mitchell, "2,000 in Plea for School Aid," *Oakland Tribune*, November 21, 1972, 1 and 10.

92. "Foundation Grant to Support Reading Centers Near Schools," *Oakland Post*, November 18, 1971, 1; "Community Involvement Encouraged," *Oakland Post*, March 2, 1972, 1; "Dr. Foster Encourages Participation in Education Picture," *Oakland Post*, March 9, 1972, 1; J. William Snodgrass, "Dr. Foster Says Oakland Is the City That Can Make It," *Oakland Post*, July 29, 1972, 3.

93. "School Chief Talks Reform."

94. "Introduction," Frederick M. Wirt, ed., *The Polity of the School: New Research in Educational Politics* (Lexington, Mass.: Lexington Books, 1975), xiii.

95. Foster, *Making Schools Work*, 52, 50.

96. Bev Mitchell, "New School Chief Urges Integration," *Oakland Tribune*, April 5, 1970, 1.

97. U.S. Senate, Senate Select Committee on Equal Educational Opportunity, Hearings, *Compensatory Education and other Alternatives in Urban Schools, Part 12* (Washington, D.C.: U.S. Government Printing Office, 1971), 5, 510.

98. For a thorough discussion of these trends, see Self, *American Babylon*, 166–74.

99. See Gary Yee, "Miracle Workers Wanted: Executive Succession and Organizational Change in an Urban School District, An Exploratory Study," EdD thesis, Stanford University, 1996, 82–86 and 186 note 73.

100. "Dr. Foster says Oakland Is the City That Can Make It," 3.

101. U.S. House of Representatives. *Hearings of the Committee on Education and Labor, Oversight Hearings on Elementary and Secondary Education, October 4 and 11, 1972* (Washington, D.C.: U.S. Government Printing Office, 1973), 439.

102. U.S. Senate Select Committee on Equal Educational Opportunity, *Part 12*, 5, 513.

103. "One Day Teacher's Strike Schedule for June 10th," *Oakland Post*, June 2, 1971, 1.

104. "Schools Will Defy a Strike," *Oakland Tribune*, October 3, 1973, 1; "Oakland School Strike Averted—Black Panther Party Negotiates Model Pact," *Black Panther*, October 27, 1973, 16.

105. See "Schools to get $255,584 for Anti-Violence," *Oakland Post*, September 15, 1973, 1. This article announces the release of these new funds in response to a grand jury report on school violence. The new funds come from the Alameda County Justice Planning Board, the county juvenile court system, and the California Youth Authority.

106. U.S. House of Representatives, Hearings before the Select Committee on Crime, *Drugs in Our Schools*, 92nd Congress, 2nd sess. (Washington, D.C.: U.S. Government Printing Office, 1973), 1,621–26.

107. Oversight Hearings on Elementary and Secondary Education, 439.

108. Elaine Reed, "A League Look at Education," *Oakland Tribune,* World of Women section, September 13, 1973, 9K.

109. "Marcus Foster Slain, Assistant Wounded," *Oakland Tribune,* November 7, 1973, 1; Richard Paoli, "Letter Boasts of Foster's Murder," *Oakland Tribune,* November 11, 1973, 1; Earl Caldwell, "Oakland 'Army' Puzzles Police," *New York Times,* November 11, 1973, 42; Earl Caldwell, "Veteran Is Charged in Killing of Oakland Educator," *New York Times,* January 12, 1974, 19.

110. "Services for Dr. Foster," *Oakland Post,* November 11, 1973, 6.

111. Press Release #557, Box P15, Ronald Reagan Gubernatorial Papers, Press Unit, Press Releases, November 1973, Reagan Presidential Library, Simi Valley, Calif.

112. I sought access to the student newspapers of the six high schools featured in Amy Stuart Wells, *Both Sides Now: The Story of School Desegregation's Graduates* (Berkeley: University of California, 2009). I also made the same request to the principals of two other high schools I encountered in my own research, Beaufort High School (in Beaufort, South Carolina) and, of course, Simon Gratz High School in Philadelphia. From all these inquiries, I received only one response, which came from Joan Barker, of the Topeka [Kansas] High School Historical Society.

113. The account of the political life of this student body confirms many of the findings of Gael Graham's fascinating study, *Young Activists: American High School Students in the Age of Protest* (DeKalb: Northern Illinois University Press, 2006).

114. For the specific date of this change, I am indebted to Joan Barker of the Topeka Historical Society (e-mail message to author, September 6, 2010). On the persistence of the feeling that there remained a "school within a school," see Wells, *Both Sides Now,* 69.

115. On the struggle between "democracy and peace" and "servitude and unrest," see the students' annual *Topeka High Sunflower* (1950), 34. On how the Korean war touched student life, see "Draft Issue Holds Wide Interest, Attracts Adventure Seeking Youngsters," in the student newspaper, *THS World,* January 13, 1951, 2. The editors also contributed to the war effort by endorsing government censorship of military news during wartime ("Freedom of the Press Also Means Suppression of the News in Emergency," *THS World,* January 26, 1951, 2).

116. On the rise of outright cheating, see Terry Smith, "An Intolerable Situation," *THS World,* February 26, 1961, 2. On a rise in student public misbehavior, see Susan Heil, "THS Assembly Behavior Needs Some Improvement," *THS World,* March 27, 1959, 2; "Rowdyism: Whose Fault Is It?" *THS World,* January 16, 1962, 2; Robert Kaufman, "Battleground," *THS World,* January 22, 1966, 2; Les Kurtz, "Trojans Seek Vandalism Solution," *THS World,* February 25, 1966, 1; "Speech Rocks Troy," *THS World,* October 14, 1966, 2; and "Recent Assembly Conduct Needs Improvement; Students Must Help," *THS World,* October 30, 1968, 4. In the fall of 1968, security police were retained to help enforce discipline ("Security Police Are Necessary," *THS World,* October 4, 1968, 3; "Class Day's Alternative of 1969's Fiasco," *THS World,* March 20, 1970, 3).

117. "For the Last Time," *THS World,* May 22, 1964, 2. The campaign for a student-led judicial process was successful. In the fall of 1972 a new system of school government was

established, merging the student government with elements of the faculty government, but this system was dismantled and replaced by a more traditional student government setup ("THS Considers StuCo Revisions," *THS World,* April 21, 1972, 1; "Plans for Student Government Drawn Up," *THS World,* November 10, 1972, 2). For a midterm report on the experiment, see "Student-Faculty Board in Review: Lack of Communication Biggest Problem in 1974," *THS World,* May 10, 1974, 7. The reference to the need for "climate control" between faculty and students on issues ranging from general comportment to hair length and the dress code is taken from the *Sunflower* (1965), 76.

118. Karen Haney, "*World* Viewpoints" column, *THS World,* October 9, 1964, 2.

119. *Topeka High Sunflower* (1963), 34. On the addition of courses in Negro history and human relations after the King assassination, see "New Courses Possible," *THS World,* April 29, 1969, 3.

120. Wells, *Both Sides Now,* 70.

121. On the absence of blacks on the staff, see Mark Gardner, "Racism in the Schools, Part I: Integration Fails at Topeka High," *THS World,* December 22, 1971, 2.

122. Frank Petroni et al., *Two, Four, Six, Eight, When You Gonna Integrate?* (New York: Behavioral Publications, 1970), 44.

123. Ibid., 136–41.

124. Scott Berridge, "Negro Students Unite, Promote 'Black Pride,'" *THS World,* September 20, 1968, 1.

125. "Faculty Discloses Results of Discipline Discussions," *THS World,* April 24, 1970, 1.

126. Frederick M. Wirt and Michael W. Kirst, *The Political Web of American Schools* (Boston: Little, Brown, 1972), 94. Sometimes student leaders at Topeka High School spoke up for greater restriction of student conduct. In the fall of 1969, the student council, with only two dissenting votes, overwhelmingly supported a resolution demanding that the administration take "more definite and united action" against a rising tide of student misconduct and replace any "indecisive and overly tolerant policies of the past" ("Student Government Ratifies Resolution," *THS World,* October 24, 1969, 2.

127. "THS Considers StuCo Revisions," 1; "StuCo's Failure Inevitable," *THS World,* April 7, 1972, 2; "Student-Faculty Committees Formed at THS," *THS World,* April 21, 1972, 2; "Plans for Government Drawn Up," 2; Student-Faculty Board in Review," 2.

128. *Topeka High Sunflower* (1979), 150; Joanne Malley, "Government Strives for Improvement," *THS World,* December 7, 1979, 2.

129. Petroni et al., *Two, Four, Six, Eight,* 14.

130. Ibid. Mexican American students were widely acknowledged as outsiders by those interviewed for the Petroni study (200–231). Although the broader-scale activism of the late 1960s brought these students a bit more into the civic circle, my own review found that their activities were not much chronicled in the *THS World* during the 1970s. For an early response to protests by Chicano students over exclusion from being homecoming royalty, see "Candidates for Royalty Picked on Racial Basis," *THS World,* December 11, 1970, 1; and "Candidates Selected to be Representative of All Ethnic Groups," *THS World,* February 5, 1971, 1.

131. Petroni et al., *Two, Four, Six Eight,* 14.

132. Ibid., 80, 102, 118.

133. Ibid., 102.

134. Ibid., 251.

135. Ibid., 253.

136. Ibid., 253–54.

137. Anemona Hartocollis, "Time for a Little Liberation at THS," *THS World,* January 6, 1972, 2; Jacob Dickinson, "Riggs Lobs Libbers," *THS World,* September 14, 1973, 2; Tom Laney, "Girls' Sports Barely Noticed," *THS World,* October 5, 1973, 2; Kris Dickerson and Linda Selgar, "District Disregards Supreme Court," *THS World,* September 6, 1974, 2.

138. "I Need to Talk to Someone . . . ," *THS World,* January 17, 1975, 4.

139. Nola Wright, "Experience Proves the Best Teacher in Child Development," *THS World,* March 29, 1974, 5.

140. Robert Redfield, "Can Rules or Tutors Educate?" address to the Parents Association of the University of Chicago Laboratory School, March 16, 1943, Margaret Park Redfield, ed., *The Papers of Robert Redfield,* vol. 2: *The Social Uses of Social Science* (Chicago: University of Chicago Press, 1963), 9–10.

CHAPTER THREE

Note to epigraph: Robert Coles, *Children of Crisis: A Study of Courage and Fear* (Boston: Little, Brown, 1967), xl.

1. At the start of their work in the South, the Coleses had to rely on family resources. This work laid the groundwork for the support of the Field, New World, and Ford foundations. Jane Hallowell Coles was a twentieth-century member of the New England "gentry class" identified by Dorothy Ross. The Hallowells were New England bankers with a strong commitment to abolition. Robert Coles's British-born father entered the upper class as a MIT-trained engineer whose smart investments in Boston real estate allowed him to set up trust funds for his two sons. Robert Coles's mother was the Iowa-born daughter of a minister; she knew the Bible exceedingly well and took great care in her children's moral and religious education. Robert Coles discussed the Coles/Hallowell family's support for his initial research in a telephone interview with the author on July 27, 2007; on Coles's parents, see also Paul Wilkes, "Robert Coles: Doctor of Crisis," in Jay Woodruff and Sarah Carew Woodruff, eds., *Conversations with Robert Coles* (Jackson: University of Mississippi Press, 1992); and Susan Hilligoss, *Robert Coles* (New York: Twayne Publishers, 1997), 1–2. On the founding generation of social science, see Dorothy Ross, *The Origins of American Social Science* (New York: Cambridge University Press, 1991), 53–55, 61–62.

2. The *Children of Crisis* series consists of *Children of Crisis: A Study of Courage and Fear* (1967); *Migrants, Sharecroppers and Mountaineers: Volume II of Children of Crisis* (Boston: Little, Brown, 1971); *The South Goes North: Volume III of Children of Crisis* (Boston: Little, Brown, 1971); *Eskimos, Chicanos, Indians: Volume IV of Children of Crisis* (Boston: Little, Brown, 1977);

and *Privileged Ones: The Well Off and Rich in America: Volume V of Children of Crisis* (Boston: Little, Brown, 1977).

3. The phrase "America's Forgotten Children" appears on the cover of the February 14, 1972, issue of *Time* along with a photograph of Coles, framed by children's drawings. The feature article is titled "Breaking the American Stereotypes." A month earlier, *Newsweek* magazine devoted the entire religion section of its January 17 issue to a detailed and deeply admiring review of volumes 2 and 3 of the *Children of Crisis* series; see Kenneth L. Woodward, "A Good Neighbor," *Newsweek*, January 17, 1972, 81–82.

4. "Breaking the American Stereotypes," *Time*, February, 14, 1972, 36.

5. Robert Coles, interview with the author, October 5, 2006.

6. Coles to Roman Leverenz, October 31, 1983, Robert Coles Papers, Box 5, Misc., University of North Carolina–Chapel Hill.

7. Robert Coles, *Doing Documentary Work* (New York: Oxford University Press, 1997), 60–61.

8. Ibid.

9. Ibid.

10. Coles, *Children of Crisis: A Study of Courage and Fear*, 3–4.

11. Ibid., 43.

12. Coles recounts his wife's criticism in an undated and unpublished essay, "The American Character: Hopes, Hates, Binds," Coles Papers, Box 14, pp. 6–7.

13. Coles, *Children of Crisis: A Study of Courage and Fear*, 33; Oscar Lewis, *The Children of Sanchez: Autobiography of a Mexican Family* (New York: Random House, 1961); Allison Davis and John Dollard, *The Children of Bondage: Personality Development of Negro Youth in the Urban South* (Washington, D.C.: American Council on Education, 1940); John Dollard, *Caste and Class in a Southern Town* (New Haven, Conn.: Yale University, 1937); Abram Kardiner and Lionel Ovesey, *The Mark of Oppression: A Psychosocial Study of the American Negro* (New York: W. W. Norton, 1951); Kenneth B. Clark, *Prejudice and Your Child* (Boston: Beacon Press, 1955). For Coles's published discussion of these works, see Robert Coles and Joseph Brenner, "American Youth in a Social Struggle: The Mississippi Summer Project, *American Journal of Orthopsychiatry* 35, no. 5 (October 1965): 909–26.

14. Coles, interview with the author, October 5, 2006.

15. Coles, *Children of Crisis: A Study of Courage and Fear*, 41, 46.

16. Ibid., 47.

17. Ibid., 48–49.

18. Ibid., 48–49.

19. Ibid., 62.

20. Ibid., 49.

21. Robert Coles to David Riesman, May 1, 1967, Coles Papers, Box 6.

22. Coles to Daniel Patrick Moynihan, September 29, 1967, Coles Papers, Box 5.

23. Coles, *Children of Crisis: A Study of Courage and Fear*, 367.

24. See Daniel Patrick Moynihan, "The President and the Negro: The Moment Lost," *Commentary* (February 1967).

25. On the circumstances of the leak, see Robert Novak, *The Prince of Darkness: 50 Years Reporting in Washington* (New York: Crown Forum Books, 2007), 134–35. James T. Patterson provides the best analysis of the long-term implications of this debate in *Freedom Is Not Enough: The Moynihan Report and America's Struggle over Black Family Life—from LBJ to Obama* (New York: Basic Books, 2010).

26. Earl Lewis, *In Their Own Interests: Race, Class, and Power in Twentieth-Century Norfolk, Virginia* (Berkeley: University of California Press, 1991), 200–204. On deindustrialization in the urban core, see especially William Julius Wilson's *When Work Disappears: The World of the New Urban Poor* (New York: Alfred A. Knopf, 1997), and *The Truly Disadvantaged: The Inner City, the Underclass and Public Policy* (Chicago: University of Chicago Press, 1987). On the political and intellectual context of the debate over the Moynihan report, see Jonathan Scott Holloway and Ben Keppel, eds., "Segregated Social Science and Its Legacy," in *Black Scholars on the Line: Race, Social Science, and American Thought in the Twentieth Century* (Notre Dame, Ind.: Notre Dame University Press, 2007), 18–20.

27. "The Observer and the Observed," in Robert Coles, *Farewell to the South* (Boston: Little, Brown, 1972), 372–73.

28. Robert Coles, *The Middle Americans* (Boston: Little, Brown, 1971); Carol Baldwin, *The Buses Roll* (New York: W. W. Norton, 1974). In this book, Coles provided the written text which accompanies photographs by Carol Baldwin and Peter T. Whitney.

29. In 1986, when Coles revisited his New Orleans materials in *The Moral Life of Children* (New York: Atlantic Monthly Press, 1986), he provided a longitudinal portrait of Hank, a New Orleans boy not discussed in the earlier *Children of Crisis* series. Hank's father was a "hard-drinking carpenter and house painter . . . militant segregationist, a constant heckler of Rudy and, not least, a member of the Ku Klux Klan" (37). As a boy of seven, Hank thought that Rudy "had been 'crazy' for continuing her mob-threatened education" but did not seem to share in his father's systematic racism (in this, Coles wrote, Hank took after his mother). Hank did not immediately adopt his father's attitudes, Coles suggested, because "all during the 1960s . . . [Hank] had enough to do during those years simply dealing with the difficulties, dangers and demands of his family's emotional life" (37). Within a few years, as Hank entered adolescence, however, he had adopted his father's combativeness, occasionally explosive temper, and racism (41–44).

30. Coles, *Children of Crisis: A Study of Courage and Fear,* 52–53.

31. Ibid., 53.

32. Ibid., 55.

33. Ibid., 57.

34. Ibid., 85.

35. Ibid., 83–84.

36. Ibid., x.

37. Ibid., xi–xii.

38. Coles qtd. in Citizens Board of Inquiry, A. Philip Randolph, and Robert Warren Spike, *Final Report on the Child Development Group of Mississippi* (1966), 6. The Citizen's Crusade Against Poverty was organized by the allies of the CDGM in organized labor and allied groups in the civil rights community.

39. Memorandum by Catherine Small Tratner, "What I've Accomplished Working with the Pre-school Children," n.d., CDGM Papers, Reel 3, Wisconsin State Historical Society.

40. Progress Report from First Baptist Center, Moss Point, Mississippi, August 9, 1966, CDGM Papers, Reel 6.

41. Allen, *Talking to Strangers*, 18.

42. Polly Greenberg, *The Devil Has Slippery Shoes: A Biased Biography of the Child Development Group of Mississippi* (New York: Macmillan, 1969), 281.

43. Ibid., 282–83.

44. "Paid Announcement of the Friends of CDGM" (announcing a general meeting in Jackson, Mississippi, to fight a cutoff of funds), CDGM Papers, Reel 12.

45. See two reviews of the Greenberg memoir by Coles: *Harvard Educational Review* 40, no. 1 (Spring 1970): 134–35, and *Social Casework* 51, no. 6 (July 1970): 431–32.

46. Gene Roberts, "In Mississippi Delta, More Pay Means Few Jobs," *New York Times*, February 13, 1967, 1.

47. U.S. Senate Subcommittee on Employment, Manpower and Poverty of the Committee on Labor and Public Welfare, *Examining the War on Poverty*, 90th Cong., 1st sess., part 1, 157–58 .

48. U.S. Senate, *Hunger and Malnutrition in America: Hearings before the Subcommittee on Employment, Manpower and Poverty of the Committee on Labor and Public Welfare*, 90th Cong., 1st sess., 26.

49. Ibid., 25.

50. U.S. Senate Subcommittee on Executive Reorganization of the Committee on Government Operations, *The Federal Role in Urban Affairs*, 89th Cong., 1,590–91.

51. On the close, personal relationship that developed as a result of this exchange, see Peter Edelman, *Searching for America's Heart: RFK and the Renewal of Hope* (Boston: Houghton Mifflin, 2000), 66–67, and Evan Thomas, *Robert Kennedy: His Life* (New York: Simon and Schuster, 2000), 339–40.

52. U.S. Senate Subcommittee on Executive Reorganization, *Federal Role in Urban Affairs*, 1598–1602.

53. Robert F. Kennedy, speech before the Child Study Association, March 6, 1967, Robert Kennedy Senate Papers, John F. Kennedy Memorial Library, Columbia Point, Boston, 4.

54. Ibid., 9.

55. Ibid., 18.

56. Robert Coles, *Eskimos, Chicanos, Indians*, xi–xii.

57. On the complicated politics of this period, Jefferson Cowie's *Stayin' Alive: The 1970s and the Last Days of the Working Class* (New York: New Press, 2010) is essential. This comparison of Coles's work to Kennedy's was inspired by Kenneth B. Clark's 1971 interview with Coles titled "Poverty Is Black and White" (obtained from the William T. Boyce Library of Fullerton College). In this interview, Coles described his deep admiration for Kennedy as well as his encounter with Kennedy voters who became Wallace voters. Coles argued that Wallace gave "cohesion to poor and middle-class white people."

58. George McGovern, who became the Democratic presidential nominee in 1972, was a key figure in the congressional investigation of hunger in the United States as chair of the U.S.

Senate Select Committee on Hunger and Human Needs. Walter Mondale, who was elected vice-president of the United States in 1976 and was the Democratic presidential nominee in 1984, conducted hearings on the problems of migrant workers as chair of the Subcommittee on Migratory Labor of the U.S. Senate Committee on Labor and Public Welfare. McGovern and Mondale provided introductory remarks to Coles's *Uprooted Children: The Early Life of Migrant Farm Workers* (Pittsburgh: University of Pittsburgh Press, 1970). Senator Edward M. Kennedy, perhaps the most important liberal voice of those years (and an unsuccessful candidate for the Democratic presidential nomination in 1980), provided an introduction to Coles's *Still Hungry in America* (New York: World, 1969).

59. Robert Coles, "Mondale of Minnesota: Champion of Powerless People," *The New Republic*, December 25, 1971, 21–23

60. Robert Coles to Walter Mondale, January 20, 1972, Coles Papers, Box 5.

61. Coles to Maria Piers, July 12, 1971, Coles Papers, Box 6.

62. Robert Coles, "Civil Rights Is a State of Mind," *New York Times Magazine*, May 7, 1967, 32. Coles's extensive collection of journalistic writing is collected in *Farewell to the South*.

63. Coles, "Civil Rights Is a State of Mind," 36, 43.

64. U.S. Senate, *Migrant and Seasonal Farm Worker Powerlessness: Hearings of the Subcommittee on Migratory Labor of the Committee on Public Welfare*, 91st Cong., 1st and 2nd sess., part 2, 334 (July 28, 1969; 1970). See also Coles's "The Poor Don't Want to Be Middle-Class," *New York Times Magazine*, December 19, 1965, which gives substantial space to the social analysis provided by the very hardworking poor of their own conditions and aspirations.

65. U.S. Senate, *Migrant and Seasonal Farm Worker Powerlessness*, 335.

66. See James T. Patterson, *America's Struggle Against Poverty* (Cambridge, Mass.: Harvard University Press, 2000), 163–66; Vincent J. Burke with Vee Burke, *Nixon's Good Deed: Welfare Reform* (New York: Columbia University Press, 1974), 117–18.

67. Robert Coles to Peter Davison, August 4, 1970, Coles Papers, Box 2.

68. Coles text in Baldwin, *The Buses Roll*, 29.

69. Ibid., 27–28.

70. Ibid., 38.

71. Ibid., 27.

72. Ibid., 37.

73. Ibid., 28–47.

74. Mike Barnicle, "Busing Puts Burden on Working Class, Black and White," *Boston Globe*, October 15, 1974, 23. On the relationship of the Boston busing program to legal trends set in motion both by electoral politics and by Supreme Court decisions, see Ronald P. Formisano, *Boston Against Busing: Race, Class and Ethnicity in the 1960s and 1970s* (Chapel Hill: University of North Carolina Press, 1991), 229; on this interview as a watershed moment in Boston politics, see Lukas, *Common Ground*, 506.

75. Barnicle, "Busing Puts Burden on Working Class, Black and White."

76. Hubie Jones, "For Blacks, Race Not Class is the Ultimate Reality," *Boston Globe*, November 1, 1974, 27.

77. C. Vann Woodward, *Tom Watson: Agrarian Rebel* (New York; Macmillan Co., 1938); Lawrence Goodwin, *The Populist Moment: A Short History of the Agrarian Revolt in America,* abridged ed. (New York: Oxford University Press, 1978); Steven Hahn, *The Roots of Southern Populism: Yeomen Farmers and the Transformation of the Georgia Upcountry, 1850–1890.* (1982; updated ed. New York: Oxford University Press, 2006); Michael Kazin, *The Populist Persuasion: An American History* (Ithaca, N.Y.: Cornell University Press, 1998); Nell Irvin Painter, *Standing at Armageddon: A Grassroots History of the Progressive Era* (New York: W. W. Norton and Co., 2013).

78. On the genesis of this political prospect, Jules Witcover's *85 Days: The Last Campaign of Robert F. Kennedy* (1969; rpt. New York: William Morrow & Co., 1988) is the essential first source while Jefferson R. Cowie follows it into the next decade in *Stayin' Alive.*

79. Robert Coles, "Ronald Reagan, Populist," *New Republic,* April 12, 1980, 16.

80. Ibid., 17.

81. Ibid., 16.

82. Ibid., 17.

83. The phrase "stepped into history's shadow" is attributed to NBC correspondent Bob Dotson, who narrated Ruby Bridges's return to William Frantz Elementary. This segment is part of *Make It Memorable* (NBC, 2002), an instructional video featuring Dotson.

84. For *The Spiritual Life of Children,* see the *New York Times Best-seller List,* February 24, 1991; for *The Moral Intelligence of Children,* see March 23, 1997.

85. Marshall McLuhan, *Understanding Media: The Extensions of Man* (New York: McGraw Hill and Co., 1964), 204–5.

86. Lynn Spigel, *Make Room for TV: Television and the Family Ideal in Postwar America* (Chicago: University of Chicago Press, 1992), 112, 100.

87. Lynn Spigel, *Welcome to the Dream House: Popular Media and Postwar Suburbs* (Durham, N.C.: Duke University Press, 2001), 33; see also Spigel, *Make Room for TV,* 37–45.

88. Spigel, *Welcome to the Dream House,* 33–34.

89. Todd Gitlin, *The Twilight of Common Dreams: Why America Is Wracked by Culture* Wars (New York: Metropolitan Books, 1995), 63.

90. Ibid., 65.

91. Gray, "Remembering Civil Rights," 350.

CHAPTER FOUR

Note to first epigraph: "Playboy Interview: Bill Cosby," *Playboy,* May 1969, 84, 175.

Note to second epigraph: Bill Cosby and Alvin F. Poussaint, M.D., *Come On, People: On the Path from Victims to Victors* (Nashville: Thomas Nelson, 2007), xvii–xviii.

1. Roy Hemming, "*Senior Scholastic* Interviews Bill Cosby: 'Down with Mental Sin,'" *Senior Scholastic,* March 18, 1965, 17.

2. "Master Mimic Bill Cosby: An Electronic Mark Twain," *Life,* March 15, 1968, 38.

3. Lawrence W. Levine, *Black Culture/Black Consciousness: Afro-American Folk Thought from Slavery to Freedom* (New York: Oxford University Press, 1977), 366.

4. Dick Gregory, *Nigger: An Autobiography* (New York: E. P. Dutton, 1964), 148.

5. Hemming, "*Senior Scholastic* Interviews Bill Cosby," 17.

6. Richard Leiby, "Reliable Source [Cosby, Saying the Darndest Things]," *Washington Post*, May 19, 2004, C3.

7. Ibid. For a thoroughly researched and thoughtfully argued discussion of Cosby's comments in 2004, see Michael Eric Dyson, *Is Bill Cosby Right? (Or Has the Black Middle Class Lost Its Mind?)* (New York: Basic/Civitas Books, 2005).

8. Patterson, *Freedom Is Not Enough*, 204.

9. "Master Mimic Bill Cosby," 39.

10. Ibid.

11. Ibid., 40.

12. Dyson, *Is Bill Cosby Right?* 5, 8.

13. Edward P. Whipple, qtd. in Daniel Wickberg, *The Sense of Humor: Self and Laughter in Modern America* (Ithaca, N.Y.: Cornell University Press, 1998), 60.

14. Ibid., 119.

15. Donna M. Goldstein, *Laughter Out of Place: Race, Class, Violence, and Sexuality in a Rio Shantytown* (Berkeley: University of California Press, 2003), 5.

16. Herbert Hyman, "Dimensions of Social-Psychological Change in the Negro Population," in Campbell and Converse, eds., *Human Meaning of Social Change*, 373–74.

17. Ibid.

18. U.S. House of Representatives Committee on Education and Labor, *Employment Practices in the Performing Arts: Hearing*, 87th Cong., 2nd sess., 61.

19. Maurice Christopher, "Colgate Next Target in Integrated Ads Push," *Advertising Age*, August 19, 1963, 1, 8. An enlargement of a sixteen-millimeter frame from that first ad accompanies this article. More on this effort to desegregate advertising is found in Maurice Christopher, "Desegregate Ads, TV, Lever Tells Agencies," *Advertizing Age*, August 12, 1963, 1, 8.

20. Daisy Fullilove Balsley, "A Descriptive Study of References Made to Negroes and Occupational Roles Represented by Negroes in Selected Mass Media," PhD diss., University of Denver, 1959, 15; Donald Bogle, *Primetime Blues: African Americans on Network Television* (New York: Farrar Straus Giroux, 2001), 74–77.

21. "*I Spy* with Negro Widely Booked," *New York Times*, September 10, 1965, 93.

22. "Race Won't Be a Theme in TV Episodes," *Ebony*, September 1965, 66.

23. "Color Him Funny," *Newsweek*, January 3, 1966, 76.

24. "The Case of the Scholarly Spy," *New York Times*, October 17, 1965, section II: 21.

25. Gerald Nachman, *Seriously Funny: The Rebel Comedians of the 1950s and 1960s* (New York: Pantheon Books, 2003), 564.

26. Mel Watkins, *On the Real Side: Laughing, Lying, and Signifying—The Underground Tradition of African-American Humor that Transformed American Culture, from Slavery to Richard Pryor* (New York: Simon and Schuster, 1995), 505.

27. Ibid., 504, 505.

28. *Bill Cosby Is a Very Funny Fellow Right!* (1963; Burbank, Calif.: Warner Archives, 1995, CD #15'8–2); *I Started Out as a Child* (1964; Burbank, Calif.: Warner Archives, 2009, CD #2–1567); *Why Is There Air?* (1965; Burbank, Calif.: Warner Archives, 2009, CD #2–1606); *Wonderfulness: The Amazing Comedy of Bill Cosby* (1966; Burbank, Calif.: Warner Archives, 2009, CD #2–1634); *Revenge* (1967; Burbank, Calif.: Warner Archives, 2009, CD #2–1691); *To Russell, My Brother, Whom I Slept With* (1968; Burbank, Calif.: Warner Archives, 2009, CD # 2–1734).

29. The childhood routines from this record are the foundation of Cosby's anthology, *Childhood* (New York: G. P. Putnam's Sons, 1991).

30. Bill Cosby, *Time Flies* (New York: Doubleday, 1987). These words are from the unpaginated introduction.

31. Bill Cosby, "An Integration of the Visual Media via *Fat Albert and the Cosby Kids* into Elementary School Curriculum as a Teaching Aid and Vehicle to Achieve Increased Learning," PhD diss., University of Massachusetts, 1976, 137–38.

32. Cosby, *Childhood*, 27, 87.

33. Alfred Lubrano, *Limbo: Blue Collar Roots, White Collar Dreams* (Hoboken, N.J.: Wiley, 2004).

34. *Black History: Lost, Stolen or Strayed?* (n.d., Xenon Home Video, XE-XX-1502).

35. *To All My Friends on Shore*, directed by Gilbert Cates (1971; Quality Home Video, 1998).

36. Cosby, "Integration of the Visual Media," 11–12.

37. Bill Cosby, *Fat Albert and the Cosby Kids* (New York: Filmation Associates, 1973), 4.

38. Ibid., 25–26.

39. Heather Hendershot, *Saturday Morning Censors: Television Regulation Before the V-Chip* (Durham, N.C.: Duke University Press, 1998), 204.

40. Bill Cosby, *The Wit and Wisdom of Fat Albert* (New York: Windmill Books/E. P. Dutton, 1973), 22, 24, 30, 42, 50.

41. On this point I am indebted to Richard Sennett and Jonathan Cobb's *The Hidden Injuries of Class* (New York: Knopf, 1972).

42. Bogle, *Primetime Blues*, 293.

43. James Baldwin, *The Fire Next Time* (1963; rpt. New York: Vintage, 1992), 93–94.

44. Bogle, *Primetime Blues*, 12.

45. Balsley, "Descriptive Study of References Made to Negroes."

46. Ibid., 11–13.

47. "Playboy Interview," 82.

48. Alex Haley, "Talking with Cosby," *Ladies Home Journal*, June 1985, 32, 167.

49. Ibid., 32.

50. "Playboy Interview," 79.

51. Bogle, *Primetime Blues*, 186–87.

52. Baldwin, *The Fire Next Time*, 93–94.

53. Herman Gray, *Watching Race: Television and the Struggle for "Blackness"* (Minneapolis: University of Minnesota Press, 1995), 27, 17–18; Adolph Reed Jr., "The 'Black Revolution' and the Reconstitution of Domination," in *Race, Politics and Culture: Critical Essays on the Radicalism of the 1960s* (New York: Greenwood Press, 1986), 80.

54. Baldwin, *The Fire Next Time*, 94.

55. Harry F. Waters, "Bill Cosby Comes Home," *Newsweek,* November 5, 1984, 93.

56. Mark Edmondsun, "Father Still Knows Best," *Channels of Communications,* June 1986, 71.

57. Ibid.

58. John Leonard, "Leave It to Cosby," *New York Magazine,* October 22, 1984, 154.

59. Ibid.

60. Terry Teachout, "Black, Brown, and Beige," *National Review,* July 18, 1986, 60.

61. Ibid., 60–61.

62. Richard Zoglin, "Prime Time's New First Family," *Time,* May 6, 1985, 88.

63. Sut Jhally and Justin Lewis, *Enlightened Racism: The Cosby Show, Audiences, and the Myth of the American Dream* (Boulder, Colo.: Westview Press, 1992), 7–8.

64. Alvin F. Poussaint, "The Huxtables: Fact or Fantasy?" *Ebony,* October 1988, 72–73.

65. "Playboy Interview," 80.

66. Ibid.

67. Ibid., 87.

68. Richard Zoglin et al., "Cosby, Inc.," *Time,* September 28, 1987, 56.

69. Jhally and Lewis, *Enlightened Racism,* 50, 53, 107–8, 119.

70. Ibid., 60–61, 78.

71. Bogle, *Primetime Blues,* 292.

72. Jhally and Lewis, *Enlightened Racism,* 50.

73. Linda K. Fuller, *The* Cosby Show*: Audiences, Impact, and Implications* (Westport, Conn.: Greenwood Press, 1992), 91–98.

74. Jhally and Lewis, *Enlightened Racism,* 50, 53.

75. James P. Comer, *Waiting for a Miracle: Why Schools Can't Solve Our Problems—and How We Can* (New York: E. P. Dutton, 1997), 27.

76. Ronald Walters, *White Nationalism/Black Interests: Conservative Public Policy and the Black Community* (Detroit: Wayne State University Press, 2003), 74–75; Sharon M. Collins, *Black Corporate Executives: The Making and Breaking of a Black Middle Class* (Philadelphia: Temple University Press, 1997), 34. Two essential discussions of the content and legacy of Reagan-era social policies are provided by Sean Wilentz, *The Age of Reagan: A History, 1974–2008* (New York: HarperCollins, 2008), 144–50, 206–7; and Lou Cannon, *President Reagan: Role of a Lifetime* (New York: Simon and Schuster, 1991), 240–79.

77. Sam Fulwood, *Waking from the Dream: My Life in the Black Middle Class* (New York: Anchor Books, 1996), 27–28.

78. Bart Landry, *The New Black Middle Class* (Berkeley: University of California Press, 1987), 194.

79. Bruce D. Haynes, *Red Lines, Black Spaces: The Politics of Race and Space in a Black Middle-Class Suburb* (New Haven, Conn.: Yale University Press, 2001), 113.

80. Landry, *New Black Middle Class,* 221.

81. Joe R. Feagin and Melvin P. Sikes, *Living with Racism: The Black Middle-Class Experience* (Boston: Beacon Press, 1994), 319. The phrase "coon counter" is reported in George Davis and Glegg Watson, *Black Life in Corporate America: Swimming in the Mainstream* (New York: Anchor Press/Doubleday, 1982), 3; on retrenchment on minority recruitment by corporations

during the Reagan years, see 49–55. For the way in which the new bureaucracy of civil rights enforcement placed many black executives in positions both more vulnerable to elimination and further away from the centers of corporate power, see Feagin and Sikes, *Living with Racism,* 157–64; and Collins, *Black Corporate Executives,* 89–96, 120–21, 133–36, 141–43.

82. Bogle, *Primetime Blues,* 5. On residential segregation, see Mary Pattillo-McCoy, *Black Picket Fences: Privilege and Peril among the Black Middle Class* (Chicago: University of Chicago Press, 1999), 25. For a model historical study of the ways in which discrimination shaped the African American migration to the suburbs, see Andrew Wiese, *Places of Their Own: African-American Suburbanization in the Twentieth Century* (Chicago: University of Chicago Press, 2004).

83. Ron Krabill, *Starring Mandela and Cosby: Media and the End(s) of Apartheid* (Chicago: University of Chicago Press, 2010), 117.

84. Ibid., 102–7, 114–17, 151–52.

85. Ibid., 21, 27, 45, 58–64. The phrase "structured absence" belongs to Louis Althusser and is applied to the South African situation by Krabill.

86. Adolph Reed Jr., *The Jesse Jackson Phenomenon: The Crisis of Purpose in Afro-American Politics* (New Haven, Conn.: Yale University Press, 1986), 19.

87. Roland Marchand, *Advertising the American Dream: Making Way for Modernity, 1920–1940* (1985; Berkeley: University of California Press, 1986), 167.

88. Michael Schudson, *Advertising, The Uneasy Persuasion: Its Dubious Impact on American Society* (New York: Basic Books, 1986), 221.

89. Ibid., 232.

90. Ibid., 233.

91. Ibid., 221. For a cultural history that charts a pursuit of abundance which begins long before twentieth-century consumer culture, see Jackson Lears's *Fables of Abundance: A Cultural History of Advertising in America* (New York: Basic Books, 1994).

92. Derrick Bell, *Silent Covenants: Brown v. Board and the Unfulfilled Hopes for Racial Reform* (New York: Oxford University Press, 2004), 79.

93. For a vividly informed discussion of these issues in the lives of real people, see Sheila Bair, *Bull by the Horns: Fighting to Save Main Street from Wall Street and Wall Street from Itself* (New York: Free Press, 2012), 66–70.

94. Gray, *Watching Race,* 82.

95. On this tradition, see Kevin K. Gaines, *Uplifting the Race: Black Leadership, Politics, and Culture in the Twentieth Century* (Chapel Hill: University of North Carolina Press, 1996).

96. John D. H. Dowling, "The *Cosby Show* and American Racial Discourse," in Geneva Smitherman and Teun A. van Dijik, eds., *Discourse and Discrimination* (Detroit: Wayne State University Press, 1988), 69.

97. Ibid., 70.

98. For a sense of Cosby's public standing just before the latest disclosures, see Mark Whitaker's biography, *Cosby: His Life and Times* (New York: Simon and Schuster, 2014). Representative of the accusations, and of the public debate that they have provoked, are the following: Beverly Johnson, "Bill Cosby Drugged Me. This Is My Story," *Vanity Fair,*

December 11, 2014, www.vanityfair.com/culture/2014/12/bill-cosby-beverly-johnson-story; David Carr, "Calling Out Bill Cosby's Media Enablers, Including Myself," *New York Times* November 24, 2014, www.nytimes.com/2014/11/25/business/media/calling-out-bill-cosbys-media-enablers-including-myself.html; and Ta-Nehsi Coates, "The Cosby Show: Declining to Seriously Reckon with Rape Accusations against Him Is Reckless," *The Atlantic,* November 19, 2014, www.theatlantic.com/entertainment/archive/2014/11/the-cosby-show/382891/; Lorne Manley and Graham Bowley, "Cosby Team's Strategy: Hush Accusers, Insult Them, Blame the Media," *New York Times,* December 28, 2014, www.nytimes.com/2014/12/29/arts/cosby-teams-strategy-hush-accusers-insult-them-blame-the-media.html?_r=0.

CHAPTER FIVE

Note to epigraph: U.S. Senate, Select Committee on Equal Educational Opportunity, *Equality of Educational Opportunity, An Introduction—Continued,* 91st Cong., 2nd sess., pt. 2, at 928W.

1. On the "neighborhood" as an important metaphor for understanding how the leaders of television saw their role, see Spigel, *Make Room for TV,* 100, 112, and *Welcome to the Dream House,* 37, 43.

2. Wilbur Schramm, Jack Lyle, and Edwin B. Parker, *Television in the Lives of Our Children* (Stanford, Calif.: Stanford University Press, 1961), 161, 181.

3. Spigel, *Welcome to the Dream House,* 203–9. On how these concerns set the stage for *Sesame Street,* see Robert W. Morrow, Sesame Street *and the Reform of Children's Television* (Baltimore: Johns Hopkins University Press, 2006).

4. Robert Andrew Carlson, "The Creation and Development of Educational Television as an Institution of Adult Education: A Case Study in American History," PhD diss., University of Wisconsin, 1968, 285, 491; see also Robert M. Pepper, *The Formation of the Public Broadcasting Service* (New York: Arno Press, 1979), 31.

5. Harold D. Lasswell, "The Future of Public Affairs Broadcasting," in Lester Asheim, ed., *Educational Television, The Next Ten Years: A Report and Summary of Major Studies on the Problems and Potential of Educational Television* (Stanford, Calif.: Stanford Institute for Communications Research, 1962), 99.

6. "Cast Entertains in Chicago, At the White House," Sesame Street *Newsletter,* December 31, 1970, 1–2, Children's Television Workshop Papers, Box 2A, Public Broadcasting Archives, University of Maryland–College Park.

7. For a further discussion of this contrast, see Robert K. Avery, ed., *Public Service Broadcasting in a Multi-channel Environment: The History and Survival of an Ideal* (New York: Longman, 1993). On the political forces that influenced the financing model for what became PBS, see Robert Blakely, *To Serve the Public Interest: Educational Broadcasting in the United States* (Syracuse, N.Y.: Syracuse University Press, 1979), 179–80, and Marilyn Lashley, *Public Television: Panacea, Pork Barrel, or Public Trust?* (New York: Greenwood Press, 1992), 7, 30.

8. John Walker Powell, *Channels of Learning: The Story of Educational Television* (Washington, D.C.: Public Affairs Press, 1962), 121–42; Joe Hall, "ETV: A Major Resource," in Asheim,

ed., *Educational Television,* 43; and Carlson, "Creation and Development of Educational Television," 235–38, 252.

9. Wilbur Schramm, *The People Look at Educational Television* (Stanford, Calif.: Stanford University Press, 1963), 35, 55.

10. Ibid., 45.

11. James Ledbetter, *Made Possible By . . . : The Death of Public Broadcasting in the United States* (London: Verso, 1997), 111.

12. Lester Asheim, "A Survey of Informed Opinion on Television's Future Place in Education," in Asheim, ed., *Educational Television,* 29.

13. Carnegie Commission on Educational Television, *Public Television, A Program for Action: The Report and Recommendations of the Carnegie Commission on Educational Television* (New York: Bantam, 1967), 92.

14. Roger Revelle, "Testimony Before the Television Advisory Panel," in Asheim, ed., *Educational Television,* 88.

15. Lawrence Dennis, "Instructional Television: A National Perspective," in Barton Lovewell Griffith and Donald W. MacLennan, eds., *Improvement of Teaching by Television: Proceedings of the National Conference of the National Association of Educational Broadcasters, University of Missouri, March 2–4, 1964* (Columbia: University of Missouri Press, 1964), 5–6.

16. Steven D. Classen, *Watching Jim Crow: The Struggles over Mississippi TV, 1955–1969* (Durham, N.C.: Duke University Press, 2004), 37, 79, 111, 119–22, 157.

17. On the conservatism of 1950s commercial television when it come to broadcasting material that might challenge existing stereotypes and arrangements, see Balsley, "Descriptive Study of References Made to Negroes." For an informative discussion of the sophisticated understandings that African American listeners and viewers brought to stereotypic entertainments, and for a sense of how progress away from stereotypes reinforced a new narrowness in portrayals of African American life, see Melvin Patrick Ely, *The Adventures of Amos 'n' Andy: A Social History of an American Phenomenon* (New York: Free Press, 1991).

18. Gray, "Remembering Civil Rights," 350.

19. Spigel, *Make Room for TV,* 37–45.

20. Spigel, *Welcome to the Dream House,* 31–34.

21. Hartford N. Gunn Jr., "A Station Manager's View of the Problems of Programming," in Asheim, ed., *Educational Television,* 142; Schramm, *People Look at Educational Television,* 55.

22. Schramm, *People Look at Educational Television,* 14–15.

23. G. Alexander Moore Jr., *Realities of the Urban Classroom: Observations in Elementary Schools* (New York: Frederick A. Praeger, 1967), 14–15.

24. Ibid., 24. Expressing similar reservations is Asheim, "A Survey of Informed Opinion," 19–20.

25. McLuhan, *Understanding Media,* 335.

26. Michael Davis, *Street Gang: The Complete History of Sesame Street* (New York: Viking, 2008), 148–49; Morrow, Sesame Street *and the Reform of Children's Television,* 87, 97–98.

27. Joan Ganz Cooney, "The Potential Uses of Television in Pre-school Education," 9, CTW Papers, Public Broadcasting Archives, University of Maryland–College Park, Box 1.

28. Ibid., 10.

29. The comments on these programs are from a résumé that Cooney sent to Lloyd Morrisett on May 13, 1966 (Carnegie Corporation Papers, Series II, Subseries III, Box 523, File 10). On Cooney's affinity for liberal politics in the 1960s, see Davis, *Street Gang,* 12, 17–23, 63–64.

30. "Address by Joan Ganz Cooney to NET Affiliate Meeting for Station Managers," New York City, October 18, 1968, 4, Children's Television Workshop Papers, Series 1, Subseries 15, Box 32, Folder 12, Public Broadcasting Archives.

31. Moore, *Realities of the Urban Classroom,* 9.

32. Schramm, Lyle, and Parker, *Television in the Lives of Our Children,* 178.

33. Carlson, "Creation and Development of Educational Television," 7–8, 12, 122–26, 109, 145, 146, 152, 235–38, 247–48, 252, 255, 536; and Pepper, *Formation of the Public Broadcasting Service,* 73.

34. U.S. House of Representatives, Hearings before the Subcommittee on Communications and Power of the Committee on Interstate Commerce, *Educational Television,* 87th Cong., 1st sess. (Washington, D.C.: Government Printing Office, 1961), 41, 63–64.

35. Hall, "ETV: A Major Resource," 41–43.

36. Carnegie Commission on Educational Television, *Public Television,* 92.

37. U.S. House of Representatives, Hearings before the Committee on Interstate and Foreign Commerce, *Public Television Act of 1967,* 90th Cong., 1st sess. (Washington, D.C.: Government Printing Office, 1967), 415.

38. U.S. Senate Subcommittee on Executive Reorganization, *Federal Role in Urban Affairs,* 89th Cong., 2nd sess., pt. 13: 2, 641 (from the statement of "urbanologist" and future senator Patrick Moynihan, who represented New York in that body between 1977 and 2001).

39. "Sesame Street," *Newsweek,* January 29, 1970, 102.

40. Bayard Rustin, *A Way Out of the Exploding Ghetto* (New York: League for Industrial Democracy, 1967), 3.

41. Robert L. Green, *The Urban Challenge—Poverty and Race* (Chicago: Follett Publishing Co., 1977), 140.

42. Jane Jacobs, *The Death and Life of Great American Cities* (New York: Random House, 1961), 182.

43. Ibid., 170, 241.

44. Senate Hearings before the Subcommittee on Executive Reorganization, pt. 1: 37.

45. U.S. Senate, Hearings before the Select Committee on Equal Educational Opportunity (Washington, D.C.: Government Printing Office, 1970), 928V.

46. Ibid., 928W.

47. Ibid.

48. Ibid.

49. Ibid.

50. Ibid.

51. Otto Klineberg, "Life Is Fun in a Smiling, Fair-Skinned World," *Saturday Review,* February 14, 1963, 77.

52. Ibid.

53. Eleanor Burke Leacock, *Teaching and Learning in City Schools: A Comparative Study* (New York: Basic Books, 1969), 78–79.

54. Murrow, *Sesame Street and the Reform of Children's Television,* 51; Hendershot, *Saturday Morning Censors,* 141–51.

55. These comments are in an unpaginated foreword to Irma Simonton Black, *Teacher's Guide to Green Light, Go* (New York: Macmillan, 1966).

56. Ibid.

57. Grace and Fred Hechinger, "There Are No Sexists on *Sesame Street,*" *New York Times,* January 30, 1972, section II: 19.

58. Ibid.

59. Theodore Clymer, "The Structured Reading Approach," in Helen M. Robinson, ed., *Controversial Issues in Reading and Promising Solutions* (Chicago: University of Chicago Press, 1961), 77.

60. See Lema L. Gitter, *The Montessori Way* (Seattle: Special Child Publications, 1970), 21; and Joan Beck, *How to Raise a Brighter Child,* (New York: Trident Press, 1967), 199–211. On the Montessori movement and the *Sesame Street* approach, see Hendershot, *Saturday Morning Censors,* 138–39.

61. Beck, *How to Raise a Brighter Child,* 25.

62. Nancy McCormick Rambusch, *Learning How to Learn: An American Approach to Montessori* (Baltimore: Halicon Press, 1962), 3; Maria Montessori and R. Calvert Orem, *A Montessori Handbook: Dr. Montessori's Own Handbook* (New York: G. P. Putnam and Sons, 1965), 9; and E. M. Standing, *The Montessori Revolution in Education* (New York: Schocken Books, 1966), 195–96.

63. Ronald and Beatrice Gross, "Let the Child Teach Himself," *New York Times Magazine,* May 16, 1965, 50.

64. Ogbu, *Next Generation,* 154–55.

65. Ibid., 259.

66. Michael Harrington, " An Unconditional War," *Wilson Library Bulletin* 38, no. 10 (June 1964): 835.

67. Francis Keppel, "Poverty: Target for Education," speech, American Association of School Administrators, February 15, 1964, in *Vital Speeches of the Day* 30, no. 16 (June 1, 1964): 511.

68. Peter B. Mann, *Sesame Street Research: A Twentieth-Century Symposium* (New York: Children's Television Workshop, 1990), 78.

69. "Report of Workshop 1: Moral and Affective Development," 11, Children's Television Workshop Papers, Public Broadcasting Archives.

70. Ibid.

71. Ibid., 3.

72. This comment is recalled by David Connell in Robert Davidson's oral history of the CTW, "The Children's Television Workshop, The Early Years, An Oral History," 83, unpublished manuscript dated 1990–92, Public Broadcasting Archives, call number PN1992.77.

73. "Report of Workshop 1," 5.

74. Ibid. On the powerful influence of the Kennedy assassination on efforts to reform television, see Hendershot, *Saturday Morning Censors,* 11, 27–34.

75. Gerald Lesser, *Children and Television: Lessons from* Sesame Street (New York: Random House, 1974), 94–95. On these deliberations, see also Richard M. Polsky, *Getting to* Sesame Street*: Origins of the Children's Television Workshop* (New York: Praeger Publishers, 1974), 13–23.

76. Barbara H. Stewart, "*Sesame Street*: A Linguistic Detour of Black Language Speakers," *Back World,* August 1973, 14.

77. Lesser, *Children and Television,* 51.

78. Ibid., 145.

79. Ibid., 48.

80. Thomas D. Cook, *Sesame Street Revisited* (New York: Russell Sage Foundation, 1975), 20.

81. Ibid., 372.

82. Ibid., 20. Following closely on these findings is Judith Huber Minton, "The Impact of *Sesame Street* on Reading Readiness in Kindergarten Children," PhD diss., Fordham University, 1972, esp. 62–66, 156–57.

83. "Television for Preschool Children," 1–2, Box 1, CTW Papers.

84. Ibid., 4.

85. Ibid., 5.

86. Ibid.

87. Ibid., 7.

88. For a searching analysis of "community action" written as it was being implemented around the country, Peter Marris and Martin Rein's *Dilemmas of Social Reform: Poverty and Community Action in the United States* (New York: Atherton Press, 1967) remains essential.

89. Westinghouse Learning Corporation and Ohio University, *The Impact of Head Start: An Evaluation of the Effects of Head Start on Children's Cognitive and Affective Development* (Bladensberg, Md.: Westinghouse Learning Corporation and Ohio University, 1969), vol. 1: 5.

90. Ibid., 8–9.

91. Ibid.

92. Hendershot, *Saturday Morning Censors,* 143.

93. Urie Bronfenbrenner, John Merrow, and Barbara Reinhardt, *Portrait of Urie Bronfenbrenner,* audio recording (Washington, D.C.: National Public Radio, 1981).

94. Urie Bronfenbrenner, *The Troubled American Family,* audio recording (New York: Psychology Today, n.d.).

95. Hearings before the House Committee on Interstate and Foreign Commerce, "Public Television Act of 1967," HR 6736, S1160, and HR4140, 90th Cong., 1st sess., 792.

96. For an evocative discussion of this reconstructive process in Mississippi television, see Classen, *Watching Jim Crow,* 1–39.

97. U.S. House of Representatives, Hearings before the Committee on Interstate and Foreign Commerce, 410–11.

98. Waldo Braden, "The Speaking of the Governors of the New South," in Calvin M. Logue and Howard Dorgan, eds., *A New Diversity in Contemporary Southern Rhetoric* (Baton Rouge: Louisiana State University Press, 1987), 204.

99. Bob W. Roland to Joan Ganz Cooney, May 13, 1968, 1, CTW Papers, Box 12A, file labeled "Mississippi."

100. Cooney to Roland, May 22, 1968, CTW Papers, Box 12A, "Mississippi."

101. "Mississippi Agency Votes for a Ban on *Sesame Street*," *New York Times*, May 3, 1970, 54. Institutional resistance from southern PBS affiliates to some programming on race and civil rights issues continued. Between 1979 and 1981, the Arkansas public television authority refused to broadcast a thirty-minute documentary on former congressman Brooks Hays, who sought to negotiate an end to the Little Rock crisis and was defeated for reelection in 1958 by an ardent segregationist for his trouble. This controversy is thoroughly documented in the clipping files of the Brooks Hays Papers at the University of Arkansas, Fayetteville.

102. "Mississippi Agency, in Shift, will allow *Sesame Street*," *New York Times*, May 26, 1970, 62.

103. Earl K. Moore to Robert Davidson, June 4, 1970, with a transcript of the press secretary's statement to Governor Williams noting the limited reception area of Jackson's ETV station, CTW Papers, Box 12A, "Mississippi."

104. For the history of this litigation, see Classen, *Watching Jim Crow*.

105. John Culhane, "Report Card on *Sesame Street*," *New York Times*, May 24, 1970, section VI: 70.

106. "Switched on School," *Newsweek*, June 1, 1970, 69.

107. Hendershot, *Saturday Morning Censors*, 175

CHAPTER SIX

Note to epigraph: Robert L. Carter, "A Reassessment of *Brown v. Board* in Bell, ed., *Shades of Brown*, 22, 23.

1. James M. McPherson, "The Dimensions of Change: The First and Second Reconstructions," *Wilson Quarterly* 2, no. 2 (Spring 1978): 135–44.

2. www.presidency.ucsb.edu/showelection.php?year=1968.

3. Those five states were Illinois (26), Ohio (26), Missouri (12), New Jersey (17), Washington (8).

4. Cashin, *Failures of Integration*, 266–75.

5. Charles and Bonnie Remsberg, "Chicago Voices: Tales Told out of School," in Mack, ed., *Our Children's Burden*, 285–88.

6. Marian Edelman, "Southern School Desegregation, 1954–1973: A Judicial Political Overview," *Annals of the American Academy* 47 (1973): 35–36; Gary Orfield, "Congress, the President, and Anti-Busing Legislation, 1966–1974," in Davison M. Douglas, ed., *School Busing: Constitutional and Political Developments* (New York: Garland Publishers, 1994), vol. 2: 2,

6–9, 11, 14–17; Orfield, *Reconstruction of Southern Education,* 94–95, 117–18, 121, 144, 168–69, 173–207. On early desegregation efforts, including some busing, see Thomas J. Sugrue, *Sweet Land of Liberty: The Forgotten Struggle for Civil Rights in the North* (New York: Random House, 2008), 449–92; Mack, ed., *Our Children's Burden*; and Robert L. Crain, *The Politics of School Integration: Comparative Case Studies* (1968; rpt. Chicago: Aldine-Transaction, 2010); David Kirby, T. Robert Harris, and Robert L. Crain, *Political Strategies in Northern School Desegregation* (Lexington, Mass.: D. C. Heath and Co., 1973). On the willingness of the Kennedy administration to settle for lax enforcement provisions in order to get a bill, see Hugh Davis Graham, *The Civil Rights Era: Origins and Development of National Policy* (New York: Oxford University Press, 1990), 80–81; U.S. House of Representatives, *Civil Rights, Part 1,* Hearings Before the House Committee on the Rules (January 9, 14, 15, 16, 1964), 131–35. For Senator Humphrey's reassurance that passage of the proposed Civil Rights Act would not require busing, see U.S. Congress, *Congressional Record,* 88th Congress (Washington, D.C.: U.S. Government Printing Office, 1964), 13, 820. Fear of busing, triggered by statements by HEW Secretary Gardner that action was needed against de facto segregation, was also expressed by northern representatives during the debate over the Model Cities Program; see U.S. Senate, *Elementary and Secondary Education Amendments of 1966,* Report 1674, 89th Congress, 2nd sess. (Washington, D.C.: U.S. Government Printing Office, 1966), 365–66; *Congressional Record,* 89th Congress (Washington, D.C.: U.S. Government Printing Office, 1966), 26, 922. Paul Rilling, a Johnson-era HEW bureaucrat, expressed regret for the laxity of desegregation policy in testimony before the Senate Select Committee on Equal Educational Opportunity, chaired by Senator Mondale (U.S. Senate Select Committee on Equal Educational Opportunity, *Desegregation Under Law, Part 3A,* 91st Congress, 2nd sess. (Washington, D.C.: U.S. Government Printing Office, 1970), 985.

7. Brown-Nagin, *Courage to Dissent,* 77.

8. Charles Lawrence, "'One More River to Cross'—Recognizing the Real Injury in *Brown*: A Prerequisite for Shaping New Remedies," in Bell, ed., *Shades of Brown,* 55.

9. On how some members of the judiciary (in this case future Carter administration attorney general Griffin Bell) became behind-the-scenes activists for token compliance, see Brown-Nagin, *Courage to Dissent,* 374–76.

10. Robert L. Carter, "The Warren Court and Desegregation," *Michigan Law Review* 67, no. 2 (December 1968): 248.

11. John Dewey, *The School and Society* (Chicago: University of Chicago Press, 1915), 15.

12. Ibid., 3.

13. This phrase is from Bell, *Silent Covenants,* 9.

14. Deidre Cobb-Roberts, Sherman Dorn, and Barbra J. Shircliffe, "Introduction: Schools as Imagined Communities," in Cobb-Roberts et al., eds., *Schools as Imagined Communities,* 5.

15. Corwin, *Sociology of Education,* 111–12.

16. Ibid., 167.

17. Lo, *Small Property versus Big Government,* 58.

18. The single most studied community in the literature of school desegregation is Charlotte, North Carolina, which is the subject of three major monographs. See Davison M.

Douglas, *Reading, Writing and Race: The Desegregation of the Charlotte Schools* (Chapel Hill: University of North Carolina Press, 1995), esp. 47–54, 224–48, and 317; Stephen Samuel Smith, *Boom for Whom? Education, Desegregation, and Development in Charlotte* (Albany: State University of New York Press, 2004), esp. 61–63, 92–106; 111–15, 170, and 215; Frye Gaillard, *The Dream Long Deferred: The Struggle for School Desegregation in Charlotte, North Carolina* (Columbia: University of South Carolina Press, 2006), esp. 47–58, 91–119, 149–56, and 192. On the social politics of busing in Boston, see Formisano, *Boston Against Busing*, esp. 70–72, 82–83, 98–103, 138–58, 176–77, and 209–12, and Lukas, *Common Ground*, esp. 240–44, 249–51, and 261–63. An excellent comparative analysis of busing in two "frost belt" cities is provided by Stephen J. .L Taylor, *Desegregation in Boston and Buffalo: The Influence of Local Leaders* (Albany: State University of New York Press, 1998), esp. 37–99 and 159–62. On New Orleans and Baton Rouge, see Carl L. Bankston III and Stephen J. Caldas, *A Troubled Dream: The Promise and Failure of School Desegregation in Louisiana* (Nashville: Vanderbilt University Press, 2002), esp. 72–75, 100–119, and 215. On Mobile Alabama, see Richard A. Pride, *The Political Uses of Racial Narratives: School Desegregation in Mobile, Alabama, 1954–1997* (Urbana: University of Illinois Press, 2002), esp. 123–48. On Charleston, South Carolina, see R. Scott Baker, *Paradoxes of Desegregation: African-American Struggles for Equality in Charleston, South Carolina, 1926–1972* (Columbia: University of South Carolina Press, 2006), esp. 158–61; 171–72; on the pressure from black parents to improve existing black schools, see 169; on the use of new regimes of testing to get rid of black teachers, see 172–78. Desegregation experiences in the West have also produced valuable studies. In addition to the work of Clarence Y. H. Lo, one should begin with Diane E. Watson, "The Effects of the Desegregation Controversy on Trustee Governance in the Los Angeles Unified School District, 1975–1980," PhD diss., Claremont Graduate School, 1987, particularly noteworthy for interviews with Bobbie Fiedler and Roberta Weintraub, two leaders of "Bustop" who were elected to the Los Angeles board, and for its scrupulously fair analysis of their views. Watson was herself an elected member of the board during the height of the busing controversy who went on to serve in the California state senate and the U.S. House of Representatives. Also essential are Donald Glen Cooper, "The Controversy over Desegregation in the Los Angeles Unified School District, 1962–1981," PhD diss., University of Southern California, 1991, and Barbara D. Jacobs, "The Los Angeles Unified School District's Desegregation Case: A Legal History," PhD diss., Pepperdine University, 1989, which provides historical background. For a comparative analysis of Los Angeles with other primarily western cities, see Harriet Elaine Glosson Adair, "Trends in School Desegregation: An Historical Case Study of Desegregation in Dayton, Ohio, Denver, Colorado, Los Angeles, California, and Seattle, Washington, 1954–1985," PhD diss., Brigham Young University, 1986; this study is distinctive for showing how economic downturns and limits on property-tax increases create fiscal crises that overwhelm and overshadow earlier priorities centered on school desegregation (see esp. 215–16, 220–21).

19. Bell, "Introduction," *Shades of Brown*, viii. See also Graham, *Young Activists*, 44, 61–81.

20. Brown-Nagin, *Courage to Dissent*, 84, 105–13, 321–22, 346–48.

21. Carter, "Reassessment of *Brown v. Board*," 27.

22. See Bell, *Silent Covenants*, 20–26.

23. On this perception, widely held among liberal and conservative members of the political establishment during the 1970s, see Cowie, *Stayin' Alive,* 99.

24. Hochschild and Scovronick, *The American Dream and the Public Schools,* 31.

25. Ibid.

26. Diane Ravitch provides an insider's account of these efforts in *The Death and Life of the Great American School System: How Testing and Choice are Undermining Education* (New York: Basic Books, 2010). On the way in which the "choice" and "charter" movements have sometimes worked against the growth and maintenance of schools as effective tutors in citizenship and collective memory, see Catherine Michna, "Stories at the Center: Story Circles, Educational Organizing, and the Fate of Neighborhood Public Schools in New Orleans," *American Quarterly* 61, no. 3 (September 2009): 529–55.

27. Michael W. Apple, *Official Knowledge: Democratic Education in a Conservative Age* (New York: Routledge, 2000), 3; Apple, *Cultural Politics and Education,* 30.

28. Apple, *Official Knowledge,* 34–35, 87.

29. Michael W. Apple, *Teachers and Texts: A Political Economy of Class and Gender Relations in Education* (New York: Routledge and Keegan Paul, 1986), 159.

30. Michael W. Apple, *Ideology and Curriculum* (London: Routledge and Kegan Paul, 1990), 57; see also 52–56 and 65–68.

31. I have been drawn to this point of view by the following teachers: Collins, *Another Kind of Public Education*; Meier, *Power of Their Ideas*; Nell Noddings, *The Challenge to Care in Schools: An Alternative Approach to Education* (New York: Teachers College Press, Columbia University, 1992); and Jane Roland Martin, *The Schoolhome: Rethinking Schools for Changing Families* (Cambridge, Mass.: Harvard University Press, 1992).

INDEX

Note: Page numbers followed by "n" indicate endnotes.

Adair, Harriet Elaine Glosson, 213n18
Adams, Virginia, 64–65
advertising: Cosby and, 97, 98, 106; cultural politics of, 106–7; social impact of, 126–27
affirmative action, 61, 122
Agee, James, 24, 38
Age of *Brown:* busing debate and, 9–11; as historical reenactment, 5, 17; ideal vs. reality and, 12; localism and challenges of follow-through, 18–25; meaning of, 2; new habits of citizenship, imagined community, and, 4–9. *See also specific topics, such as* desegregation
Alabama Educational Television Commission, 135–36, 141
algebra as gateway or barrier, 47
Ali, Muhammad (Cassius Clay), 95
"allegiant subjects," 33
Allen, Danielle S., 2, 5–6, 30–31, 76
All in the Family (TV), 113, 116
Almond, Gabriel, 32–33
Althusser, Louis, 205n85
American Council on Education, 135
American Federation of Teachers, 54
"America's Forgotten Children" (Galvin, Adams, and Newman), 64–65
Anderson, Benedict, 9, 18
Annual Conference on Reading, University of Chicago, 46–47
Apple, Michael W., 5, 178
Arkansas public television authority, 211n101
Arkin, David, 8, 9
Asheim, Lester, 135
Askew, Reuben, 10–11

Bair, Sheila, 205n93
Baker, R. Scott, 213n18
Baldwin, James, 110, 113, 115, 122
Balsley, Daisy Fullilove, 111, 207n17
Bank Street Readers, 147–48
Barnicle, Mike, 87
Beals, Melba Pattillo, 182n8
Beck, Joan, 149
Bell, Derrick, 3, 12, 127
Bell, Griffin, 212n9
Berkeley, CA, 86–87
"Bill Cosby Comes Home" (Waters), 115–16
Bill Cosby Is a Very Funny Fellow Right! (Cosby), 99
black and brown colors in Coles's analysis of children's drawings, 69, 73

"Black and White" (song; Arkin and Robinson), 7–9
Blackburn, Robert, 55
"Black Friday" (Till case), 23
"Black History: Lost Stolen or Strayed?" (*Of Black America* episode), 102–4
"Black Monday," 22
blackness, 99, 121
Black Panther Party, 51, 54
Black Power, 59–60, 61, 104
Black Power: The Politics of Liberation in America (Ture and Hamilton), 26–27
black student organization, Topeka High School, 59–60
"Bleeding Kansas," 57
Bogle, Donald, 111, 113, 125
Bonilla-Silva, Eduardo, 184n35
Booth, John Wilkes, 166
Boston, 85–86, 87
Bridges, Ruby: Coles and, 69, 73, 78–79, 81, 89; cultural images of, 23, 24; Kennedy (Robert) on, 81; Presidential Citizens Medal awarded to, 90
British Broadcasting Corporation (BBC), 134–35
Bronfenbrenner, Urie, 159
brown and black colors in Coles's analysis of children's drawings, 69, 73
Brown-Nagin, Tomiko, 23, 33, 168, 176, 212n9
Brown v. Board of Education: as cornerstone moment, 4–5; Cosby statements on 50th anniversary of, 94; cultural impact of, 23–24; Dewey's pragmatism and, 173; implementation and compliance, issues of, 19; murder of Emmett Till and, 22–23; on racism, 133. *See also* Age of *Brown*
The Buses Rolled (Coles), 72–73
busing debate, 9–11, 85–87, 175, 176, 212n6

Caillois, Roger, 187n81
Carmichael, Stokely (aka Kwame Ture), 26
Carnegie Corporation Commission on Education Television, 135, 142, 151
Carson, Claybourne, 42
Carter, Jimmy, 48, 88–89
Carter, Robert L., 165, 171–72, 176
Cashin, Sheryll, 168
Cates, Gilbert, 104
CBS Reports, 7–8
A Chance at the Beginning (TV), 140
Charlotte, NC, 212n18
Charron, Katherine Mellen, 44
charter schools, 178, 214n26
cheating, 58
Chicago, 168
Chicano activists, 154
Child Development Group of Mississippi (CDGM), 74–77, 160
Children of Crisis (Coles), 64, 66, 67–68, 73–74, 78, 81, 83, 90, 103, 171
children's drawings, Coles's study of, 68–69, 73
Children's Television Workshop (CTW), 132–33, 139, 152–57
Citizens' Councils movement, 22–23
Citizen's Crusade Against Poverty, 198n38
citizenship: new habits of, 6, 9, 76; unequal national-unity conception of, 5–6
Civil Rights Act (1964), 124–25, 168
Clark, Kenneth B., 66–67, 68–69, 106, 145
Clark, Mamie, 68–69, 106
Clark, Septima, 43–48
class, socioeconomic: black middle class, 124, 127–28; *Cosby Show* and classism, 125; racial discrimination, racial interaction, and, 60–61; suburbia and, 174–75. *See also* working class, African American
Classen, Steven D., 137
Clinton, Bill, 90
Clyburn, James E., 47–48
Cobb, Charles E., Jr., 47
Cobb-Roberts, Deidre, 18
Coffin, William Sloan, 7

Cold War, 25–29, 38
Cole, Nat King, 98
Coleman, James S., 36, 39–40
Coles, Jane Hallowell, 64, 68, 69, 72, 73, 196n1
Coles, Robert: "America's Forgotten Children" (*Time*) and, 64–65; background of, 27, 64, 196n1; *Boston Globe* interview with Mike Barnicle, 87; *The Buses Rolled,* 72–73; on busing, 85–87; *Children of Crisis,* 64, 66, 67–68, 73–74, 78, 81, 83, 90, 103, 171; children's drawings, work with, 68–69, 73, 103; Cold-War national culture and, 27–28; colloquy with Robert Kennedy, 79–82; congressional testimony, 79, 84; cultural exchange and, 65–66; as cultural politician, 169; cultural role of, 2–4; as diplomat and go-between, 65; essay for *New York Times Magazine,* 83–84; as goodwill diplomat during Reagan's populism, 88–89, 163; Hank, longitudinal portrait of, 198n29; honors received by, 89–90; on hunger crisis, 77–78; Jimmy profile, 73; *The Middle Americans,* 72–73; as modernizer, 26–27; "Mondale of Minnesota," 83; *The Moral Intelligence of Children,* 90; Moynihan Report and, 70–72; Mrs. Patterson profile, 74; *New Republic* writings, 82–83, 88–89, 91; "The Observer and the Observed," 72; as participant symbol, 170–71; political contacts and friendships, 82–83; "Poverty Is Black and White" (interview), 199n57; Project Head Start, CDGM, and, 74–77; Ruby Bridges and, 69, 73, 78–79, 81, 89; *The Spiritual Life of Children,* 90; theory of racism and, 68; on Wallace, 199n57; white Americans, efforts to understand, 84–86; whiteness, white privilege, and, 67
"color blindness": Cosby's comedy and, 98–99; *Cosby Show* and, 125–26; mass media and, 137
Columbia, South Carolina, 46
Come On, People (Cosby and Poussaint), 93
Comer, James P., 122
commercials. *See* advertising
Committee on Education of the "State Convention of the Colored People" of New York State, 15–16
commons, 57–62
community, virtual, 151
community development corporations (CDCs), 144
Congress of Racial Equality, 106
Cooke, Thomas D., 156
"coon counters," 124–25, 204n81
Cooney, Joan Ganz: background of, 27; Cold-War national culture and, 27–28; congressional testimony, 132, 144–45; Cosby compared to, 143; CTW and, 132–33, 161; as cultural politician, 169; cultural role of, 2–4, 170; earlier programs by, 140; on Mississippi network, 161; as modernizer, 26–27; as pioneer, 158; as political power broker, 170, 172; reports to Carnegie, 139; *Sesame Street* and, 140–41, 147; TV as medium and, 139
Cornielle, Anne, 55–56
corporate model of education, 178
Corwin, Ronald, 174–75
Cosby, Bill (William H., Jr.): advertisements for Coca-Cola and Jell-O, 97, 98, 106; *To All My Friends on Shore* (film), 104–5; audience solidarity and, 162; background of, 27; "Black History: Lost Stolen or Strayed?" (*Of Black America* episode), 102–4; Cold-War national culture and, 27–28; "color-blind" comedy and, 98–99; comedy albums, 99–100; *Come On, People* (Cosby and Poussaint), 93; as complicated and contradictory figure, 95–96; Cooney compared to, 143; *Cosby Show* (TV), 106–10, 112–13, 115–23, 125–29, 171; CTW compared to,

Cosby, Bill (*continued*)
139; as cultural politician, 94, 97, 122–29, 169; cultural role of, 2–4; desire to teach, 93–94; doctoral dissertation on *Fat Albert*, 101, 105–6; *Fat Albert and the Cosby Kids* (TV), 100–102, 105, 107–8, 171; on Gregory and Clay, 95; humor as vehicle and, 96; *I Spy* (TV), 97–98, 112; Los Angeles Rodney King riots and, 128; as modernizer, 26–27; nation building and, 96–97; as participant symbol, 171; *Playboy* interview (1969), 93, 112, 119; Reagan compared to, 120; Reagan's conservative counterrevolution and, 114, 115, 117–18, 122–23, 126; serial rapist accusations and loss of cultural presence, 129–31; stand-up comedy, 94; statements on 50th anniversary of *Brown v. Board*, 94; on television as medium, 112; as Victorian reformer, 96, 108–9, 128–29; *The Wit and Wisdom of Fat Albert* (book), 108
Crossroads Africa, 7–8
cultural education, 15–16
cultural exchange, 65–66

Dahlke, H. Otto, 189n26
Davis, Allison, 68
Davis, George, 204n81
Davis, Ossie, 5
Davis, Sammy, Jr., 9
Death at an Early Age (Kozol), 38
debt and predatory lending, 127–28
Dellums, Ron, 55
Dennis, Lawrence, 135
de Schweinitz, Rebecca, 2–3
desegregation: busing, 9–11, 85–87, 175, 176, 212n6; in Chicago, 168; Hochschild and Scovronick on, 177; imagined Humphrey presidency and, 167–68; localism and, 18–19; new habits of citizenship and, 6; opposition as continuation of existing trend, 175; of sports teams, 57. *See also* integration
Detroit, 34–35
Dewey, John, 14, 172–73
Dewey, Thomas E., 141
Dollard, John, 68
Dotson, Bob, 201n83
Douglas, Davidson M., 48
Douglas, Stephen A., 13
Douglass, Frederick, 1, 5, 10, 13, 16–17, 108, 130, 165
Dowling, John D. H., 129
drug abuse in Oakland schools, 54–55
Du Bois, W. E. B., 130, 166
Dyson, Michael Eric, 95, 202n7

Eastland, James, 75–76
Eckford, Elizabeth, 23
Edelman, Marian Wright, 77, 175
Edelman, Peter, 79
Edmundson, Mark, 116
education: Albany, NY, convention on liberating potential of, 15–16; charter schools, 178, 214n26; Dewey on, 14, 173; Douglass on, 5; fundamental weaknesses in American system of, 38–40; "going to school" vs. "getting schooled," 173–74; Lincoln on importance of, 14; social organization of, 173. *See also* school systems and public education
educational television (ETV). *See* Children's Television Workshop; public (educational) television; *Sesame Street*
elites, African American, 60, 61
Ely, Melvin Patrick, 207n17
Emergency School Aid Act (1972), 186n69
Ernst, John, 14–15
Escobar, Arturo, 25
Evans, Walker, 24

Fairclough, Adam, 33, 191n65
Farm Security Administration, 38
Fat Albert and the Cosby Kids (TV), 100–102, 105, 107–8, 171
Faubus, Orval, 19
Fiedler, Bobbie, 213n18
Fischer, John H., 4
Food Stamp program, 84
Formisano, Ronald P., 200n74
Foster, Marcus: assassination of, 55–56; Cosby and, 108; on disadvantaged families, 155; doctoral dissertation of, 192n80; in Oakland, 48, 50–57; at Octavius V. Catto Remedial Disciplinary School, 192n80; at Simon Gratz High School, Philadelphia, 48–50
The 400 Blows (film; Truffaut), 190n34
Frazier, E. Franklin, 103
free blacks, 14–15
Freedom Summer and Freedom School movement, 40–42, 46, 75, 80, 150
Freeman, Alan David, 11–12
Freyer, Tony A., 19
Fulwood, Sam, 123–24
funding and financing of schools: declining enrollments and, 53; electoral politics of property taxes, 24–25; Foster in Oakland and, 52–54; increasing numbers of students and, 36; politics of, 52–53; private-sector partnerships for, 56–57; property tax and fiscal overburden, 35–37. *See also* resource scarcities and inequities

Galvin, Ruth Mehrtens, 64–65
games, 187n81
Gardner, John, 168, 212n6
Geertz, Clifford, 30, 31, 187n1
Gitlin, Todd, 92
Gitter, Lena, 75
Goldstein, Donna M., 96
Good Times (TV), 113
Goodwin, Lawrence, 88
governance of schools: Topeka High School and, 60, 194n117; trend toward student activism, 60
Graham, Gael, 194n113
Graham, Hugh Davis, 212n6
Gray, Herman, 92, 115, 128, 137
Great Society: Coles-Kennedy colloquy and, 81; high point of, 71; public television and, 134; *Sesame Street* and, 144, 152, 156, 157; sociopolitical challenges of, 86. *See also* Project Head Start; War on Poverty
Green, William C., 49
Greenberg, Polly, 76
Gregory, Dick, 94, 95, 99
Gross, Neal Crasilneck, 189n26
Guinea, Republic of, 7–8
Gullah language, 44

Hahn, Steven, 88
Haley, Alex, 112
Hall, E. N., 15
Hall, Ruby Bridges. *See* Bridges, Ruby
Hallowell, Jane, 170
Hamilton, Charles V., 26
Hammer, Emmanuel, 103
Hansberry, Lorraine, 185n47
Hanushek, Eric A., 39
Harding, Vincent, 42, 122
Harlem: The Winter After (TV), 140
Harrington, Michael, 41, 150, 163
Hawks, Esther Hill, 45
Haynes, Bruce D., 124
Hays, Brooks, 211n101
Head Start. *See* Project Head Start
Hearst, Patricia, 55
Hemphill, Robert W., 142
Hendershot, Heather, 107, 158, 163
Henry, Jules, 38

Highlander Folk School, Johns Island, South Carolina, 43–45, 190n51
Hill, Norman, 97
Hinman-Smith, Daniel Peter, 40
Hirsch, Ernest A., 60–62
historical reenactment: Age of *Brown* as, 5, 17; culture-wide exercise of, 167; mass-production model of education and, 178; Septimia Clark and, 45
Hochschild, Jennifer, 176–77
Holt, John, 38–39
Horton, Myles, 190n51
housing segregation. *See* residential segregation
Hudson, Judith C., 40
humor as vehicle, 95. *See also* Cosby, Bill
Humphrey, Hubert H., 167–68
hunger crisis, Coles on, 77–78
Hurlbert, Raymond, 141
Hyman, Herbert H., 96–97

imagined community: "Black and White" (song) and, 8–9; Dewey and, 172–73; localism and, 18–19
individualism, 169
innovation, rhetoric of, 178
integration: Bell on equal educational opportunity and, 12; *Brown v. Board* and, 4–5; Carter on views of, 165; corporate model as de-integrative strategy, 178; Cosby, advertising and, 126; Cosby and, 96; Foster and, 53; Riles on strategies of, 11; *Sesame Street* and, 172; shallow conception of, at Topeka High School, 62; technological, on television, 111; television and, 137, 152–53; virtual, limits of, 162. *See also* desegregation
"An Integration of the Visual Media via Fat Albert and the Cosby Kids into Elementary School Curriculum as a Teaching Aid and Vehicle to Achieve Increased Learning" (Cosby), 105
interracial contact: class and income as related to, 60–61; Lincoln on separateness, 13; *Sesame Street* and, 162
In the Heat of the Night (film), 114
I Spy (TV), 97–98, 112
I Started Out as a Child (Cosby), 100

Jackson, Jesse, 117, 123, 126, 134
Jacobs, Jane, 144
Jhally, Sut, 118, 120–21
Johns Island, South Carolina, 43–45
Johnson, Lyndon B., 36, 58, 89, 114, 156
Johnson, Paul, 75–76, 160
Jones, Hubie, 87

Kain, John F., 39
Kardiner, Abram, 68
Kaufman, Bel, 24, 38
Kazin, Michael, 88
Kennedy, Edward M., 82, 200n58
Kennedy, Jacqueline, 167
Kennedy, John F., 24, 167
Kennedy, Robert F.: assassination of, 167; CDCs and, 144; Coles, colloquy with, 79–82; death and electoral performance of, 88
Keppel, Francis, 150–51, 168
Killian, James R., 135
King, Martin Luther, Jr.: assassination of, 57, 59, 115, 117, 122; rioting after assassination of, 128; in school libraries, 167
King, Rodney, 128
Klineberg, Otto, 146, 147, 148
Kluger, Richard, 182n8
knowledge gap, *Sesame Street* and, 156, 159, 172
Kohl, Herbert, 38, 151
Kohn, Hans, 28
Kozol, Jonathan, 24, 38
Krabill, Ron, 125, 205n85

labor, free blacks on, 14
Landry, Bart, 124

land use, Philadelphia's Simon Gratz High School and, 49–50
language, black, 154
Lawrence, Charles, 168
Lawrence, Sara (later Lightfoot), 21–22, 23–24
Leacock, Eleanor Burke, 146–47
Lear, Norman, 113
Lears, Jackson, 205n91
Ledbetter, James, 135
Lee, Harper, 23–24
Leonard, John, 116–17
Leonard, Sheldon, 98
Lesser, Gerald, 148–49, 153, 154–55
Lever Brothers, 97
Lewis, Earl, 71
Lewis, John, 22, 23–24, 28–29
Lewis, Justin, 118, 120–21
Lewis, Oscar, 68
Lightfoot, Sara Lawrence, 21–22, 23–24
Lincoln, Abraham, 1, 10, 13–14, 16, 20–21, 165–66
Lipsitz, George, 17, 184n47
Littlefield, Valinda, 191n55
Lo, Clarence Y. H., 36–37, 175
localism and local control: *Brown v. Board* compliance and, 19; imagined community and, 18–19; public television and, 135–36, 141–42, 161–62, 211n101; resource inequalities magnified by, 174
Los Angeles: anti–property tax campaigns in, 36–37; Rodney King riots, 128
Lovelace, Valerie, 154–55
Lubrano, Alfred, 102
Luce, Henry, 91
Lukas, J. Anthony, 182n8

magical thinking, 166–67
magnet schools, 11–12
Maloney, Joseph F., 189n26
Mandela, Nelson, 125
Marchand, Roland, 126
Mark of Oppression (Kardiner and Ovesey), 68
Marris, Peter, 210n88
Martin, Trayvon, 17
Marx, Karl, 28
mass-production model of education, 178
Matthews, Donald R., 31–32
McAdam, Doug, 27, 41–42
McGovern, George, 82, 83, 199n58
McLuhan, Marshall, 138–39, 153, 156
McPherson, James, 166
Meier, Deborah, 5
Mexican American students as outsiders, 195n130. *See also* Chicano activists
Michna, Catherine, 214n26
The Middle Americans (Coles), 72–73
middle class, black, 124, 127–28. *See also* class, socioeconomic
Missell, M. Hays, 6
Mississippi: ban of *Sesame Street* and reversal, 161–62; Child Development Group of Mississippi (CDGM), 74–77, 160
Mississippi Commission for Educational Television, 161
Mondale, Walter, 24–25, 82–83, 84, 144, 186n69, 200n58
Montessori movement, 149–50
Montgomery, G. V. (Sonny), 142
Moore, Alexander G., 138, 141
Morrisett, Lloyd, 151
Morrow, Robert, 147
Moses, Robert P., 47
Moynihan, Daniel Patrick, 70–72, 143
Moynihan Report, 70–72, 152
Mr. F., case of, 33
Myers, S., 15

NAACP, 12, 175–76
Nachman, Gerald, 98–99
National Educational Television (NET), 135, 137–38

nation building: in American schools, 1960s and 1970s, 37–40; black middle class and, 124; Cosby and, 96–97; future of, 177–79; on home-front of Cold War United States, 25–29; NAACP and, 175–76; Septima Clark's South Carolina and, 43–48
negative social and cultural messages: black and brown colors in Coles's analysis of children's drawings, 69, 73; Coles on, 68–69; *Sesame Street* and constructive images vs., 153; stereotypes eschewed in *Cosby Show,* 116
Newman, Nancy, 64–65
newspapers, student, 58–60
Niemeyer, John, 147
Nixon, Pat, 134
Nixon, Richard M., 24, 114, 167, 168
No Child Left Behind Act, 56, 178
Novak, Robert, 71

Oakland, CA, 48, 50–57
Obama, Barack, 123
"The Observer and the Observed" (Coles), 72
Of Black America (TV documentary), 102–4
Ogbu, John U., 38, 150, 155
Oldendorf, Sandra Brennemen, 45
Orfield, Gary, 19
Ovesey, Lionel, 68

Painter, Nell Irvin, 88
Palmer, Edward, 154–55
participant symbolism, 169–72
Patterson, James T., 94, 182n8
Peterson, Paul E., 188n18
Petroni, C. Lillian, 60–62
Petroni, Frank, 59, 60–62, 195n130
Philadelphia, 48–50
Playhouse 90 (TV), 111
Poussaint, Alvin F., 93, 118
poverty: CDGM and, 76–77; Coles and, 41, 74; Cooney and, 140; Cosby's portrait of, 100; *Fat Albert* and, 107; hunger crisis, Coles on, 77–78; Lesser on, 155; public television and, 136, 139; stereotype of choice or laziness, Coles on, 84; textbooks and, 146, 148. *See also* War on Poverty
Poverty, Anti-Poverty and the Poor (TV), 140
preschool and early learning, 149–51
Press, Andrea L., 121
Progressive education, Dewey on, 173
Project Head Start: CDGM and, 74–76; public television and, 140, 141, 150, 157; sympathetic critics of, 158
property taxes, 24–25, 35–37
Prothro, James W., 31–32
Public Broadcasting Act (1967), 134, 160
Public Broadcasting System (PBS), 134. See also *Sesame Street* (TV)
public (educational) television: audience solidarity and, 162–63; BBC vs. PBS, 134–35; *A Chance at the Beginning,* 140; in classrooms, 138–39; definition of, 142; early television and, 133–34; *Harlem: The Winter After,* 140; Head Start and, 140, 141, 150, 157, 158; local and state debates over, 141–42, 161–62, 211n101; mission and cultural role of, 136–37; Montessori movement and, 149–50; NET, 135, 137–38; partner countries and coproduction disparities, 163; *Poverty, Anti-Poverty and the Poor,* 140; as preschool learning, 149–51; *Science House,* 138; social reconstruction through TV, 144–49; *Speak-Out in East Harlem,* 140; strong local option, 135–36; techniques of, 139–41; textbooks and readers and, 145–48; virtual reconstruction, limits of, 159–64. See also *Sesame Street* (TV)
Purcell, Theodore, V., 27–28

racial diplomacy, end of, 33–34
racism: *Brown v. Board* decision on, 133; Coles and theory of, 68; Coles on, 73,

82; Cosby on institutional racism, 95, 105–6; *Cosby Show* and, 117–18, 125; educational equality and, 12; *Fat Albert* and, 102; Klineberg's discrediting of scientific racism, 146; Moynihan Report and, 71; new abolitionists and awareness of, 41; perceptions of both parties distorted by, 73; psychological damage done by, 68, 103–4, 106; Reagan and, 114; Second Reconstruction and complexity of, 31; Topeka High School interviews and, 61
Rafferty, Max, 11, 36
Rambush, Nancy McCormick, 150
Ravitch, Diane, 214n26
Reagan, Ronald: on assassination of Foster, 56; Clark's criticism of, 48; coded language used by, 114; Cosby and, 114, 115, 117–18, 120, 122–23; election and reelection of, 82, 88–89, 114, 115, 122; Foster in Oakland and, 52; programs cut by, 122–23; seen as giant step backward, 126
Reconstruction, First: coming together of white and black in, 12; Lincoln's announcement of, 20–21; Sea Islands, NC, and, 45; South Carolina and, 43
Reconstruction, Second: American South as underdeveloped area and, 31–34; federal system and, 19; ideal vs. reality and, 12; Kennedy-Coles colloquy and, 81; public television and, 148–49; *Sesame Street* and, 133; South Carolina and, 43; Warren's announcement of, 20–21
Reconstruction, virtual, 159–64. *See also* public (educational) television
Redfield, Robert, 63
redlining and exclusion in television, 91
Reed, Adolph, Jr., 126
Rein, Martin, 210n88
residential segregation: *Cosby Show* and, 125; Lipsitz on, 17; Northern, 168; school attendance zones and, 174; television and, 91
resource scarcities and inequities: localism and, 174; political hurdles and, 35; private-sector partnerships and, 56–57; in South Carolina, 44. *See also* funding and financing of schools
Revelle, Roger, 135
Revenge (Cosby), 100, 105
Riesman, David, 70
Riles, Wilson, 11
Rilling, Paul, 212n6
Ring, Natalie J., 188n5
Rist, Ray C., 38
Robeson, Paul, 130
Robinson, Earl, 8, 9
Robinson, Helen N., 146, 192n67
Rockwell, Norman, 24, 89
Roland, Bob, 161
Rose, Willie Lee, 45
Rothschild, Mary Aikin, 42
Rustin, Bayard, 143

school bonds, voter resistance to, 53
School Lunch program, 84
school systems and public education: antiquated systems outside the South, 34–37; compulsory attendance, consequences of, 35–36; corporate, mass-production model of, 178; culture-wide debates on meaning of, 3. *See also* education; funding and financing of schools
Schramm, Wilbut, 141
Schudson, Michael, 126, 127
Schulman, Bruce J., 188n5
Science House (TV), 138
Scovronick, Nathan, 176–77
Sea Islands, South Carolina, 43–45
segregation: Highlander Folk School and, 44; informal, 62; as Northern in origin, 168; psychological damage done by, 68, 103–4, 106; as symptom of white supremacy, 165. *See also* racism; residential segregation

Senate Select Committee on Equality of Educational Opportunity: Cooney testimony, 132, 144–45; Mizzell testimony, 6; Mondale on, 25, 186n69; Riles testimony, 11
Serling, Rod, 111
Sesame Street (TV): color line broken by, 106; Cooney on mandate of, 140–41; effectiveness debate and criticism of, 156–58; knowledge gap and, 156, 159, 172; Mississippi ban and reversal, 161–62; as neighborhood, 132, 151; planning and coalition-building for, 152–54; as social program, 154–59; social reconstruction and, 145, 147–48, 158, 162–63; techniques, 139–41; as urban renewal, 143–44
Simon Gratz High School, Philadelphia, 48–50
Sirhan Sirhan, 167
Smith, Alfred E., 32
Smith, Howard K., 7
Smith, T. V., 187n81
Smith, William R., 160, 161–62
the South: Child Development Group of Mississippi (CDGM), 74–77, 160; Coles's portrait of white southerners, 72; increased religious tolerance in, 32; new politics and language of unity, emergence of, 160–61; public television and, 135–36, 141, 161–62; teacher pay in, 48; as underdeveloped area, 31–34
South Africa, 125
South Carolina, 43–48, 142
South Carolina Community Relations Program, American Friends Service Committee, 6
Speak-Out in East Harlem (TV), 140
Spencer, John P., 51–52
Spiegler, Charles G., 36
Spigel, Lynn, 91, 137, 206n1
sports teams, desegregation of, 57
standardized tests, consequences of, 56
Stennis, John, 75–76
student conduct and Topeka High School, 195n126
student government at Topeka High School, 58, 60, 194n117
student newspapers, 58–60
Student Non-violent Coordinating Committee (SNCC): northern volunteers and social advantage, 32, 41–42; Zinn on "new abolitionists," 8, 40–41
suburbia as class phenomenon, 174–75
Susman, Warren I., 29, 187n81
Symbionese Liberation Army, 55

taxes. *See* property taxes
taxes, property, 24–25, 35–37
Taylor, Stephen J. L., 212n6
teacher memoirs, 38–39
teacher pay, 48
teaching materials, 44
Teachout, Terry, 117
television: *All in the Family,* 113, 116; *Of Black America,* 102–4; conservatism in, 137; Cosby and advertising on, 97, 98, 106; Cosby on medium of, 112; *Cosby Show,* 106–10, 112–13, 115–23, 125–29, 171; *Fat Albert and the Cosby Kids,* 100–102, 105, 107–8, 171; fatherhood images in, 116; first ad featuring and African American, 106; *Good Times,* 113; *I Spy,* 97–98, 112; *Playhouse 90,* 111; role of, 91–92, 110–11; social role, sense of, 160; whiteness and the color barrier, 106. *See also* public (educational) television; *Sesame Street*
Television Advisory Panel, U.S. Office of Education, 135
textbooks and readers, 145–48
36 Children (Kohl), 38
Till, Emmett, 22–23, 111
To All My Friends on Shore (film), 104–5

To Kill a Mockingbird (Lee), 23–24
Topeka High School, Kansas, 57–62, 194n117, 195n126
Topeka High World (student newspaper), 58–60, 62, 195n130
Topp, William R., 15
To Russell, My Brother, Whom I Slept With (Cosby), 100
Townsend, J. H., 16
Truman, Harry, 89
Ture, Kwame (aka Stokely Carmichael), 26
Twain, Mark, 9

underdeveloped area, American South as, 31–34
University of Chicago Annual Conference on Reading, 46–47
University of Chicago Laboratory School, 63
uplift, racial, 128–29
Up the Down Staircase (Kaufman), 38

Verba, Sidney, 32–33
Victorianism, 95, 108–9, 128–29
virtual integration, limits of, 162
voter disenfranchisement, 35
voter participation, 32–33, 45

wages, 77
Wallace, George C., 23, 167, 168, 199n57
War on Poverty: Coles and, 77–78; Montessori movement and, 150; Project Head Start and, 74–76, 141; public television and, 134. *See also* poverty
Waters, Harry F., 115–16
Watkins, Mel, 99
Watson, Diane E., 213n18
Watson, Glegg, 204n81
Weaver, Pat, 91
Weintraub, Roberta, 213n18
West, John, 48
Whitby School, Greenwich, CT, 150
white flight, 34–35
whiteness and white privilege, 67, 106
white supremacy, segregation as symptom of, 165
Whitfield, Stephen, 22
Why Is There Air? (Cosby), 100
Wickberg, Daniel, 95
Wiese, Andrew, 205n82
The Wit and Wisdom of Fat Albert (Cosby), 108
Wonderfulness (Cosby), 100
Wood, Robert R., 48
Woodward, C. Vann, 88
working class, African American: black elite criticism of, 60; Coles on, 87; Cosby and, 27; Cosby on, 94–95, 104, 109; *Cosby Show* and, 121; *Fat Albert* and, 105; racial friction with working-class whites, 61; recession and, 124
Wright, Marian (later Edelman), 77, 175
Wright, Richard, 24

Yonkers, NY, African Americans in, 124

Zinn, Howard, 3, 8, 27, 28, 40–41, 170
Zoglin, Richard, 117, 120